'Dan Plesch comprehensively analyses the threats that we face in the twenty-first century, and offers clear proposals to make the world a safer and better place for all its citizens. He rightly looks beyond the current focus on military solutions to complex international security problems. In a time when neither beauty queens nor politicians seem to worry about the survival of future generations, this book is a sober reminder that we live in a fragile system, which is in urgent need of some challenging maintenance.'
Air Marshal Lord Garden, Wells Professor, Indiana University

'Dan Plesch is not only well informed; his work is engaging and readable. His comprehensive knowledge of the strategic issues which we now face demands that any self-respecting student of war and peace reads this book.'
Peter Kilfoyle MP, former Defence Minister

'Dan Plesch addresses the contemporary world crisis caused by the Anglo-American attack on Iraq and the so-called "war on terror" with authority, clarity and directness. Recalling how previous insurgencies were overcome by the winning of hearts and minds as well as scrupulous observance of the law, he exposes the neo-conservative fantasies that are taking the world to the brink of disaster. In condemning corporate greed, structural inequality and oil dependency, he challenges the West to put its own house in order before imposing its will on the rest of the world.'
Malise Ruthven, author of Islam in the World

D0273949

For Lindsay and Susannah

DAN PLESCH was born at Keele in Staffordshire and grew up in London. He studied history at Nottingham University and qualified as a social worker at Bristol University. In the early 1980s he was active in the Campaign for Nuclear Disarmament and began helping organise the Glastonbury festivals. In 1987 he founded the British American Security Information Council (BASIC) which he directed from Washington DC until 2001, when he was appointed Senior Research Fellow at the Royal United Services Institute for Defence and Security Studies. In 2003 he then became an Honorary Fellow of Birkbeck College, University of London and Visiting Senior Research Fellow at the University of Keele. He has written for the *Guardian*, the *Independent*, the *New York Times*, the *Observer*, *Tribune*, the *Washington Post* and the *Washington Times*. He has regularly provided live political and military analysis of evolving news stories for the BBC, CNN, ITN and other news media. He lives in London with his wife and daughter.

THE BEAUTY QUEEN'S GUIDE TO WORLD PEACE

MONEY, POWER AND MAYHEM IN THE TWENTY-FIRST CENTURY

DAN PLESCH

POLITICO'S

First published in Great Britain 2004 by
Politico's Publishing, an imprint of
Methuen Publishing Limited
215 Vauxhall Bridge Road
London SW1V 1EJ

10 9 8 7 6 5 4 3 2 1

Copyright © Daniel Plesch 2004

Daniel Plesch has asserted his right under the Copyright, Designs & Patents Act, 1988, to be identified as the author of this work.

A CIP catalogue record for this book is available from the British Library.

ISBN 1 84275 110 7

Printed and bound in Great Britain by Bookmarque Ltd, Croydon, Surrey

This book is sold subject to the condition that it shall not by way of trade or otherwise be lent, resold, hired out, or otherwise circulated without the publishers' prior consent in writing in any form of binding or cover other than that in which it is published and without a similar condition being imposed on the subsequent purchaser.

Contents

Private Frazer: 'I knew it – we're doomed – doomed!'
Captain Mainwaring: 'Be quiet, Frazer – I'm trying to think.'

From the BBC sitcom *Dad's Army*[1]

Foreword and acknowledgements

In Joseph Heller's satirical novel *Catch-22* his (anti)hero, Yossarian – an American bomber pilot in the Second World War – complains that the Nazis are trying to kill him, personally. His friends assure him that it is just the way war is – there is nothing personal in it. He doesn't agree. And neither do I. Unless we stop it, some stupid war will likely get us all killed. Consequently, I have ended up spending most of my working life in and around pressure groups trying to prevent first nuclear and then other forms of war. I have been fortunate in my colleagues and in the foundations that provided grants to support my research and advocacy.

We have now come to a point where much that we have achieved in international law, disarmament and social security seems unsettled and even under threat. At the same time we seem to be running out of positive ideas and, even worse, growing fatalistic. A researcher I happened to talk to recently, remarked that he had run out of indignation. But there is still an awful lot to be indignant about, so I would be delighted to learn about other people's plans for how we extricate ourselves from the present mess in international security, and it is only because I have found very few other hopeful ideas that I have taken the presumptuous step of offering my own. In choosing what to focus on, a lot had to be left out in order to provide, in one volume, both a diagnosis and a prescription. I hope that they can be improved on.

Many other issues, from improving intelligence cooperation between governments to improving the effectiveness of pressure groups, sit amongst the topics that have had to be set aside for now. If you would like to learn more please visit my website www.danplesch.net.

*

I have many people to thank for their help and I hope I have not left anyone out. If despite their best efforts there are mistakes, they are mine. Tony Rudolf of the Menard Press invited me to write *Sheriff and Outlaws in the Global Village* in the aftermath of 9/11and Karen Bartlett, while Director of Charter 88, commissioned, *Getting a Grip on Globalisation*. These two pamphlets were prototypes for parts of this book. Rear Admiral Richard Cobbold and my colleagues at the Royal United Services Institute for Defence and Security Studies stimulated my thinking on many issues in the two years after 9/11. Professor Robert Jenkins of Birkbeck College, University of London, Professor Alex Danchev of Keele University and Tarak Barkawi at Cambridge University's Centre for International Studies gave me the opportunity to road test the policy agenda I have outlined here. General Lee Butler, formerly head of the US Strategic Command, taught me much about the mythology of deterrence. Jamie Lowther and Brigadier Wight reminded me of the importance of General Kitson. Karel Koster and Malise Ruthven provided very useful advice. John Pike provides the world with a wealth of primary source material on military issues at www.globalsecurity.org. Lord Phillips of Sudbury has been very encouraging about making limited liability an issue. Professors David Fisk,

Tom Burke and Michael Grubb and the Energy Futures Coalition all helped me get to grips with renewable energy issues. Dr Trevor Findlay of VERTIC, Otfried Nassauer of BITS and both Tariq Rauf and Fiona Simpson of the IAEA provided very helpful comments on the SCRRAP proposal. Martin and Sandra Butcher have helped me keep my feet on the ground in twenty years working on the problems of Weapons of Mass Destruction. Through the years I have been indebted to Professor Sir Joseph Rotblat for holding up the light at the end of the tunnel. Nick and Sue Webb helped me understand how to deal with the world of publishing. Miranda McCabe very kindly provided a school teacher's perspective on the draft text. Sean Magee and John Schwartz gave me the contract and encouragement to write this book and John and his colleague Emma Musgrave helped me pin down the text when it showed signs of escaping me.

Dan Plesch
June 2004

Introduction

One crisis after another explodes across our television screens: 9/11, Iraq, weapons of mass destruction, terrorism, globalisation, world poverty – we can't keep up. We've barely yelled 'Stop! Don't do that!' when along comes the next disaster.

This book is about practical ways of creating a peaceful world. The problem is not that we have to persuade people that peace is desirable: if it wasn't a common desire, beauty queens wouldn't express their hope for world peace the way they do. The problem is to find a practical way of turning what appears to be an impossible dream into practical action.

A long time ago, at the end of the Cold War, there was a brief, romantic moment when it seemed that world peace was within sight. These hopes were dashed, the United Nations became weaker than ever, weapons of mass destruction piled up and corporate power devastated the environment and individual freedoms. Now, after Bush's extremism and the emergence of global terrorism, we seem further away than ever from the sort of world we want.

In 2005, there will be another round of global meetings where people will be trying to make a positive impact. Britain will host both the World Social Forum of activists from around the world and the annual G8 summit meeting of the world's largest economic powers. Meanwhile, in New York, the United Nations will hold a global conference on nuclear proliferation. The sixtieth anniversary of the end of the Second World War and the first use of nuclear weapons, on Hiroshima and Nagasaki, also fall in 2005.

This book is intended to help the public debates and decision-making at these and future meetings and provide a guide for people looking for a new course of action in a very confusing world. They are intended to provide practical ways of building peace, freedom and prosperity while neutralising the naïve and bombastic politics of neo-conservatives; isolating violent religious extremism and cutting the corporations down to size. To create the change we want, we need a diagnosis of the ills we suffer and a comprehensive treatment plan. The first part of this book provides the diagnosis. The second part describes a treatment programme.

First of all, however, I want to summarise the main ideas of the book, and then discuss some myths about the United States that get in the way of clear consideration of current problems. These myths are that the US is either predominantly good or bad and that its economic and military strength makes it all-powerful.

What this book is about

As we consider the mind-wrenching problems of war and peace, it is encouraging to realise that, nowadays, we usually think of war as a bad thing, and we think of peace as the normal and desirable state of affairs. The idea that war is bad certainly wasn't universal in the past. War was often portrayed as a glorious and profitable activity until the World War of 1914–18. The change in attitude provides a good foundation for thinking that we can continue to make peace normal and war taboo.

Two great philosophers, Thomas Hobbes and Immanuel Kant, are often portrayed as the exponents of the two traditionally opposed views of world affairs. Hobbes's view was that 'the condition of man ... is a condition of war of everyone against everyone.'[2] The Hobbesians argue that humans and the countries they run are inevitably anarchic and selfish. Kantians argue that we can aspire to make the world a peaceful place. This is a simplification of these philosophies, but it serves to highlight the long-standing dispute over whether humanity can progress or is bound to behave as Hobbes suggests.

The main point of Chapter 1 is that changes in the world brought about by industrialisation and globalisation have turned peace from being a desirable optional extra into a practical necessity. Industrialisation produced the first revolution in military affairs. By the end of the First World War, industrialisation had made warfare so destructive that world leaders tried to prevent future wars by creating the League of Nations. At the height of the Second World War, having seen the failure of states to make the League of Nations stop Benito Mussolini and Adolf Hitler, the American and British governments made a second attempt at an international organisation to preserve peace: the United Nations that we have today. After 1945, nuclear weapons supplied a further reason to ensure international cooperation to prevent war and the annihilation of civilisation in a nuclear holocaust. The logic of survival means that notions of peace that were once ideals have become necessities. Global anarchy is not an option. Hobbesians must become Kantians or face extinction.

Globalisation has been around for centuries. Paul Hirst and Grahame Thompson provide a timely reminder of how globalised the world was, a century ago, before the First World War in their book *Globalisation in Question*.[3] Today, global corporations, the speed of transportation, the internet and global mobile phones have brought an interrelated global culture. And within that interrelated culture a global guerrilla war has been launched by Al-Qaeda. This is neither a war between countries nor a war within a country, but a war waged by groups of people in many countries against many countries. The fact that this war is both global and internal makes it the second revolution in military affairs.

In a multicultural world, in which religion is not confined to a particular nation or skin colour, the war launched by Al-Qaeda is similar to guerrilla wars that used to be confined to single countries. There are many ways of fighting a guerrilla war. I was discussing the ideas in this book with a retired SAS officer and I observed that his own approach to counter-terrorism amounted to ninety-five per cent social democracy and five per cent 'Kill them'. 'No,' he replied, 'not five per cent, one per cent.' What is especially interesting is that the British Army's textbook approach emphasises that redressing grievances, having the greatest political consensus and operating within the rule of law are essential to success.

These principles are not being used today by the UK and the US. We hear far too much about the military and security aspects of counter-terrorism and all too little about what should be the other ninety-nine per cent. This does not mean that the military and security aspects are unimportant, just that without the proper context they are useless.

Both industrialisation and globalisation have changed the basis of warfare from one where war and the armed forces could provide victory to one where the military have a role to play but there must be a political solution. The revolution of industrialisation was recognised by Winston Churchill and Franklin D. Roosevelt when, while preoccupied by their urgent need to beat Hitler, they still found it necessary to declare a vision of the future where 'for realistic as well as spiritual reasons, nations must come to renounce the use of force.'[4]

Today, it is common to hear people say that the United Nations is a nice idea but it does not work. But the seemingly chaotic world we now face is neither natural nor inevitable. Churchill and Roosevelt experienced both the failure of the League of Nations and the terror of Hitler and they realised that it was essential to try again. Who are we to abandon what they started?

*

The second chapter moves on from the assessment that international cooperation is now a practical necessity and outlines the main threats to peace. These threats are Invasion, Death, Destruction and Destitution.

For the first time since the fall of the Roman Empire more than 1,500 years ago, invasion is no longer a threat to the people of Europe. It never has been for the United States. In much of the rest of the world, the demise of the colonial empires in the period after 1945 also marked the end of an era of invasion and occupation. Invasions have become rare. Today, for smaller states facing Western displeasure, invasion under President Bush's doctrine of pre-emption has re-emerged as a danger.

Death and destruction are still a huge problem for many nations and the world as a whole. Weapons of mass destruction built up during the Cold War exist in large numbers and can still destroy civilisation. New rivalries between, for example, the US and China may emerge. And now there is the added risk that atomic, biological or chemical weapons may be used not just by governments in a third world war, but also by terrorists.

For billions of people worldwide, destitution, brought about by economic injustice and lack of development, creates a real and pressing threat to peace. When contemplating the (supposed) threat from radical Islam, remember that a central tenet of the code of social conduct developed by Mohammed was wealth-sharing and social security, and that continues to be an important part of the attraction of Islam.

Poverty is a huge source of daily suffering and contributes to fighting over resources all over the world. The major industrial powers compete to control resources that will sustain their economies, especially oil. Looming over the existing destitution is the threat of devastation by global warming, especially to the millions of poor people living in areas threatened by rising sea levels caused by the melting of the polar ice caps.

Confronted by this intimidating list of threats, the challenge is to come up with effective ideas for change. These are outlined in Part 2.

*

My overall strategic approach is discussed in Chapter 3. I draw guidance from the 'millennium goals' agreed by the United Nations in 2000 and the British textbook approach to fighting a guerrilla war. There are a number of key priorities: finding new ways to advance economic justice and sustainable development in the face of corporate power; revitalising democracy by reforming international institutions; creating awareness of the historical achievements that brought the freedoms we enjoy today; defusing the struggle for control of the world's oil and gas supplies through an emergency programme of renewable energy; and creating a comprehensive system to regulate and remove weapons of mass destruction.

*

Chapter 4 outlines a new way to advance the agenda of economic justice and sustainable development. It shows that the current attempts to make corporations socially responsible are making insufficient progress. However, a look at the regulations giving shareholders legal immunity from liability for the actions of the companies they own, reveals a critical contradiction. Shareholders, more than any other section of society, benefit from protective government regulation. Their protection is enshrined in the limited-liability laws that give them power but no responsibility.

Self-styled 'free market' supporters insist that the business model should become almost the only accepted way of organising public services. Regulations limiting the free market must, they argue, be set aside. In fact, this approach relies upon dividing the world into first-class citizens – the shareholders – who are effectively above the law, and the rest, who have neither any legal rights to sue shareholders nor, the way deregulation is going, any protections of their own against the power of corporations.

In countries with weak legal and social structures supervising business activity, such as the new democracies of eastern Europe and Latin America, limited liability is a device to legalise the theft and corruption that went on under the old dictatorships. Economic reform must now focus on restoring equality before the law by abolishing limited liability, or at least balancing limited liability with equal protections for other sections of society. It is a matter of human rights.

A political campaign to deregulate shareholder privilege will also help those working for fair trade, environmental protection, union rights, sustainable development and human rights within the US, Europe and the other industrialised powers as well as in the developing world. It can bring together disparate political forces without requiring formal links or agreements. Were it possible to sue the shareholders, one can be sure that they, or their insurers, would make much stronger demands upon that company to behave responsibly.

The demand to make shareholders equal before the law is based on a core principle of liberal democracy and will strengthen democratic societies against attack, especially from those who argue against the injustice and inequalities within democracies in order to attack democratic society itself.

The reform of limited liability should form the organising focus of efforts for economic justice and to reduce the pervasive sense of economic grievance between rich and poor. Making the rich accountable for their financial actions will provide a legal basis for balancing power with responsibility. It is a tool for redistributing wealth based upon equal human rights rather than on asking the rich to behave nicely.

This key economic reform will be most effective if it is accompanied by improvements in the way we organise democracy. Money and political power are the vital elements of the way society is organised and reforms in each area should support each other.

*

Chapter 5 looks at the lack of democracy at an international level. Democracy is a vital part of building world peace, keeping governments accountable to their people. Democratic states have a good record of staying at peace with one another. Improved democracy is a necessary part of the reform of global institutions, making their actions more legitimate and defusing the argument of the enemies of democracies that, in practice, democracy is a sham. This chapter diagnoses our failure to modernise democracy to keep up with globalisation and prescribes a range of reforms to the way international institutions carry out their business. When parliaments were first created back in the Middle Ages, representatives were chosen by each *county*. In an interconnected world, we need to elect representatives directly from each *country* to the key global decision-making institutions. This upgrade will plug our democratic power into the places that matter. The chapter ends by looking at weaknesses in democracy in Britain and proposes that more key public offices be elected.

It is too easy to be cynical about democracy: easy to forget how much worse off we would be without legal rights and the ability to vote out a government. Governments in democratic countries are, for example, often worried that if they raise taxes they will be voted out. Do not forget that, without democracy, rulers taxed people into destitution and seized their possessions by force to pay the bills.

Look forward into the middle of the century to, say, 2050 – about as far forward as the Second World War is behind us. Is it not obvious that in a globalised world, with more and more decisions being made at global level, we should be directly electing the people our country sends to represent us? As soon as a significant group of nations starts to elect their representatives at the United Nations, the International Monetary Fund and the World Trade Organisation, the culture of these organisations will change and become more open. With many countries electing their representatives to the United Nations, that institution will increase its legitimate authority and be better able to resist those who attack its existence.

Together with reform of shareholders' special status, democratic election of international institutions would provide a mutually supporting strategy to reduce the influence of the small numbers of the wealthy and powerful. Elected representatives can better advocate the restoration of equal rights before the law through the removal of shareholders' privileges.

*

A strong democratic society is important in its own right. It is also essential as a base from which to build the policies that will provide the social strength and flexibility to stand up to attacks on democracy, whether from people carrying out guerrilla warfare or from those who would reject international law. Chapter 6 examines the lack of interest in democracy, especially in Britain, from a historical perspective.

The history of famous battles forms a vital part of preparing soldiers to fight. As we face new threats to democracy itself, it is vitally important that we use the same type of examples to inspire our democratic politics. For people to be enthusiastic about democracy, they need to appreciate as examples and role models those who won our democratic rights in the first place. Our history is full of kings, queens and generals, but the leaders who overthrew slavery and first campaigned for the vote and equal rights are mentioned only in passing, if at all. Millions of people signed the great democratic petitions of the Chartists and the Suffragettes. There should be a national project to reconnect people with the ancestors who gave us the freedoms we enjoy today. In this way we can regain some confidence by building on their achievements.

The economic and political reforms I have outlined are intended to reduce and remove the causes of war and reinforce the authority of the UN. They are political tools that can have an impact in the short term, but also, in the long term, decisively strengthen many specific campaigns and goals adopted by the UN and other organisations, down to community level.

*

Within the framework of long-term political and economic reform, a number of other strategies can more specifically reduce and manage war and the causes of war. The two most pressing causes are the struggle for resources and the uncontrolled build-up of weaponry.

The struggle for control of the world's oil and gas is by far the most important resource battle today, affecting people all over the world. The world economy relies upon oil for transport and plastics. Of these, air travel and plastics take a small share; the vast majority of production is for cars and trucks. Two-thirds of the world's oil reserves are found around the Persian Gulf; this has generated a history of war and uncertainty in the region. The military cost of the struggle for control of oil is very high, while sudden crises have raised prices and caused economic recessions around the world. A future larger war in the Gulf could result in a near collapse of the industrial economies, which at present cannot exist without oil. At the same time the use of gas as fuel for producing electricity is rapidly increasing; this too is in short supply, from countries with a history of war and instability.

Dependence on oil and gas is a source of strategic instability and national and international insecurity.

The solution is obvious and has already begun to be implemented: to replace oil and, to a degree, gas with renewable energy. Concern over global warming has already produced an upsurge in renewable energy production, if a little late. Adding the security argument to the environmental case for renewable energy provides a powerful combination for policy change. Added investment in renewables will bring down their cost and increase their popularity, making them an economical and socially attractive resource in the developing world. Cheap, low-tech and decentralised electricity supplies will reduce global poverty and destitution. Along with the reform of limited liability, renewable energy will have near-universal economic benefit to both developing and industrialised societies.

*

The chapter on weapons describes a programme for the comprehensive regulation of proliferation and the scrapping of armaments. Until the turn of the century, there had been astonishing concrete achievements in disarmament and arms control. Nuclear testing is now under a global ban. France's testing in the Pacific was the last by the major powers. India and Pakistan each test-fired a handful of nuclear devices in 1998. But since then, for the first time since 1945, years have gone by without any nuclear explosions at all. Thousands of tanks, guns and missiles had been chopped up under strict verification. A range of regulations covering aspects of weapons of mass destruction had been agreed by the UN and continue to operate. In

Iraq, UN inspections were highly effective in containing Saddam Hussein's weapons programmes, despite the protestations of the critics.

Unfortunately, these achievements have been mostly forgotten. Public expectation at the end of the Soviet-Western confrontation was that nuclear weapons would be got rid of in an accelerating process of disarmament. This did not happen. Instead, during the 1990s, the debate on disarmament by all countries was reduced in focus to looking only at the spread of weapons – proliferation – and ignores the stockpiles already held. Even standard undergraduate textbooks discuss nuclear weapons under the title of Proliferation rather than under headings such as Disarmament and Arms Control. Nevertheless, unreported debates at the UN continue in which the majority of states demand that the few nations with nuclear weapons reach an agreement to scrap them all. Indeed, as recently as 2000, the five main nuclear powers gave an 'unequivocal' commitment to the world to do just that, but have done nothing to implement it.

A comprehensive plan of weapons regulation and destruction is practical. Such a plan would involve taking the most effective, tried and tested measures from existing treaties and adapting them into a template that covers all types of weaponry. One of the unique results of the existing treaties is that, for the first time in history, almost every nation on earth has a group of government officials whose job is to make disarmament agreements work. This undeservedly obscure network is a global resource of great value. These centres of excellence need to be developed and expanded to support a new and comprehensive programme of disarmament.

A comprehensive approach to controlling weaponry is essential because partial approaches are inadequate. While the major powers hang onto their weapons and argue that smaller nations have no right to them they have all the credibility of alcoholics denouncing teenage drinkers. A comprehensive approach will tackle both ends of the problem and make it far easier to gain political support against attempts at deception by some countries.

A positive international context of disarmament will remove much of the incentive for nations, whether North Korea, China or the US, to develop new weapons, and provide the basis for unified international pressure on nations that try to do so.

Taken together, the proposals in this book have the potential to move forward the causes of peace, justice and sustainable development around the world, using the simple arguments that all should be equal before the law; that we should increase democratic representation internationally; that we should replace oil and gas dependency with renewable energy; and that we should regulate and scrap all kinds of weapons.

Misunderstandings

To help get to grips in more detail with the huge issues I have just summarised I want to peel away some misunderstandings.

First let's chuck out two extreme approaches. One version runs something like this: 'It is an evil world out there, the UN is a fine idea but at the end of the day it is only the US and Britain who can pin on the sheriff's badge and save the world. The US does not want to be the world's policeman, only with reluctance does it saddle up to tackle the outlaws. And we know who they are, the terrorists, the enemies of freedom, the "Outlaws".' This argument was made popular in Washington by Richard Haass in his 1998 book The *Reluctant Sheriff*.[5]

But the US and Britain do not go rushing out every time someone calls 999. Not for five years in the Balkans, not over the millions of dead in the Congo, or the dictatorships of central Asia, the so-called 'Stans', or, despite thirty-five years of Security Council Resolutions, in the case of occupied Palestine. And as Haass makes clear, the legal authority that makes the sheriff legitimate does not need to come from the UN or anywhere else. Indeed, Haass forgets that in the American tradition sheriffs are usually elected by the people.

So it is a mistake to think that the problems in US policy either began with President Bush Junior, or that they will end when he leaves office. There has been a long discussion in the United States about how it should use what is regarded as its dominant (hegemonic) power.

One US Democrat has outlined a multilateral strategy with which the US could manage its global power. This writer, Zbigniew Brzezinski, who was President Carter's National Security Adviser, wrote in his work *The Grand Chessboard*:[6]

> *For America, the chief geopolitical prize is Eurasia. Now a non-Eurasian power [the US] is pre-eminent in Eurasia – and America's global primacy is directly dependent on how long and how effectively its preponderance on the Eurasian continent is sustained.*
>
> *To put it in a terminology that hearkens back to the more brutal age of ancient empires, the three grand imperatives of imperial geostrategy are to prevent collusion and maintain security dependence among the vassals, to keep tributaries pliant and protected, and to keep the barbarians from coming together.*

As early as 1993, with the Soviet Union only two years in the past and the liberation of Kuwait under a clear UN mandate a very recent event, President Clinton's officials at NATO headquarters outside Brussels circulated an informal paper called 'With the United Nations Whenever Possible, Without When Necessary?'.[7] It argued that 'NATO should set the decision-making parameters for the United Nations and not the other way around.' The paper argued that the legal authority of a UN mandate needed to be 'demystified' because the interests of other states with veto power in the Security Council were 'simply too diverse to expect that they will always succeed in generating the mandates necessary ... A debate has definitely begun about the wisdom of having tied NATO so tightly to the United Nations' apron strings'. One could see this paper as predicting the weakening of the UN or, as I think is the case, as describing a policy of weakening the UN and giving the US, through its control of NATO, the ability to act alone.

The military strategy underpinning this approach was established in the 1990s by the Pentagon under the title 'Full Spectrum Dominance'. This colourful phrase is much repeated in other documents such as the US military's Joint Staff document, *Vision 2020*. This lays out plans for winning any conflict anywhere on earth, from guerrilla war to war in space. For US defence planners, the latest project is to establish dominance in space warfare and in missile wars. This is the so-called 'Star Wars' concept, which is discussed in more detail later.

Now, while it is mostly the case that the self-styled sheriff acts more like rentacop for the rich than an accountable police force, this does not mean that there are no other threats to safety, freedom and democracy, nor does it mean that the US or UK inherently present the main problem. French and Russian complicity with Saddam was far greater than that of Britain and the United States. If not the United States, who would prefer Russia, China or France, or Al-Qaeda for that matter, as a world superpower?

The second myth that we need to dispose of is the idea that the US is the most evil force in the world – a sheriff in the tradition of the evil Sheriff of Nottingham in the Robin Hood stories. In this fiction, Al-Qaeda and other guerrilla groups are freedom-fighters. It is absurd to romanticise and support political violence. Stateless groups that turn to killing and destruction rarely have sufficient cause to do so and should be brought to justice. But not to the justice-free zone of Guantanamo.

An obsession with US imperialism overlooks the US role in creating first the League of Nations and then the United Nations. It ignores the US role in the defeat of Nazism and resisting Stalin. Much of the record has been mixed – the Marshall Plan of economic assistance was a boon to much of western Europe after the Second World War but did not exactly benefit people under General Franco's dictatorship in Spain. The Cold War took two sides to make it happen. But to hear some people talk, it is as if the US fought with Hitler, not against him, and that Stalin never murdered tens of millions of his own citizens. Nor do the most ardent critics of US imperialism explain why the US did not incinerate the Soviet Union when it had first a monopoly of nuclear weapons from 1945–9 and then a huge superiority for more than a decade after that.

There is a broader, more genuinely cooperative, approach to be found in the US. The success of the liberal political soap *The West Wing* was that it represented America as many people want it to be. You can find 'West Wing' politics all over the United States and in major institutions such as the Ford Foundation and the Carnegie Endowment for International Peace. US social movements have made a great global contribution to democratic politics, women's and gay rights and anti-racial discrimination.[8]

It is worth noting the following statement before the attack on Iraq:

> *America must steer away from actions that could produce the unintended results of fracturing those very institutions that have helped keep peace since World War II. Allowing a rush to war in Iraq to create divisions in those institutions and alliances that will help sustain American security and world stability is a short-sighted and dangerous course of action.*
>
> *In order for America to address the differences between ourselves and our allies, we must understand those differences. We don't enhance our relationships and bridge differences by impugning the motives of our friends. Let us not forget, they too are democracies. They too are accountable to their people and respond to the judgment of their citizens. Isn't that the essence of our noble purpose as democratic governments? We must listen and learn, then forge a coalition based upon our common interests.*
>
> *The diplomatic challenges before us should not weaken our resolve to obtain a second United Nations resolution that threatens serious consequences for Iraq's continued defiance of United Nations resolutions. While time may be short, the diplomatic option has not yet played out. It will take more hard work, and the military option should*

remain on the table. The world has additional time, and we
should not short-circuit what has begun through legitimate
United Nations channels. This responsible course will
maximize the force of world opinion and bring it to our
side.

The speech was from Senator Chuck Hagel, a member of Bush's own Republican Party. Hagel went on to argue that the UN should have the lead role both in Iraq and in a new UN-sponsored conference on the Middle East.

So, rather than either idolising or vilifying US policy, what is important is to help improve it and the political ideas in Part 2 are as applicable, if not more so, in the US as elsewhere.

From Enron to Pentagon

The extremely conservative policies of the Bush administration have provided ample evidence that, far from being supreme in the world, the US, under the most determined 'go it alone' leadership ever seen in Washington, has delivered a policy of anarchic incompetence. As the Bush administration cannot make the vaunted supremacy work, the supremacy is not what it may seem.

There are strong parallels between the Bush administration's foreign policy and the hyped-up stock market boom of the late 1990s. Both shared a false belief that regulation was simply an obstacle to success, which would be guaranteed by the latest technology. The 'new economy' has parallels in a supposed 'revolution in military affairs'. The attention given to these false ideas created a distraction from long-standing problems.

On economic issues US conservatives objected to environmental and financial rules; in foreign policy they sought to do away with international law altogether. The 'new economy' of the internet was supposed to have removed the economic cycle altogether, while war was supposed to have been transformed by precision weapons and a military internet.

The challenge to international law comes from a long-standing and, at present, dominant group in US politics. John Bolton, Under Secretary of State for George W. Bush, argued before he was appointed that 'treaties are "law" only for US domestic purposes. In their international operation, treaties are simply "political", and not legally binding.'[9] He argues this even though the relevant article of the Constitution clearly places treaties on an equal footing with the Constitution itself and laws passed by Congress: 'This Constitution, and the laws of the United States which shall be made in Pursuance thereof; and all Treaties made, or which shall be made, under the Authority of the United States, shall be the supreme Law of the Land...'[10] That is to say, treaties are legally binding and as most lawyers and US administrations have assumed, they are supreme unless they are formally revoked. Bolton and his ilk argue that treaties have no force if a court or Congress argues they do not. Robert Kagan simply argues that nations favour international law when they are weak and as they become strong they discard it. He explains the threat this poses to the EU:

That is one reason Europeans were so adamant about preserving the universal application of the International Criminal Court. For the United States to demand immunity, a double standard for the powerful, is to

> *undermine the very principle Europeans are trying to establish – that all nations strong and weak, are equal under the law, and must abide by the law. If this principle can be flouted ... then what happens to the European Union, which depends for its existence on common obedience to the laws of Europe? If international law does not reign supreme, is Europe doomed to return to its past?*[21]

It is this ideology that led the US to pursue a policy of renouncing or setting aside a stack of treaties regulating armaments and the environment. The now familiar list includes the Kyoto protocol to control global warming, and various agreements and negotiations on biological weapons, missiles, AK-47-style small arms and nuclear weapons-testing. Opponents of the UN sneered at the work of its inspectors in Iraq and when the rest of the world declined to follow the US lead, the UN itself was declared a useless talking shop.

By going to war in Iraq without UN support, the US played into the hands of its enemies and lost the support of vital allies. For the first time since the Second World War, Germany opposed US policy. Even Mexico and Canada, two allies highly dependent on US economic and political ties, refused to go along. Turkey and Saudi Arabia, two vital allies of the US in the Middle East, unexpectedly blocked the US from using bases in their countries because there was no UN support. This lack of support contributed to the poor US control of the country after the fall of Baghdad and the subsequent continuing low-level war. The unexpected continuation of the war immediately became a major political headache for the White House.

So even in the supposedly tough-minded logic of the Bush team, lack of legal authority cost them dear. Indeed, as soon as the guerrilla war broke out in Iraq in the summer of 2003, the line from Washington changed. Suddenly the US wanted the UN in Iraq, and was urging it to do more. When Ayatollah Sistani insisted on a rapid transfer of power to Iraqis and on early elections, it was to the UN that the US turned. When it came to negotiating on weapons of mass destruction with Libya and Iran, it was UN inspectors operating under a UN treaty[12] that were called in. And in the case of Iran, it is European diplomacy and the economic opportunities with the EU that have produced some progress. In February 2004 President Bush gave a detailed speech on non-proliferation. The whole speech was focused on improving UN treaties, even though this was all to be done by other states. Bush is even finally adopting Greenpeace's position that nuclear power plants have a direct connection to nuclear weapons, something the West's nuclear industry refused to accept for decades.

This is not to say that the President had a change of heart. But, like every other nation, the US under George W. Bush turned to the UN when it was in trouble.

In Britain, by contrast, the Prime Minister has gone out of his way to reassert the doctrine of pre-emptive war. He continued to explicitly reject the system of non-interference in other people's countries established as a principle of international affairs after the devastating religious civil war in Europe that came to an end with the Treaty of Westphalia in 1648. Before looking briefly at the Afghan and Iraqi campaigns it is worth pausing a moment to reflect a little longer on the implications of deregulating international affairs. Tony Blair argued:

> *In a speech in Chicago in 1999, where I called for a doctrine*
> *of international community, where in certain clear circum-*

stances, we do intervene, even though we are not directly
threatened, I said this was not just to correct injustice, but also
because in an increasingly inter-dependent world, our self-
interest was allied to the interests of others; and seldom did
conflict in one region of the world not contaminate another. ...
So, for me, before September 11th, I was already reaching for
a different philosophy in international relations from a tradi-
tional one that has held sway since the treaty of Westphalia in
1648; namely that a country's internal affairs are for it and
you don't interfere unless it threatens you, or breaches a treaty,
or triggers an obligation of alliance ... All this was before
September 11th.[13]

Blair went on to argue that the combination of repressive regimes
with weapons of mass destruction and terrorism required the option
of pre-emptive interference and, if necessary, war. It is left to Henry
Kissinger, a man who carried out covert interventions in several Latin
American and south-east Asian states to put the case for old-style
Westphalian regulation:

The abrupt abandonment of the concept of national sover-
eignty...marked the advent of a new style of foreign policy
driven by domestic politics and the invocation of universal
moral slogans ... The new [post-Westphalian] discipline of
international law sought to inhibit repetition of the
religious wars of the seventeenth century during which
perhaps 40 per cent of the population of Central Europe
perished in the name of competing versions of universal
truth. Once the doctrine of universal intervention spreads

*and competing truths contest we risk entering a world
where, in G. K. Chesterton's phrase, virtue runs amok.*[14]

Virtue has indeed run amok. The US and the UK invented for themselves the unilateral right to enforce UN resolutions over Iraq. Then,
days before Blair's speech, the Bush administration carried out a coup
in Haiti. Bush announced on the White House lawn:

> *President Aristide resigned. He has left his country. The
> constitution of Haiti is working. There is an interim
> President, as per the constitution, in place. I have ordered
> the deployment of marines, as the leading element of an
> interim international force, to help bring order and
> stability to Haiti. I have done so in working with the inter-
> national community. This government believes it essential
> that Haiti have a hopeful future. This is the beginning of a
> new chapter in the country's history. I would urge the people
> of Haiti to reject violence, to give this break from the past a
> chance to work. And the United States is prepared to help.
> Thank you.*[15]

Jean-Baptiste Aristide had been elected overwhelmingly in Haiti's
first free election. He said that he was evicted at gunpoint. Former US
President Jimmy Carter confirmed that 'as you probably know, the
US Ambassador announced in advance that Aristide would either
leave in a Gulfstream aeroplane or a body bag.'[16] Listening to Blair
speak a few days later, I imagined for a moment that he would follow
the logic of his argument and dispatch a task force to liberate Haiti
from the US Marines. Where there is a case to intervene, for example

to suppress genocide, the conditions for legal, UN-based intervention are outlined in Chapter 3.

In Iraq the policy of setting aside the UN failed, and so too did the overreliance on smart weapons. This US approach does not have a track record of military success against terrorism, despite the short-term victories in Afghanistan and Iraq.

The US-led Afghan and Iraq campaigns were characterised by a belief that technology had changed age-old rules for ever. The claims were based on long-range precision weapons, electronic surveillance and target acquisition. First seen in the first Gulf War in 1991, the video footage of the missile reaching its target was a defining image of this approach. But in the Kosovo war of 1999, US warplanes blew up lots of Serb dummy tanks but barely a dozen real ones after months of bombing. Meanwhile, US intelligence told political leaders that the bombing had successfully smashed the Serb forces. In fact, success only came when traditional static strategic targets such as bridges and factories were attacked in the heart of the country. Then precision strikes worked, as the factories were easy to hit and precise bombing meant that civilian casualties could be minimised, preserving the humanitarian dimension of the war.

In Afghanistan a quick change of government was made in Kabul in early 2002 using smart missiles combined with commando forces working with the Northern Alliance – a loose grouping of local warlords previously defeated by the Taliban. The Taliban themselves had no modern weapons and quickly withdrew into the mountainous areas of south-east Afghanistan. A significant success was achieved in shutting the camps in which tens of thousands of Al-Qaeda fighters were trained. However, despite all the technology, neither Osama bin Laden nor Mullah Omar were accounted for and Al-Qaeda dispersed to continue the fight elsewhere. Subsequently a high-profile attempt to ambush Al-Qaeda in the mountains (Operation Anaconda) was itself comprehensively ambushed by Al-Qaeda.

The largest material change in Afghanistan has been the restarting of heroin production. Afghan production dominates the world market and, despite having an army on the ground, the US appears to have abandoned the war on drugs in order to win support from these warlords for their presence in the country. It may be the export of heroin to the West is itself a form of culturally destabilising warfare. I have heard stories that the heroin is packaged with labels saying 'only for Westerners'. True or not, what I find curious is that in conversations that I have had with British officials and conservative US newspaper editors I have found total denial that anyone in Afghanistan could be that sophisticated.

What is more, the division of US and allied forces into two separate commands[17] – one in south-east Afghanistan, answerable to US Central Command in Florida, the other in Kabul, answerable to NATO HQ in Brussels, breaks a fundamental principle of military operations, namely to have one commander. Consequently, while the Taliban and Al-Qaeda operate all over the country, those who are sworn to defeat them have deliberately disorganised themselves.

Now painstakingly, new efforts at nation-building and counter-insurgency are gathering pace, but they are traditional and low-tech approaches, long despised by the prophets of high-tech solutions. The US may find it far harder to leave than to get in. Even Hillary Clinton stated during a visit to Afghanistan that 'Taliban and Al-Qaeda forces are trying to wear down our staying power. I believe we need more troops to be able to provide that security.'[18]

Elections are expected in 2004 in Afghanistan, as is a renewed US offensive against bin Laden and allied forces. The outlook is uncertain with attacks on US and NATO forces increasing in 2004.

In Iraq the failures and consequences have been far greater than in Afghanistan. To list US failures in Iraq only briefly: there were no weapons of mass destruction; the Iraqis did not react with joy at being liberated; despite the prediction of a joyous welcome, many Iraqis fought and thousands died by their obsolete tanks under typically stupid orders from Saddam and atrocities committed by American soldiers at Abu Ghraib prison have shattered Iraqi and world confidence in the occupying forces, and undermined the American claim that it was liberating the Iraq from oppression. The war has played into Al-Qaeda's hands and the rule of international law has been damaged.

Perhaps most importantly, the lack of troops and planning helped create the bad political situation that the US now faces. As it is still unclear who caused this confusion, it is worth spelling out that the troops had no orders from President Bush and Donald Rumsfeld, as this document makes evident. The following extracts are taken from the official report by the US 3rd Infantry Division of the battle leading up to the fall of Baghdad.[19] The 3ID was the unit of some 18,000 soldiers that attacked up the west bank of the river Euphrates before driving east past Kerbala to Baghdad.

> *Higher headquarters needs to understand the immediate need and impact of the local police in the aftermath of war. The people wanted police and needed security. But we had no plan to accomplish this...*
>
> *Over the course of the war, many components of the national infrastructure especially electricity, water, and sewage*

utilities were damaged or destroyed. Much of the damage was as a result of looters and vandals in the immediate aftermath of regime fall and all would have to be rebuilt. This was most immediately apparent at Baghdad International Airport (BIA). Although this airport and numerous other objectives around Baghdad were specified, the division had been given no plan to occupy the city and transition to SASO [Stability and Support Operations]. Multiple military and interagency organizations vied to set up operations at BIA, but the [force] controlling BIA was too engaged in continuing combat operations to coordinate this adequately ...

Recommendation: If the final objective of an operation includes restoring utilities operations to an existing infrastructure, the tactical unit occupying the ground needs to understand the plan and organization that will execute the restoration of utilities within the goal of a safe and secure environment.

Additionally, higher-level plans and teams designated to rebuild civilian infrastructure need to be clearly established, made known to all units involved, and must be on the ground immediately. This is particularly important for non-military agencies charged with the political authority to make decisions with potentially long-ranging impact, such as designating which personnel we will recognize and work with.

In the first few months of the occupation, the US replaced its first civilian commander, General Jay Garner, with Jerry Bremer and then changed Bremer's line management from the office of the Defense Secretary to the White House. However, there was still no single US command in Iraq as the military and the Coalition Provisional

Authority had separate sanction from the government in Washington. US planning remains confused and aggressive.

From having no plan, the US first envisaged an administration lasting years, but in response to the insurgency and pressure from the Shia, this collapsed into a few months, with the intent of getting Iraq off the US news come election day. At the time of writing, the Bush administration has again run to the UN to try to mediate a deal with Shia leaders, who want immediate elections.

The reliance on precision and high-tech weaponry resulted in the President choosing a far smaller force than his army generals recommended. In February 2003, the Army Chief of Staff, Eric Shinseki, told members of the Senate Armed Services Committee: 'Something of the order of several hundred thousand soldiers are probably ... a figure that would be required. It takes a significant ground force presence to maintain a safe and secure environment, to ensure that people are fed, that water is distributed, all the normal responsibilities that go along with administering a situation like this.'[20]

The US force that took Baghdad was led by the army's 3rd Infantry Division and the Marines' 1st Division. This force won through the use of traditional heavy firepower and rapid-manoeuvre warfare as pioneered by the British Army in 1918 and later branded as the Blitzkrieg. They rapidly overcame Iraqi forces and occupied Baghdad, but, as is clear from the 3rd Infantry Division's own reports,[21] they relied on massive tanks and brute firepower to defeat and kill the Iraqis. These tank units had been insisted on by the army and Marine generals in the face of Rumsfeld's belief that, as in Afghanistan, precision weapons and lightly armed forces would win through. A week into the war the *Washington Post* reported: 'More than a dozen officers interviewed, including a senior officer in Iraq, said Rumsfeld took significant risks by leaving key units in the United States and Germany. That resulted in an invasion force that is too small, strung out, undersupplied and awaiting tens of thousands of reinforcements that will not get there for weeks.'[22]

In the reality of battle, a key US unit, the 101st Air Assault, was not used in its high-tech role but instead had to be used first to protect the forces going into Baghdad from being surrounded and then to carry out street battles in the towns and cities along the river Euphrates. The 3rd Infantry's vaunted Apache assault helicopters proved to be vulnerable to lightly armed Iraqi troops, in much the same way as medieval knights in armour fell to bows and arrows. Precision weapons were used in abundance and destroyed many Iraqi troops and equipment, but at the heart of the precision guidance system was also a very imprecise weapon – the cluster bomb – which many countries have tried to outlaw. Its use caused heavy civilian and military deaths and injuries, and these are still continuing as many unexploded bombs lie around waiting for someone to touch them. On many occasions precision weapons slammed into buildings where Saddam and his henchmen were supposed to be hiding, but without success because the weapons were useless without good intelligence.

Present US high-tech supremacy is really not much more than an update of the supremacy enjoyed at Omdurman or in Iraq during the interwar period. In the 1920s and 1930s British RAF biplanes dropped 250lb bombs into Iraqi and Afghan villages to ensure compliance, while in the nineteenth century the European empires were able to inflict huge casualties against people without firearms. For example, on 2 September 1898 British forces fought the army of the Islamic leader Mahdi Mohammed Ahmed at Omdurman, killing an estimated ten thousand for a few hundred British, primarily through the use of machine guns. Today, the third world has firearms and obsolete Western heavy weapons, and the West needs a higher level of technology to achieve much the same result.

The revolution in military affairs turned out very much like an old-fashioned blitzkrieg. The army's tank-heavy forces had been derided by Rumsfeld and many US officials and writers. They had been encouraged by seemingly easy victories in the first Iraq war and in the Balkans and believed that technology had given a new kind of power to the US. Having sold the public and themselves on the idea that a quick victory would be followed by rejoicing in the streets and a peaceful democratic Iraq, coalition leaders now found themselves engaged in an old-fashioned guerrilla war. The idea that the US could 'shock and awe' opponents into defeat with minimum force targeted at structural weaknesses in the enemy society has proved to be an illusion.

Militarily, the US lacked troops and planning for a guerrilla war. Rumsfeld rejected the US Army's demand for an occupation force of three hundred thousand that would have been able to secure Iraq's borders – so preventing foreign fighters entering the country and ensuring sufficient stability to enable prompt elections.

The assessment of the Iraq invasion as a strategic disaster stretches across the Atlantic and into the heart of conventional military thinking. Jeffrey Record of the US Army's Strategic Studies Institute observed: 'Of particular concern has been the conflation of Al-Qaeda and Saddam Hussein's Iraq as a single, undifferentiated terrorist threat. This was a strategic error of the first order because it ignored critical differences between the two in character, threat level, and susceptibility to US deterrence and military action. The result has been an unnecessary preventive war of choice against a deterred Iraq that has created a new front in the Middle East for Islamic terrorism and diverted attention and resources away from securing the American homeland against further assault by an undeterrable Al-Qaeda.'[23]

At the time of writing the number of US dead is approaching one thousand. It is worth noting that in 1920 British forces suffered 312 dead and killed 8,450 Arabs when suppressing the Arab insurrection[24] – a comparable ratio to the present war in Iraq, despite the high-tech, supposedly casualty-reducing weapons that now exist. In contrast to the British, whose 100,000-man force was mostly gone within a year, the US Army has now got almost half of its entire fighting power still committed to Iraq and unable to act elsewhere.

This criticism of the limitations of Pentagon planning under Rumsfeld must not be overstated. First, the US does enjoy an enormous superiority in the type of weapons used in major battles, and even in guerrilla war in towns for example, the use of infra-red night sights turns darkness from a condition favouring the ill-equipped guerrilla into one favouring the high-tech soldier. The two fundamental points, though, are (1) that the technology does not mean that politics, diplomacy, spies, bribes, deserts, cities, jungles and simple rifles can all be ignored, and (2) that the latest technology is a continuation of the industrialisation of warfare. In small wars against the weak, technology is powerful but, as is explained in the next chapter, it proved so powerfully self-destructive in the world wars of 1914–18 and 1939–45 that the victors attempted to outlaw war altogether. Back in Iraq, the US's supposedly overwhelming global military force is starting to look much like other ill-starred and badly planned military adventures in which old-fashioned fighting and politics become the tools of both sides.

Meanwhile, Iraq has become a focus of activity for those who want to kill Americans. The failure of strategy has been colossal. The present US government does not see the need for a change of strategy. The response of the Bush administration to the experience in Iraq is to order more high-tech equipment and a larger army. This is comparable to the inability of the British Army to see that their red coats made easy targets when fighting the American revolutionaries in the 1770s and the Boer farmers of South Africa one hundred years later. We look at such blunders with disdain and believe ourselves to be superior. Nowadays it is our whole societies that are the easy targets, and ordering more troops into the mountains of Afghanistan the equivalent of ordering fresh red coats. Only when the might of the British Empire faced defeat in South Africa did it finally abandon red for khaki, more than a century after its defeat in the woods of North America. No amount of new jargon such as 'asymmetric warfare' can substitute for a radical reassessment of threats and responses.

Before leaving the self-styled 'realist' advocates of unilateral US and British military power it is worth noting that they chose not to carry out campaigns against Pakistan or Saudi Arabia. The first was a military dictatorship supplying nuclear-weapons technology around the Islamic world and the second was the spiritual and financial home of Al Qaeda. Chicken? Blowhard? Naïve? All three.

Just as the hype over Enron concealed underlying industrial problems in US industry, so the collapse of the idea of high-tech US supremacy has distracted attention from the major threats to peace. The role of the US is just one part of the global dynamic. The US is unlikely to suffer a collapse as envisaged in Emmanuel Todd's *After the Empire*, nor, despite the apparent consensus in official Washington about the inevitability of US hegemony, is the US going to run the planet. Indeed recent experience indicates that the claims of many, such as Robert Kagan, that US military power alone would enable the US to dominate the world now look simply naïve. The perils of the Pentagon-led Enron-style rejection of regulations – in this case international law – are discussed in more detail in the following chapter.

Beyond the military weaknesses in US power are potential further problems in the US economy and society. There is an argument that the US federal budget is too much in deficit, the US public and US business too much in debt, and that the nation as a whole is so reliant on borrowing foreign capital that it (and with it the world) risks a major recession. In this event the far-flung US military and the regimes that it supports around the world will all, suddenly, look extremely overstretched.

At the same time as the international system is under threat from Washington's present policy direction, a new kind of war, global guerrilla war, has been started. This is a truly new aspect of globalisation and is discussed in detail below. These two immediate challenges have distracted attention from the previously existing critical issues. These can be listed as the political, economic, environmental and military aspects of globalisation and the age-old problems of international rivalry and poverty. International institutions from the World Bank to the UN face problems of lacking democratic legitimacy. International corporations seem uncontrollable. Environmental damage threatens the very air we breathe. The bombs and missiles of the Cold War still loom in the background.

The approaches to the new and old security problems being pursued by the major powers continue the overly military policies that became firmly established in the Cold War. This obsolete approach still dominates military spending and the way foreign policy is carried out. It is like thinking that all you need to police a city is a riot squad with no need for police on the beat, community development and crime prevention. If the riot squad is all that is available then it will be called out every night. Much of the debate about global security centres on the equivalent of ordering up more riot shields, while those who argue for a bit more community action and neighbourhood watch are still at the edges of decision-making.

We are constantly told that today's threats of fundamentalism, weapons of mass destruction and rogue states are greater than those of the past. It is even said that the Soviet leaders were rational and easy to deal with. At the time, of course, we were told that they were bent on world domination and had no respect for human life. Indeed the Soviet Union had murdered millions of its own citizens, had thousands of hydrogen bombs and a global system of support. Imagine a comparison in the commercial world. Visa and MasterCard dominate the credit card business. Let us assume MasterCard went bankrupt, and within a couple of years the management at Visa were asking for more money and complaining they were under threat from a few store cards such as Nectar. The share price would collapse and there would be a great management shake-up. But in foreign policy we are told that it is all too secret and too difficult for 'ordinary people' to understand, and so we must just follow along. What a load of nonsense.

Part one

The mess we're in

One

The Revolutions in Military Affairs

Self-destructive war and guerilla war in the global village

Admiral Cunningham: *'The United Nations will never be any use to anyone.'*

Winston Churchill: *'I don't know why you say that; it is the only hope of the world.'*

From the diaries of Lord Moran, Churchill's doctor, 22 September 1944[1]

During the last century the pace of technological change has produced two revolutions in warfare. The first was the industrialisation of warfare. The second has been the development of global guerrilla war. The first revolution produced the result that civilisation could destroy itself. Consequently, as *Wargames*, a movie about nuclear weapons, concluded, the only way to win is not to play. In this situation cooperation becomes a necessity and not an optional extra. The second revolution requires effective means of waging counter-guerrilla war at a global level. There are various approaches to the problem, the most effective requiring a strong sense of political agreement in the population as a whole. There is a military component, but there is no military solution to guerrilla warfare, or terrorism, as it is so often called. Each of these is discussed more fully in my description of the threats to peace in the next chapter, but here I just want to show the revolutionary change that occurred and the attempts to reinvent politics to keep up with the technology.

Live together or die together

It should be clear that developing global governance is not an optional extra. Creating a legitimate sheriff working for a legitimate village council is the great challenge of the age. The League of Nations was not created on a whim – because world leaders had nothing better to do once the First World War was over. It was created because the mass suffering, economic devastation and collapse of the Austro-Hungarian, German, Russian and Turkish empires made people realise that the industrialisation of warfare had made war too costly and self-destructive. In that war, the mass production of rapid-firing 'machine' guns, and the mass use of high-explosive artillery shells, poison gas and defensive barbed wire produced the horrific images of trench warfare that haunt the history of the period to this day.

The League failed when it did not stop Italy conquering Abyssinia, and because it lacked support from the US, the UK and France. The US's lack of support came about through its return to isolation, while Britain and France failed to live up to their own obligations on disarmament. In China, Japan and Germany liberal internationalists seeking justice at an international level found themselves ignored by the major powers and their credibility collapsed at home, allowing those who favoured using war as a political tool to take power once again.

People only think of the League these days because the Bush administration coined the phrase 'Abyssinia moment' to describe the potential for failure of the UN in Iraq and what President Bush called a deliberate decision to be irrelevant. It is worth noting that the Iraq/Abyssinia comparison does not work. Benito Mussolini did actually invade Abyssinia, and sanctions were ineffective in curbing him. Saddam Hussein was expelled from Kuwait by the United Nations in 1991 and in 2003 he did not actually have active weapons of mass destruction because the UN was effective in containing him.

The self-destructive nature of war was a lesson again learned the hard way in the Second World War – even before the invention of nuclear weapons. The war took the destructive power of industrialised warfare to new levels. Bomber aircraft and tanks were added to the major weapons and the power of weapons increased vastly. By 1945 there were bombers able to fly thousands of miles carrying tons of high explosives and larger and more destructive weapons of all kinds. Using these types of weapons alone large cities were almost completely destroyed. The human, material and financial cost was colossal. More than fifty million people were killed.

At the height of the war, Winston Churchill and Franklin D. Roosevelt made a declaration of common principles. It was August 1941; the US was not in the war because most of the Republican Party did not want to get involved.

The Atlantic Charter was issued in a meeting between the two leaders at sea off Canada. Churchill had arrived aboard HMS *Prince of Wales*, only recently repaired after being damaged in the battle to sink the Nazi battleship *Bismarck*.

The summer of 1941 was probably the lowest point of European civilisation since the Dark Ages, at the end of the Roman Empire. Adolf Hitler was master of Europe and had attacked the Soviet Union six weeks earlier. Millions of Russian troops had already been killed or surrendered and the Panzers were expected to crush Russia in a few weeks – the Nazi defeat at Stalingrad was far in the future. Churchill and Roosevelt expected that if the Soviets collapsed then all of Hitler's attention would be turned on Britain, while in the Far East, Japanese armies were already moving into Indochina.

What did Churchill and Roosevelt say? Did they declare that in future they wanted the right to wage pre-emptive war when they even suspected a threat – as President Bush and Prime Minister Blair declared after 9/11? Did they claim that, the League having failed, unilateral actions were the way of the future? No. In the Atlantic Charter[2] they outlined a future where, for realistic as well as spiritual reasons, nations must renounce the use of force, and outlined a world of free trade, social security and labour rights. The Atlantic Charter is listed as the first 'basic' or 'antecedent' document in the archives of both the UN and of NATO.

It is easy to be cynical about such declarations, but consider Nelson Mandela's reaction:

> *Change was in the air in the 1940s.* The Atlantic Charter of 1941, *signed by Roosevelt and Churchill, reaffirmed faith in the dignity of each human being and propagated a host of democratic principles. Some in the West saw the charter as empty promises, but not those of us in Africa. Inspired by the Atlantic Charter and the fight of the Allies against tyranny and oppression, the ANC created its own charter, called African Claims, which called for full citi-*

zenship for all Africans, the right to buy land and repeal of all discriminatory legislation.[3]

The future British Prime Minister, Clement Attlee, was at the time Churchill's deputy. He recalled in his memoirs:

I got a telephone call at two o'clock in the morning from the ship where Winston and Roosevelt were meeting in Placentia Bay, Newfoundland. I was still up – never got to bed very early. I called a Cabinet at three o'clock in the morning, and by four we were able to send our reply with a new clause on social security which we wanted among Allied aims. Peter Fraser [the Australian Prime Minister] was helpful on that.[4]

It is interesting to note in passing how a British Prime Minister called home from his meeting with the US President to ensure that the full Cabinet approved the statement he was about to make. It is hard to imagine this happening now in a system where the Prime Minister has taken ever more unilateral power.

The Atlantic Charter August 1941 (emphasis added)

- The President of the United States of America and the Prime Minister, Mr. Churchill, representing His Majesty's Government in the United Kingdom, being met together, deem it right to make known certain common principles in the national policies of their respective countries on which they base their hopes for a better future for the world.
- FIRST, their countries seek no aggrandizement, territorial or other;

- SECOND, they desire to see no territorial changes that do not accord with the freely expressed wishes of the peoples concerned;
- THIRD, they respect **the right of all peoples to choose the form of government under which they will live**; and they wish to see sovereign rights and self-government restored to those who have been forcibly deprived of them;
- FOURTH, they will endeavor, with due respect for their existing obligations, to further the enjoyment by all States, great or small, victor or vanquished, of **access, on equal terms, to the trade and to the raw materials** of the world which are needed for their economic prosperity;
- FIFTH, they desire to bring about the fullest collaboration between all nations in the economic field with the **object of securing, for all, improved labor standards, economic adjustment and social security**;
- SIXTH, after the final destruction of the Nazi tyranny, they hope to see established a peace which will afford to all nations the means of dwelling in safety within their own boundaries, and which will afford assurance that all **the men in all the lands may live out their lives in freedom from fear and want**;
- SEVENTH, such a peace should enable all men to traverse the high seas and oceans without hindrance;
- EIGHTH, they believe that **all of the nations of the world, for realistic as well as spiritual reasons, must come to the abandonment of the use of force**. Since no future peace can be maintained if land, sea or air armaments continue to be employed by nations which threaten, or may threaten, aggression outside of their frontiers, they believe, pending the establishment of a wider and permanent system of general security, that the disarmament of

such nations is essential. They **will likewise aid and encourage all other practicable measures which will lighten for peace-loving peoples the crushing burden of armaments**.

Franklin D. Roosevelt, Winston S. Churchill

Are we expected to believe that Osama bin Laden, Saddam and Kim Jong Il of North Korea were and are such great threats that we must abandon the values used to beat Hitler?

Richard Perle, a cheerleader for American conservatives, and variously dubbed 'Darth Vader' and 'the Prince of Darkness', wagged his finger at me in a TV debate and told me that the US did not fight the Second World War to create the UN. Perle is wrong about the UN. The war was not just fought to create the UN; it was fought by the UN. On 1 January 1942, three weeks after the Japanese attack at Pearl Harbor, there was a 'Declaration by United Nations' from twenty-six countries, some small and far from the war, some under Nazi occupation and some leading the war effort.

Declaration by United Nations, January 1942

A Joint Declaration by the United States, the United Kingdom, the Union of Soviet Socialist Republics, China, Australia, Belgium, Canada, Costa Rica, Cuba, Czechoslovakia, Dominican Republic, El Salvador, Greece, Guatemala, Haiti, Honduras, India, Luxembourg, The Netherlands, New Zealand, Nicaragua, Norway, Panama, Poland, South Africa, Yugoslavia

The Governments signatory hereto,

Having subscribed to a common program of purposes and principles embodied in the Joint Declaration of the President of the United States of America and the Prime Minister of the United Kingdom of Great Britain and Northern Ireland dated August 14, 1941, known as the Atlantic Charter.

Being convinced that complete victory over their enemies is essential to defend life, liberty, independence and religious freedom, and to preserve human rights and justice in their own lands as well as in other lands, and that they are now engaged in a common struggle against savage and brutal forces seeking to subjugate the world,

DECLARE:

1. Each Government pledges itself to employ its full resources, military or economic, against those members of the Tripartite Pact: and its adherents with which such government is at war.

2. Each Government pledges itself to cooperate with the Governments signatory hereto and not to make a separate armistice or peace with the enemies.

The foregoing declaration may be adhered to by other nations which are, or which may be, rendering material assistance and contributions in the struggle for victory over Hitlerism.

Done at Washington, January First, 1942

Thereafter, the US President's own statements and official documents amongst the United Nations continuously referred to allied forces as part of United Nations forces. For example, the US Air Force chronology of the Second World War records: 'TUESDAY, 17 MARCH 1942 SOUTHWEST PACIFIC AREA (5th Air Force): General Douglas MacArthur arrives in Australia to assume command of United Nations forces in the SWPA.'[5] In October 1942 President Roosevelt broadcast:

> *In expanding our shipping, we have had to enlist many thousands of men for our merchant marine. These men are serving magnificently. They are risking their lives every hour so that guns and tanks and planes and ammunition and food may be carried to the heroic defenders of Stalingrad and to all the United Nations' forces all over the world.*[6]

Countless official documents and press stories from the Second World War refer to the role of UN forces in fighting the war and administering the liberated territories. A selection is given in Appendix I.

Extracts from three key documents referring to the UN are given here. These are the instructions given to General Dwight D. Eisenhower to liberate Europe; his own message to troops on D-Day; and the final surrender document of Nazi Germany.

Directive to Supreme Commander
Allied Expeditionary Force (emphasis added)

Issued February 12, 1944, by the Anglo-American Combined Chiefs of Staff, this directive formally authorized General Dwight

D. Eisenhower to implement the invasion plans of Operation Overlord.

1. You are hereby designated as Supreme Allied Commander of the forces placed under your orders for operations for liberation of Europe from Germans. Your title will be Supreme Commander Allied Expeditionary Force.
2. Task. **You will enter the continent of Europe and, in conjunction with the other United Nations, undertake operations aimed at the heart of Germany and the destruction of her armed forces.** The date for entering the Continent is the month of May, 1944. After adequate Channel ports have been secured, exploitation will be directed towards securing an area that will facilitate both ground and air operations against the enemy.

* * *

7. **Relationship to United Nations Forces in other areas.** Responsibility will rest with the Combined Chiefs of Staff for supplying information relating to operations of the Forces of the U.S.S.R. for your guidance in timing your operations. It is understood that the Soviet Forces will launch an offensive at about same time as OVERLORD with the object of preventing the German forces from transferring from the Eastern to the Western front. The Allied Commander in Chief, Mediterranean Theater, will conduct operations designed to assist your operation, including the launching of an attack against the south of France at about the same time as OVERLORD.

General Eisenhower made specific reference to the United Nations in his address to the troops of the invasion force, read out to them by their officers on the ship's public-address system as they waited, tense and seasick, for the assault to begin. In real life this is what the people portrayed in films such as *Saving Private Ryan* and *The Longest Day* would have heard.

The Times reported D-Day as a landing by the armies of the United Nations and stated in an editorial that 'four years after the rescue at Dunkirk of that gallant defeated army without which nucleus the forces of liberation could never have been rebuilt, the United Nations returned yesterday to the soil of France.' *The Times* made more than 3,500 references to the United Nations in its news reports, features and editorials between the founding declaration in January 1942 and the end of the Second World War in August 1945.

Message from General Eisenhower (emphasis added)

SUPREME HEADQUARTERS ALLIED EXPEDITIONARY FORCE

Soldiers, Sailors and Airmen of the Allied Expeditionary Force!

You are about to embark upon the Great Crusade, toward which we have striven these many months. The eyes of liberty -oving people everywhere march with you. In company with our brave Allies and brothers in arms on other Fronts, you will bring about the destruction of the German war machine, the elimination of Nazi tyranny over the oppressed peoples of Europe, and security for ourselves in a free world.

Your task will not be an easy one. Your enemy is well trained, well equipped and battle hardened. He will fight savagely.

But this is the year 1944! Much has happened since the Nazi triumphs of 1940–41. **The United Nations have inflicted upon the Germans great defeats, in open battle, man to man**. Our air offensive has seriously reduced their strength in the air and their capacity to wage war on the ground. Our Home Fronts have given us an overwhelming superiority in weapons and munitions of war, and placed at our disposal great reserves of trained fighting men. The tide has turned! The free men of the world are marching together to Victory!

I have full confidence in your courage and devotion to duty and skill in battle. We will accept nothing less than full Victory! Good luck! And let us beseech the blessing of Almighty God upon this great and noble undertaking.

General Dwight D. Eisenhower
Order of the Day
June 6, 1944

At the end of the war in Europe, the Nazi High Command surrendered. They were flown to Eisenhower's headquarters in Reims, France, on 7 May 1945. Article IV of the surrender document emphasises the authority of the UN over Germany: 'This Act of Military Surrender is without prejudice to, and will be superseded by, any general instrument of surrender imposed by, or on behalf of, the United Nations and applicable to Germany and the German Armed Forces as a whole.' It should also be mentioned that the original outline of the principles for a new world were outlined by Roosevelt in his 'Four Freedoms' speech in January 1941, which laid out the hope for 'a world founded on four essential human freedoms'. These were freedom of speech and expression; freedom of religion, freedom from want and freedom from fear.

Now, it is clear that at this time the UN was an idea that was to be implemented by the countries that were fighting the war – the United Nations – after the victory, although even while the fighting continued the United Nations Rehabilitation and Relief Administration had been created to provided humanitarian assistance in the liberated areas. The famous conferences at Dumbarton Oaks and Bretton Woods on which created the framework for postwar cooperation were officially United Nations conferences. Article III of the UN Charter makes clear that the meeting in San Fransico in 1945 that created the Charter was itself a UN conference on international organisation. The link between the wartime United Nations and the post war organisation is unambiguous.

Neither the Four Freedoms nor the Atlantic Charter nor the declaration of 1 January 1942 was utopian. They reflected strongly held national interests and hard political calculation. Nevertheless, the Atlantic Charter and the UN reflected a realistic understanding that some kind of international system was needed and, what is more, it reflected the understanding of politicians that this is what people around the world understood and also wanted.

The main point to understand is that the desire to build the UN was based on hard calculated analysis that in order to survive, civilisation needed to develop a global system of security. Both Churchill and Roosevelt had lived through the collapse of the first such attempt in US President Woodrow Wilson's League of Nations and they were determined not to give up. Roosevelt ordered the creation of a major effort within the State Department to work out the structures of a postwar world in conjunction with the other united nations. The story of this effort has recently been told in the highly readable book *FDR and the Creation of the U.N.* by Townsend Hoopes and Douglas Brinkley.[7]

In placing the UN in its rightful historical place as the banner under which nations fought, we should not exaggerate the idealism of the time. I spoke to a British admiral who served as a midshipman aboard HMS *Prince of Wales* during the meeting between Roosevelt and Churchill. He told me that for him and his shipmates the real point was that Churchill had failed to get America into the war, and they had neither known nor cared about any declarations.

I have gone out of my way to make this argument because it is all too common to assume that the history of the Second World War belongs to conservative Hobbesian political thinking. Indeed, President Bush's 'Axis of Evil' speech was a deliberate attempt to associate his war on terror with the war against the original Axis of Nazi Germany, Fascist Italy and imperial Japan in the Second World War. Conservative commentators, especially in the US Republican Party, never tire of warning of the dangers of appeasement, as if this was the only history class they ever attended. Forgotten is the US Republican refusal to back the League of Nations, or to support the UN in the first place, and of course also cast aside is the role of the UN in rallying and unifying allied forces in the war effort.

Ignoring the wartime history of the UN makes it easier to discard the UN today. The case for letting anarchy reign was put bluntly by John Bolton in a speech to the conservative/libertarian Federalist Society:[8]

Now significantly, UN Secretary Kofi Annan has specifi-
cally said, 'Unless the Security Council is restored to its
pre-eminent position as the sole source of legitimacy on the
use of force, we are on a dangerous path to anarchy.' These
sorts of statements, which the Secretary General and others
have made over the past several years, are unsupported by
over 50 years of experience with the UN Charter's
operation. The case of Kosovo and the previous administra-
tion alone proves this point.

Though we should note that Bolton is careful to base his argument
on the operation of the Charter, rather than on its text. This is the
exact opposite of the way the Federalist Society members argue that
the US Constitution should be interpreted only in the original and
not as it has been applied.

After 1945 the imperative to create a new international system was
reinforced by the invention of atomic weapons and, from the early
1950s, by hydrogen or thermonuclear weapons. As Churchill put it
in July 1945:[9] 'Fire was the first discovery, this is the second.' These
arms reinforced the new reality, that civilisation can self-destruct
through war, and this was an underlying theme throughout the
confrontation between the West and the Soviet Union from the late
1940s to the late 1980s.

It was the great physicist Albert Einstein who politely pointed out
that 'the unleashed power of the atom has changed everything except
our modes of thinking.'[10] It is fashionable amongst military strategists
to talk of the latest in high-tech precision weapons and computers as
having created a revolution in military affairs but, significant though
these weapons are, they have had a trivial impact compared to the

self-destructive nature of the industrialisation of warfare between 1914 and 1945, culminating in the creation of weapons of mass destruction. As Churchill remarked:

> If it were proved that a very large number of hydrogen explosives could, in their cumulative effect, be detrimental to the health or even the life of the whole human race (without a need for a declaration of war upon itself), the effect would certainly afford a new common interest between all men rising above their military, political or even ideological differences.[11]

Alongside discussions around the UN on peace and security there was a much wider discussion during the Cold War about how to adjust to the new reality and, for those who are interested, the Swedish government's Palme Commission report on common security remains a key study. Written in 1982 at the height of the later Cold War, it lays out the new logic of an interdependent world.

> We are totally agreed that there is no such thing as a nuclear war that can be won. An all-out nuclear war would mean unprecedented destruction, maybe the extinction of the human species. A so-called limited nuclear war would almost inevitably develop into total nuclear conflagration. Different war-fighting doctrines are therefore a grave threat to humanity. The doctrine of deterrence offers very fragile protection indeed against the horrors of nuclear war.
>
> It is therefore of paramount importance to replace the doctrine of mutual deterrence. Our alternative is common

security. There can be no hope for victory in a nuclear war,
the two sides would be united in suffering and destruction.
They can survive only together. They must achieve security
not against the adversary but together with him.
International security must rest on a commitment to joint
survival rather than on a threat of mutual destruction.

This revolution in human circumstances is as fundamental to human understanding of our place in the world as was the Copernican revolution of the early modern era. Nicholas Copernicus first suggested that the Earth revolved around the Sun, and that the Earth was not the centre of the universe. It was more than a century before his ideas took hold and there was no looming death penalty hanging over the world for a failure to understand the new ideas. What we might call the Einsteinian revolution risks our destroying ourselves before we figure out a way to live together.

One of the most noted sceptics of this view is Professor Colin Gray, an intellectual leader for many of those who oppose treaties controlling weapons. Gray derides those who warn of 'Apocalypse Soon', and recommends that strong nuclear and other forces are all that are needed. And yet, almost in passing, even Gray concedes the argument. He observes: '"One world or none" is not the range of choice before humankind – which is fortunate, since in that case the smart money would have to be on "none".'[12] As he concludes his explanation of the other options he observes that 'nuclear pessimism tends to be a self-negating prophecy. The lesson, one could argue, is that American and Soviet guardians of the nuclear peace were so aware of the scale of the danger that the danger remained strictly hypothetical.'[13] This is where he ends up contradicting himself by arguing that because the 'American and Soviet guardians' were aware that the choice was indeed 'One world or none' they refrained from nuclear war and chose coexistence. Others believe that we survived the Cold War confrontation more by luck than good judgement.[14] The problem of managing a world with weapons of mass destruction is discussed in Chapter 8.

By the 1970s it was also becoming clear that the impact of industry on the environment through global warming and the destruction of the ozone layer could also have a suicidal impact on humanity. It was only at the end of the twentieth century that the evidence became so overwhelming that a UN conference agreed the Kyoto protocol to cut down emissions of the gases, mostly from cars, that cause global warming.

New technologies may bring even greater power of destruction than nuclear weapons, continuing the pattern of the last couple of hundred years. For example genetic engineering conjures up the idea of bio-weapons targeted at specific ethnic groups. Nanotechnology, the Prince of Wales warns us, may turn the world into grey sludge as it is devoured by robots as small as bacteria. Cyber-warfare may create computer viruses that crash the banking system, the nation's defences or the controls of nuclear power plants.

It is easy to be paralysed by paranoia. But the closer these threats are to home and the more difficult they are to face up to, the more it is necessary to choose between building social consensus as a means of minimising and isolating the number of people interested in making such attacks.

The creation of the interconnected reality – what was often called the 'global village' in the 1960s and 1970s – is the most significant development that took place in the twentieth century. It is a change that has come to be called globalisation. Francis Fukuyama famously suggested that the end of communism and the triumph of liberal democracy marked the 'end of history'. But globalisation marks not the end of history but the beginning of a unified human story. The way we are going it will be a short story with a tragic ending.

Guerrilla war in the global village

The world was first shrunk to village size by missiles and telecommunications, which were built by national governments and large corporations. Now small violent groups are finding ways to fight globally in what is called international terrorism. I prefer the term 'strategic' or 'global guerrilla war'. The events of 9/11 showed how vulnerable the vital organs of centralised industrial society are to the military equivalent of the flick knife. For those who noticed, Chernobyl and then the Provisional IRA attacks on the Baltic Exchange and Canary Wharf in London provided early examples of this kind of strategic vulnerability.

I use the word 'guerrilla' or the phrase 'armed groups' rather than 'terrorist'. This is not because I have any sympathy with bin Laden and his associates but because 'terrorist' is an emotive and unclear word. Some people have been members of terrorist groups and gone on to lead democratic nations. Members of the Irgun wing of the Zionist movement and parts of the South African ANC come to mind. Other people in and out of government have perpetrated terrible acts against civilians and neither deserved nor received political rehabilitation. More neutral words such as 'guerrilla' make things clearer. The problem is too serious to call people names.

11 September was the first successful attack by a guerrilla force on a major power in modern history. It was the first time a Western power centre has been attacked since European states began the colonial period with the conquests of America, Africa, Australasia and much of Asia. (The Japanese attack on Pearl Harbor only reached a far outpost of US power.) We used to think of the dangers of invasion and death and destruction as occurring in war between armies fighting across borders or in civil wars inside particular countries. The attacks of 9/11 should be seen as marking a new kind of war, one where stateless groups can carry out crippling attacks almost anywhere. This new form of warfare is a consequence of globalisation and especially of the concentrated – large is beautiful – forms of organisation that have been created in modern, Western-style society. This new form of war lacks groups of troops and lines of battle. It is far more like a guerrilla war on a global scale. In a world that globalisation has shrunk into the proverbial village, 9/11 ushers in a new era: civil war in the Global Village.

One significant series of attacks were carried out by the Provisional IRA in the mid-1990s. The IRA attacked the financial heart of the City of London with truck bombs. Two of these used against the Canary Wharf and Baltic Exchange office blocks caused billions of pounds of damage. More importantly, many City leaders and former British government officials believe that the attacks produced a radical change in the policies pursued in Ireland by John Major's Conservative government. The change occurred because City leaders and government officials believed that many financial institutions would abandon London for Frankfurt in an attempt to find a physically and psychologically secure working environment. This in turn would have a devastating effect on the UK economy as a whole which relies heavily upon so-called 'invisible' earnings from the financial-services industry. Although the IRA demands and the entire Northern Ireland problem are provincial in comparison to the global issues raised by 9/11 and subsequent events, they do indicate the potential for carrying out strategic attacks by small groups using home-made weapons. Both these IRA attacks can be called strategic, not because of the type of weapons that they used, but because the effects of the attacks impacted vital organs of the society that was attacked.

Most individual acts of what we have come to call terrorism have killed or held hostage a few dozen people with the objective of shock and news coverage. The attacks of 11 September included the psychological element but also physically destroyed centres of US power and were timed to hurt the US economy. The US has put the economic cost at $639 billion. The scale of the attacks on centres of power makes it appropriate to call them strategic.

Notes from the Al-Qaeda classrooms of Afghanistan reveal an imaginative range of other targets and weapons. No one can be sure how many more attacks are planned. Future attacks might use nuclear, chemical or biological weapons.[15] Al-Qaeda operates globally; its supporters originated in and operate from dozens of countries. Some are from within Western societies, including those such as the American John Walker and the Briton Richard Read, who were attracted to its cause from a non-Islamic background. It has or had sections responsible for finance, weapons procurement, propaganda, recruitment, training and communications. The attacks demonstrated the sophistication of planning and execution that would normally be associated with a developed state apparatus. Al-Qaeda functions or functioned not only in the US but also in many parts of Europe, the Middle East and Asia. A quick survey of the websites of major newspapers shows how many countries the network is publicly known to operate in, and the wide variety of actions it has taken or might take in the future. No one can know how many other groups and governments will see this new form of warfare as a means of responding to Western and especially US conventional military power.

In the period since 9/11 there has been a succession of attacks attributed to Al-Qaeda and like-minded groups. They mostly have an element of strategic impact, rather than merely a horrific act of destruction. The cases in India, Morocco, Kenya, Saudi Arabia and Indonesia all involved disgusting loss of life but in most cases they also had an economic and social impact.

The economic impact has resulted from attacking luxury business and tourist targets in Morocco, Kenya, Indonesia and Turkey. These attacks hurt one of the main sources of foreign currency in these states, as fewer people wish to go as tourists to states where they may be blown up. This in turn weakens the economy and the sense that the national ruling elite is in control. At the same time the social impact is intended to demonstrate an attack against the luxurious lifestyle of the visitors in contrast to the impoverished and necessarily ascetic life of the millions of other people in the surrounding cities.

With blows against the rich, decadent and anti-Islamic elites it appears that the attackers are aiming to build wider popular support for their cause. There can indeed be little success for a movement intent on leading the vanguard of a revived and purified Islam if it does not create an army of followers, an analysis made very usefully in Jason Burke's book on the movement.[16] How successful these attacks are at destabilising regimes and mobilising populations is not yet clear. Such developments take time. What is clear is that the forces used, even as suicide attackers, are very small. Western strategists such as Harlan Ullman are committed to achieving strategic change with minimal force. Ironically, the suicide attackers exemplify that approach. In terms of Western forces, the attackers are no more than squads of special-forces troops. But the consequences of their actions are, in response to rumours of their having anti-aircraft missiles, the cancellation of all commercial airline flights to a country; in response to the destruction of a crowded disco, the collapse of a tourist industry.

Following 9/11 the US changed its national strategy, sank billions into civilian defence, disrupted the habits of countless airline passengers, and produced an industry of people thinking up what Al Qaeda might do next. The Western military spends a lot of time discussing the idea that it is essential to get inside the enemy general's decision cycle, making him change his plans and start ordering and counter-ordering his troops. So far Al-Qaeda seems to have done this quite successfully. How successful this movement may become, and indeed whether it can actually win, is discussed in Chapter 2. For now I want to establish that this form of warfare is new and revolutionary in its impact. In the language of the military it requires a global strategy of counter-guerrilla warfare.

Two

Apocalypse soon?
Could Al-Qaeda win?

How can we persuade the young generation to cast aside the
culture of violence when they know that it is on the threat
of extreme violence that we rely for security?
Joseph Rotblat, Nobel Peace Prize laureate 1995

War is organised violence between countries. Organised violence
inside countries is civil war. Nowadays, other phrases such as 'armed
conflict' or 'peace enforcement' are sometimes used.

Peace is living without violence and the fear of violence. But there are
other threats to our security, including poverty, homelessness and forced
migration. These different forms of destitution are huge problems in
themselves but are also important causes and results of violence.

We are all afraid sometimes. We may even have been attacked or
had our homes invaded by burglars. We no more want our country
broken into than our homes and we are concerned if it happens
elsewhere, partly out of compassion for those attacked and partly out
of concern that we may be next.

Thinking about international relations in personal terms is not as simple minded as you might think. Some experts, including Henry Kissinger, think of countries as individual people with their own personalities. In fact in law, nations are mostly treated as if they were a legal person. In the days of kings and emperors, territory and the people living there were the legal property of the monarch. In the phrase of the French King Louis XIV: 'I am the state.'

It is also useful to think in personal terms because, for many people, war and violence do affect them all too personally, as victims, soldiers or just as shocked bystanders watching on TV. Gun crime is a now feature of most societies. A nuclear missile can be part of some diplomatic play between nations at the UN, but it could also land on your head. A terrorist bomb might hit our local shopping centre as well as an army base overseas. There is also a connection between the way we behave as a nation in the world and the way we expect people in our own country to behave. Nobel Peace Prize winner Professor Sir Joseph Rotblat explains:

> *I am particularly concerned about the effect on the young generation. We all crave a world of peace, a world of equity. We all want to nurture in the young generation the much-heralded 'culture of peace'. But how can we talk about a culture of peace if that peace is predicated on the existence of weapons of mass destruction? How can we persuade the young generation to cast aside the culture of violence when they know that it is on the threat of extreme violence that we rely for security?*

Rotblat's observation deserves to be carefully considered by all those engaged in the vital work to combat violence on our streets. On the other hand, if the world out there is a vicious place, should we steel ourselves to commit extreme violence to protect our children and ourselves? Can what we do to protect ourselves be seen as a potential threat to someone else? These are some of the hard choices that have to be made when considering issues of war and peace.

Thinking about international affairs in personal terms also concentrates the mind on the job faced by real-life decision-makers in Downing Street, Washington or at the United Nations. What do you actually do if you have the responsibility for taking decisions on national security? If you arm yourself with nuclear weapons are you prepared to use them, to accept responsibility for the death and devastation caused? Or do you believe that by having them we never have to use them, that all we have to do is bluff? But we should not take the comparison between individuals and nations too far. Nations are huge entities with millions of people. There are real differences even in the way we think about violence. Deciding that other people should go out and kill and destroy for us or for a political leader is very different from actually doing it ourselves. In some ways it is easier to have others do it, and easier to let emotions rip if we do not ourselves feel the consequences. It is also easier not to think through the complexity of real decision-making.

Invasion, Death, Destruction, Destitution: these are the threats that people have faced since warfare was invented. They are also the means by which societies have enriched and empowered themselves at the expense of others. Destitution is often a result of natural acts such as crop failure or the weather, but in today's world it is mostly a product of the inequalities of wealth and power and the failure of the strong to meet the challenges laid out in Franklin D. Roosevelt's Four Freedoms, in the Atlantic Charter and in UN documents ever since.[2]

The threat of invasion

Today there is no threat of invasion to Britain and Continental

Europe. The armed forces of Britain and the other countries of Europe along with part of those of the United States are deeply entwined with each other in the organisations of the European Union and NATO. Generals command troops from other EU countries. Troops from Britain, France and Germany serve side by side in the Balkans. Treaties allow all the countries of Europe, including Russia as far as the Ural mountains, to inspect each other's armed forces. Even if the people of one Western country decided one day to attack another, there would be years of warning while they untangled themselves from these arrangements.

Defence Expenditures in 2001 in millions of US dollars

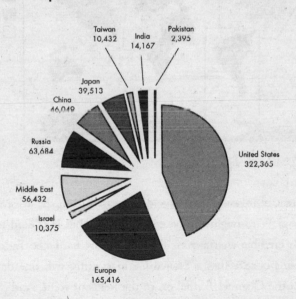

Taiwan
10,432

India
14,167

Pakistan
2,395

Japan
39,513

China
46,048

Russia
63,684

Middle East
56,432

Israel
10,375

Europe
165,416

United States
322,365

*Belgium, Czech Republic, Denmark, France, Germany, Greece, Hungary, Italy, Luxembourg, Netherlands, Norway (non-EU), Poland, Portugal, Spain, Turkey (non-EU), United Kingdom
**including Egypt, Iran, Iraq, Saudi Arabia, Syria
SOURCE: Military Balance 2002–2003, vol. 102.

This state of affairs has not existed before at any time since the fall of the Roman Empire 1,500 years ago. Indeed the United States with its allies in the EU and NATO has vast military supremacy against all other countries put together and the US policy still divides the world up into military sectors assigned to the responsibility of a general, each of whom has the job of 'shaping' his region of the world to suit US interests.

United States Military Commands

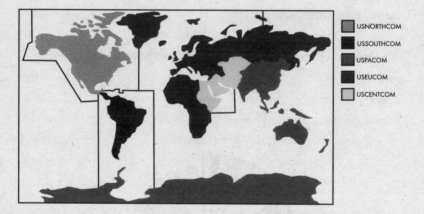

SOURCE: www.army.mil/organization

The threat of invasion may have disappeared from the West, but for how long? Who might the potential enemies be? It is hard to come up with credible alternatives. Even the most hardened Eurosceptic would not believe that a Franco-German army will one day burst through the Channel Tunnel on to the fields of Kent. And even the most paranoid anti-American would not conceive of a US attack on Britain in some far-fetched future scenario. The peoples of the Arab world have no industry with which to build major weapons and are divided among themselves and the Russians have too many problems of their own to worry about invading us, although Russian politicians remain concerned that NATO is now carrying out military exercises on its borders. Nevertheless in Asia, particularly, potential and growing rivalries between countries could produce war involving huge destruction, even if the likelihood of armies crossing frontiers and occupying territory is low.

But, while the threat of invasion does not exist for the West, this is not the case for other countries. The US, NATO and the EU are all committed to building bigger and better armed forces that can reach far and wide across the world. These rapid-reaction forces are at present almost exclusively Western. They have various purposes including securing vital Western interests such as supplies of raw materials, humanitarian intervention and helping allies. These will be discussed when we look at responses to threats. For now, I just want to establish that to some countries these forces can be seen as representing a threat of invasion. President Bush's strategy of pre-empting potential attacks has highlighted these trends.

The Bush administration has amplified the most negative aspects of US international policy – go-it-alone militarist solutions that discount the role of international law. The contrast and also the underlying problem in Washington's approach to the world were well illustrated in the following report from the US government radio station, Voice of America:

> *Many observers agree that pre-emption is not a new policy. But a distinction must be made, says retired US Army General William Odom, Director of National Security Studies at the Hudson Institute. He notes the new standard says preventive*

war can be carried out even if there is uncertainty as to the enemy's intentions or targets. Furthermore, General Odom argues that a superior military force in and of itself negates the need for pre-emptive military strikes. 'Today, it seems to me, because the United States has so much power, and there is no country capable of doing any kind of substantial damage to us, that the argument for pre-emptive strikes is very weak.' [3]

Richard Perle and David Frum have a new book, *An End to Evil*,[4] which explains how to win the war on terror. Frum is the Bush adviser credited with inventing the 'Axis of Evil' line. They reassert the policy of pre-emption even after the failure to find WMD in Iraq:

It was never quite clear how 'imminent' would have been imminent to suit these critics. Should we have waited until one month before Saddam got a nuclear bomb or weaponised smallpox? One week? The intelligence services are very human, imperfect institutions. If we wait to protect ourselves until the CIA determines that it is five minutes to midnight, we will run the ugly risk of discovering that we have waited too long. Certainly we waited too long in the case of Osama bin Laden.

The message from Perle and Frum is clear: if we even think there is a threat we will attack.

The threat of death and destruction

Actual invasion may no longer exist as a threat to the West, but the threat of death and destruction is real, not just in the West but in other parts of the world. The world wars of 1914–18 and 1939–45 brought the Industrial Revolution to the battlefield with horrible consequences including poisonous chemicals fired in artillery shells. Since then, new technologies have magnified the potential for destruction. By the 1950s three inventions – the long-range bomber, the long-range missile and nuclear weapons – changed the way force could be used and made the world a much smaller place. Put together, these weapons created the ability to attack across continents in a few hours or, with missiles, a few minutes. Nuclear weapons combined with a missile meant that a single weapon could destroy entire cities with blast, heat and radiation. A single hydrogen bomb could produce an explosion equivalent to several million tons of normal high explosive. Or to put it another way: one nuclear bomb had as much explosive power as all the high explosive used between 1939 and 1945.

These great stocks of weapons of mass destruction have never been used, but in the meantime other weapons are in use all the time. In small wars around the world tanks, artillery and warplanes are being used. The weapons in most widespread use are the handguns and rifles responsible for most military and civilian deaths in wars and civil wars around the world. These so-called 'small arms' have been used to kill millions. According to the International Action Network on Small Arms,

> small arms abuse causes violent death, injury, and psychological trauma to hundreds of thousands of people each year. These casualties occur in the context of national and regional conflicts (each with its own political, economic, social, religious and ethnic dimensions and expressions) as well as in

abusive law enforcement practices, violent repression of demo-cratic rights and violations of the right to self-determination. The easy availability of small arms is also directly linked to the increase in violent crime, domestic assaults, suicides, and accidents. In the context of political conflict, small arms help fuel violence and insecurity which breeds the sort of fear and instability which has led to the existence of millions of refugees and internally displaced persons. Many of these human-made tragedies could be prevented by controlling access to and availability of small arms – domestically and internationally – within the broader framework of measures to tackle the root causes of conflict.

The 11 September attacks, the anthrax letter attacks in Washington and the subsequent US-led military actions and further terror attacks have created concerns bordering on panic about the use of WMD. The Iraq war has made these issues – until recently the concern of just a few anoraks and boffins – front-page news for weeks. Before 11 September, I could never have imagined sitting in a TV studio providing live commentary on the evidence of the Director of the International Atomic Energy Agency (IAEA) to the UN Security Council. The title itself would usually be enough to make people's eyes glaze over.

Will future terrorist attacks include nuclear, chemical or biological weapons? Will there be a nuclear response from the US? Will another nuclear power be attacked, such as Russia? Will there be a nuclear war over Kashmir or Korea? All these problems raise the larger issue of what should be done about WMD.

Weapons of mass destruction come in three types: nuclear, biolog-ical and chemical. All three can be fitted to many types of what the military call 'delivery systems', which include missiles, aircraft, vehicles and maritime vessels. Nuclear weapons have been preferred to chemical and biological weapons because they destroy things as well as people and because they are more reliable.

Biological and chemical weapons

Biological and especially chemical weapons are far more difficult to turn into WMD than nuclear weapons. For a start they do not blow up or burn anything. They kill living things through poison and disease. Chemical weapons are far less effective killers than nuclear weapons or even powerful conventional weapons. For most military uses such as artillery shells or aircraft bombs the effect from a single chemical weapon can be confined to a few hundred metres and can fail if the wind or temperature are wrong. The killing power of high-explosive shells is much more reliable. During the Cold War, the US built and deployed thousands of nuclear artillery shells that had power equal to the Hiroshima bomb and could be fired a dozen miles or so from standard artillery guns. These were vastly more powerful than any chemical weapon. Chemical weapons are, however, much easier to build than nuclear weapons and their possession does produce a great deal of fear in the mind of an enemy, which is why they are often called the poor man's WMD. While no one should minimise the potential of chemical and especially biological weapons, it is worth considering that Winston Churchill gave far more attention to the hydrogen bomb than any other threat, even though he had been a front-line soldier in the First World War when chemical weapons were in use and had, in the Second World War, been prepared to use anthrax biological weapons on Germany if the need arose.

Of the many study and research centres concerned with biological weapons, I have found those at the Department of Peace Studies at Bradford University and the Henry L. Stimson Center, based in Washington, DC, to be the most informative and accessible. 'The Threat of Deliberate Disease in the 21st Century' by Professor Graham Pearson of Bradford University[5] is a useful summary of the biological threat.

No country admits to having chemical or biological weapons, though some states, mainly in the Middle East, are believed to have some chemical weapons. Countries without any weapons of mass destruction argue at the UN for them all to be eliminated through verifiable and enforceable treaties. Chemical and biological weapons are banned under separate conventions. The chemical-weapons ban is supported by 145 states and has a verification and enforcement mechanism. The biological ban has neither mechanism, thanks to President Bush's veto of an agreement creating them.

Nuclear weapons

China, France, Russia, the UK and the US have for many years publicly acknowledged having nuclear weapons. The US and Russia still possess tens of thousands of weapons, more than ninety per cent of the world's stockpile. Belgium, Germany, Greece, Italy, the Netherlands and Turkey all have arrangements through NATO to use US nuclear weapons in wartime.

Israel has reportedly had nuclear weapons since the 1960s; India and Pakistan exploded some in tests in 1998. Some industrialised states such as Japan and Germany could make them if they chose to. Other countries, including Taiwan, South Korea, Argentina, Brazil and Sweden, abandoned nuclear-weapons programmes before they actually made the bomb. South Africa, Belarus, Ukraine and Kazakhstan unilaterally disarmed. Iraq had a nuclear-weapons programme but it appears to have had no WMD or WMD factories at the time it was attacked by the US and UK on the grounds that it had them.

North Korea is in negotiation with its neighbours and the US about its nuclear-weapons programme. Although attacked verbally by US Republicans for many years and featured in the Axis of Evil, since the aftermath of the Iraq war the US appears less than enthusiastic towards the idea of a short successful war with North Korea. While North Korea appears to have some nuclear capacity it seems to be weak and there is no indication that it is intended for anything more than a means of preventing US attack. In his book *Disarming Strangers,* Leon Sigal of the US Social Science Research Council makes a compelling case that political infighting in the US has consistently prevented a stable solution to the crisis in Korea. This theme is continued in the journal of the International Institute for Strategic Studies, where two former US Air Force officers wrote: 'Most Korea specialists believe the North Korean regime is neither irrational nor crazy ... in some cases inaccuracies in translation [by the US] produced policy debates based on false premises or incorrect interpretations.'[6]

Iran and Libya, long accused by the US and UK of having WMD programmes, have both publicly given up their preparations for nuclear weapons factories. The IAEA [the UN's International Atomic Energy Agency] is apparently eliminating these in 2004. but the Iranians may have hidden some nuclear materials.

In the aftermath of revelations over supplies from Pakistan to Iran and Libya of machine tools for producing nuclear materials and bombs, a great deal of attention is being given by the international community to other states that may have been trading in these materials. Theoretically, industrialists involved in India's bomb programme might have been involved. States with a long-standing but low-level interest in nuclear weapons also include Saudi Arabia, Egypt and Turkey.

The five traditional nuclear-armed states have all agreed in principle to nuclear disarmament under the Nuclear Non-proliferation Treaty but they all state that nuclear weapons are the guarantee of their own security. In 2000 all these states gave an 'unequivocal' undertaking to the world at a UN conference on proliferation that they would negotiate the complete elimination of nuclear weapons. Since then they have taken no action to achieve this. The US engages in two main forms of WMD proliferation. The first, legally permitted, is to export WMD missiles and technology to the UK – and the UK returns the compliment as best it can. The second is the undertaking to use its nuclear weapons on behalf of other countries – mainly NATO members – so that even Slovakia will now have a nuclear-backed military policy. Belgium, Germany, Greece, Italy, the Netherlands and Turkey have contingency plans for the US to give them nuclear weapons in wartime, in violation of the Non-proliferation Treaty. The five all encourage other nations not to acquire nuclear weapons, but this amounts to 'do as I say, not as I do', Today, for the architects of US policy, the potential of small third-world countries to build some part of this capability – including chemical and biological weapons – has created the need to pre-empt them. For many other countries the retention of thousands of nuclear weapons by the major powers remains the greatest threat to the world.

The US and the USSR built tens of thousands of nuclear weapons and thousands of intercontinental missiles and other shorter-range systems[7] with which to fire them. At the end of the Cold War, many were destroyed, but huge quantities still remain. These are kept ready to fire at a few minutes' notice. Britain, China and France each keep a few hundred warheads, and India, Israel and Pakistan have also built nuclear weapons and missiles, though not with intercontinental ranges.

The US has around 10,600 nuclear weapons and Russia 8,600 in their armed forces with many thousands more in storage or awaiting destruction. Since the end of the Cold War, many Russian and US weapons have been removed from military units and weapons systems in stand-by status, thousands have been dismantled. Nevertheless, the destruction of the nuclear weapons themselves is not required under current arms control treaties, which also cover the systems the weapons are fitted to, such as missiles and warplanes.

According to the *Bulletin of the Atomic Scientists*, under present planning the US will have some 3,000 nuclear weapons available for its armed forces in 2012, with another 8,000 intact weapons in reserve. The Bush administration recently announced that it would use a loophole in the Moscow Treaty signed with President Putin to increase the total number of nuclear weapons it would retain beyond the announced levels of up to 2,400. The *Bulletin*'s 'Nuclear Notebook' states that although 'Russia has not released information about the size of its stockpile, it could shrink to as few as 1,000 strategic warheads and no more than 1,000 tactical warheads over the next 10 years.' Thousands more would remain in reserve.

The British government declared in July 1998 that there would 'be fewer than 200 operationally available warheads'. However, Britain should not be counted as a nuclear state in the same way as the others since it imports its WMD from the US. Imports include the lease-purchase of Trident missiles, nuclear materials, warhead design, manufacturing assistance and engineering. France, which has produced more than 1,260 nuclear warheads since 1964, currently has about 350, down from 540 in 1992. China is estimated to have an arsenal of around 400 nuclear warheads. India and Pakistan, the world's two newest declared nuclear powers, have fewer than a hundred nuclear warheads between them, most of which are not yet operationally deployed. It is estimated that India has produced enough fissile material for 45–95 nuclear warheads but may have assembled only 30–35, and that Pakistan has produced fissile material sufficient for 30–52 weapons and assembled 24–48 warheads. Both countries are thought to be increasing their stockpiles. Israel has neither confirmed nor denied possession of nuclear weapons, although US intelligence reports for many years have labelled Israel a de facto nuclear power. Some unofficial reports estimate Israel's arsenal to have as many as two hundred warheads, the first of which reportedly was assembled in 1967.

World nuclear bomb stocks (approximate figures)

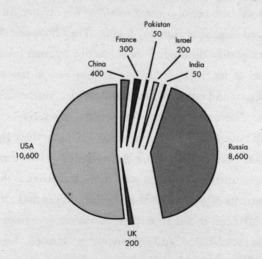

Pakistan
50

France
300

Israel
200

China
400

India
50

USA
10,600

Russia
8,600

UK
200

SOURCE: Natural Resources Defense Council, www.nrdc.org.

The potential for nuclear destruction by governments is still huge. Each nuclear weapon is about ten times as powerful as the Hiroshima bomb. Think of a country you know and what two, twenty or two hundred Hiroshimas might do to it. Imagine American and Russian capability to fire thousands of these weapons in one hour, and of India, Pakistan, Israel and China also with their fingers on the nuclear button.

It is possible to imagine civilisation continuing even after the horrors of several more Hiroshimas, but the use of thousands of nuclear weapons would not only produce immediate horror on the places bombed, but also very large quantities of lethal long-term radiation around the world, and the potentially huge climatic effects known as nuclear winter. The term derives from the dramatic lowering of temperatures as the sun is blocked out by immense amounts of dust sucked into the upper atmosphere by the rising heat of nuclear explosions. Smaller-scale effects of this type have been observed from large volcanic eruptions.

A decision to fire these weapons could come as part of a deliberate plan or, as so often happens, in a confusion of plans, mistakes and accidents. The threat of a nuclear holocaust was a great cause of public anxiety in the later part of the last century. People found it intolerable to have to live under the threat of such devastation. Indeed it was without precedent in human history, a dramatic form of globalisation in which much of the world could be transformed into a smoking ruin in a few minutes by the actions of a few people using nuclear technology. Today the political confrontation with Soviet communism no longer exists, but weapons built for that confrontation remain, and are ready to go.

Today, politicians and the media no longer consider the problems of a major nuclear war even though the potential remains intact.

Public attention has turned to the issue of some states newly acquiring nuclear and also chemical and biological weapons. This is called the problem of proliferation. The discussion of proliferation has become so prevalent that there is little attention paid at all in the West to the problems posed by existing stockpiles amongst the Western powers and in Russia and China. Before looking at the problems of chemical and biological WMD and of terrorism let's spend a moment considering the unconsidered.

Don't forget World War Three

It is possible that even having survived the Cold War we may yet be plunged into World War Three. A war involving Russia, China, the US and other powers is quite possible in the coming years. The following analysis highlights growing tensions in Asia involving China, the US and Japan. War is not likely in the near future, as there are many sane people working for stronger political and economic ties. Nevertheless it has become a dangerous fashion to pretend that simply because there are no obvious tensions today, there will be none tomorrow.

It is normal to completely discount the Russian threat today. US conservatives who for so long hyped the Russian threat now no longer talk of it. Russia may still have a lot of nuclear weapons able to reach the US, but it is left to peace groups such as the Physicians for Social Responsibility in Washington DC, to publish studies showing that millions could still die if the missiles from just one Russian submarine hit the US.

Conventional wisdom has it that the Russians accepted the eastward expansion of NATO to include the Baltic states a few miles from St Petersburg and is now both close to the West and no longer capable of mounting serious resistance to US power.

There are two reasons for caution. The first is that US and Russian political leadership and direction are uncertain, and, more importantly, there are now several countries in which both Russia and the US station troops. In Georgia and in several central Asian republics new US bases are located in one part of the country while Russia keeps its old military presence in another base. This creates a series of potential flashpoints between the two most heavily armed nuclear powers. Throughout the Cold War, the US and USSR were careful to ensure that their armies never had a chance of coming into contact with each other by being in the same country at the same time.

Since the collapse of the Soviet Union there have been two serious incidents between the US and Russia. The first occurred in January 1995, when Boris Yeltsin was awoken by a false report that the US had launched a nuclear missile attack on Russia and was told that he should order Russian forces to be launched. The second occurred in 1999 when, during the war in Kosovo, the US ordered British forces to forcibly remove Russian troops from the main airbase in Kosovo. The British General Mike Jackson refused to obey the order. Both crises were defused. Both indicate that even in times of peaceful relations crisis is not that far away. If two near-war incidents are going to occur at this rate in the future – i.e. one every six years – the chance of war by error is far too high.

A possible war between the US and China may be of greater concern than a US–Russian confrontation. China has become the third state on the planet – after the Soviet Union and the US – to launch a manned spacecraft. Such a successful introduction of advanced technology by a developing country might be thought a cause for international celebration – but that is not how the militarists in Washington are seeing it. There, it has been used as further evidence of a 'China threat', while China's own proposal – for a treaty banning weapons from space – has been rejected.

It is US national strategy to prevent any state from rivalling American power in the way that the Soviet Union once did. But some Washington strategists now see China's huge population and growing economy as challenging American hegemony. China is now becoming integrated into the global economy through the World Trade Organisation and this encourages the view that peaceful cooperation may well prevail. However, for some strategists every Chinese achievement becomes a threat and every form of cooperation appeasement. China is also cooperating with the EU on space technology through the creation of a joint project called Galileo that will operate a new form of the American Global Positioning System. Galileo will provide greater choice and independence for states, companies and consumers but is strongly opposed by Washington, which seeks to retain its monopoly.

One influential organisation in Washington that has highlighted rivalry with China is the Project for the New American Century (PNAC). This was a study group supported by many members of the Bush administration. It stated that for the US the 'focus of strategic competition' has shifted from Europe to East Asia. In a discussion of potential strategic competitors to the US, President Bush's national-security strategy explains some of the political rationale for fearing China:

> *A quarter century after beginning the process of shedding the worst features of the Communist legacy, China's leaders have not yet made the next series of fundamental choices about the character of their state. In pursuing advanced*

military capabilities that can threaten its neighbours in the
Asia-Pacific region, China is following an outdated path.

The reality of Chinese power is very different from the theories of the Washington threat creation industry. Take the idea of an attack from the mainland on Taiwan. According to the International Institute for Strategic Studies, Beijing has just sixty ships in its navy – only twice the number of tiny Taiwan and a fraction of US strength. China's real priority is to have enough power to prevent a return to the humiliations of the colonial era. It is too easy to forget that in the mid-nineteenth century Britain used gunboats to force China to import opium, and then took control of China's overseas trade. Other foreign powers joined in and the US kept a fleet operating in China's rivers up until the Second World War, when they were forced out by the Japanese invasion.

Today, the US has thousands of nuclear weapons and other missiles able to attack China, while Beijing has little to fire back with. Washington is determined to keep it that way. One of the PNAC members explained to me that 'the US has never accepted a deterrent relationship with China, the way we did with Russia.' To the US military, any space programme it does not control is a challenge to its formal policy of dominating space militarily. For its part Chinese military strategy has copied the US and it too regards space as a vital battleground in any future war.

There are two or three potential flashpoints in US–China relations. The most well known are over North Korea and the island of Taiwan. The dispute over North Korea's nuclear-weapons programme is a complex one. But in respect to the impact on US–China relations it is important to note that some US analysts regard the North Korean programme as having been encouraged by China as a tool to pressure the US and Japan, while the Chinese have repeatedly stated that a US attack on North Korea would mean war. In addition some US opinion-formers, notably the columnist Charles Krauthammer, argue that the US should encourage a Japanese nuclear programme as a means of responding to what they see as Chinese and North Korean intimidation. It is not necessary to become involved in the details of 'who hit who back first' in these disputes to see the potential for deliberate and accidental conflict. Under President Clinton, the US already came close to mobilising its forces for a war with North Korea back in 1994.[8]

Another area of dispute is over the island of Taiwan. Historically part of China, it has kept separate after Chairman Mao's communist victory on the mainland in 1948. Ever since then the US has been Taiwan's protector. The government in Beijing has always asserted that if Taiwan formalised its separation by declaring itself to be a separate country rather than, as at present, merely a rival government of China, Beijing would regard any such formal declaration of independence as an act of war. A worldtribune.com article of 17 October 2003 showed how space war and the confrontation over Taiwan are connected:

> China's military is exploring new space-based weapons, a senior Pentagon expert said.
>
> Lt. Col. Mark Stokes, a key China specialist, told a conference that China's military plans to use space weapons in any conflict involving Taiwan ...
>
> 'Space assets will play a major role in any future use of force against Taiwan and in preventing foreign intervention in a Taiwan scenario,' Stokes said.
>
> Space assets are 'important force multipliers that can help to even the playing field when you go up against a techno-

logically superior adversary' ... He said the deployment of aircraft carrier battle groups near Taiwan in 1996, following Beijing's test firing of short-range missiles near the island, 'removed any doubt in Beijing that the PLA would require the ability to deter or complicate US intervention in a Taiwan Strait conflict.'

China's military is developing space-based command and control systems, Stokes said. Its dual-use space and missile industry is 'striving to achieve ballistic missile accuracies of less than 50 meters.'

China has some 450 short-range missile targeted on Taiwan. 'Beijing is making substantial advancements in its long-range precision strike capability based on an arsenal of increasingly accurate and lethal conventional and land-attack cruise missiles,' he said.

China also is working on technical countermeasures aimed at defeating US missile defense programs and is developing a new generation of solid-fuel intercontinental ballistic missiles, he added.[9]

If you look closely at the argument you can see that he argues not that China has the ability to interfere with US defence of Taiwan, but that a US deployment of an aircraft-carrier removed any doubt that China 'would require the ability to deter or complicate US intervention', i.e. it does not have that ability today. Similarly he states that China is 'striving to achieve ballistic missile accuracies of less than 50 meters' while, as is well known, the US has long had weapons with an accuracy of less than a single metre. And at the strategic level of weapons Stokes claims that China 'is working on [i.e. does not yet have] countermeasures aimed at defeating US missile defence programs'; similarly China 'is developing [i.e. does not yet have] a new generation of solid-fuel intercontinental ballistic missiles', a capability that the US has had for half a century.

The likely reply from the Pentagon to the Chinese space programme is an intensification of the 'Son of Star Wars' project, part of which is being built at Fylingdales in Yorkshire. Opaque government statements and briefings from officials indicates that Tony Blair has already agreed to some of these American missiles coming to Britain. The 'Son of Star Wars' missile defences would be able to neutralise a Chinese deterrent, but, in fact, are better suited to shooting down satellites (including manned spacecraft) than incoming missiles because satellites follow a predictable path across the sky.

President Bush launched a new space initiative in January 2004, which included the idea of putting humans on Mars. In an interview with the *New York Times*,[10] Joan Johnson-Freese, an expert on the Chinese space programme at the Naval War College in Rhode Island, said the Bush administration had no choice but to respond to China's recent successes with its own space initiative: 'The success allowed China to reach out to other countries and they've been responding favorably, so we could not do nothing,' she said. 'While a space race is not a foregone conclusion, it is a possibility.'

In contrast to the US explicit commitment to 'space dominance' in Pentagon policy documents, the Chinese have been campaigning for a UN treaty banning weapons in space. The Chinese draft treaty should be welcomed or, at least, if China's peaceful protestations are merely bluff then that bluff should be called. There are few new technical problems in creating a verifiable inspection regime for a ban on weapons in space. Right now, there are no weapons above our heads. It is not necessary to put a UN weapons inspector like Hans Blix in a space suit to carry out inspections. There are only a handful of space launch and missile defence sites around the world. Satellites and other space vehicles are tiny, so it is easy to check if a ray gun is hidden inside. This approach should form part of the SCRRAP concept discussed in the chapter on controlling weaponry.

Center for Defense Information report
Washington DC, February 2004

For the first time in recent history, the US Air Force has formally published a list of planned space weapons programs, including both anti-satellite weapons (ASATs) and terrestrial strike weapons. The 'US Air Force Transformation Flight Plan,' November 2003 but only recently posted on the Air Force web site (www.af.mil), cites space as a major capability for enabling 'transformation' of the service from its Cold War past to a modern force capable of meeting the threats of today and tomorrow.

* * *

Most of the actual ASAT and space weapon projects are being designed for deployment in the 2015 and beyond timeframe, apparently based on technology research being started over the next five years. The programs of most potential concern include:

- Air-Launched Anti-Satellite Missile
- Ground-Based Laser

- Orbital Transfer Vehicle
- Space-Based Radio Frequency Energy Weapon
- Space Maneuver Vehicle
- Space Operations Vehicle
- Hypervelocity Rod Bundles [Rods from God]

So far, US behaviour over arms talks gives ample evidence to those dubious of its peaceful intent. Even President Clinton vetoed UN talks on a space weapons ban. In the absence of any sensible policy from Washington, the UK and its EU partners must engage in direct talks with the Chinese.

Before moving on from the sleeping problem of war between major states, let us look in a little more detail at the issue of a Japanese bomb. This possibility is an additional reason for Russia and China – and, indeed, you and me – to be worried about the knock-on effects of the Korean nuclear crisis. Inside Washington it is a problem given serious consideration by security researchers.[11]

The idea of Japanese nuclear weapons seems extraordinary because people think that Japan has been pacifist since the atomic bombing of Hiroshima in 1945. Japan is indeed a world leader in supporting the UN and it is also a strong supporter of UN peace efforts, especially those that control the spread of rifles and handguns in the third world. At the same time there has been a long debate in Japan about whether to build the bomb, and, today, pressures at home and from overseas are edging Japan towards the nuclear option.

Pressures to take a stronger military stance have already resulted in Japan having the world's fourth largest defence budget and a larger navy than Britain. In 2002, government officials raised the issue of

Japanese nuclear weapons. In June, Yasuo Fukuda, the chief Cabinet secretary, confided to Japanese reporters that 'depending on the world situation, circumstances and public opinion could require Japan to possess nuclear weapons'. Shinzo Abe, the deputy Cabinet secretary, said later that it would be acceptable for Japan to develop small, strategic nuclear weapons. Later, officials backtracked, leaving speculation that they had committed a deliberate diplomatic faux pas designed to air the issue.

This was not the first time that Japanese officials had raised the question of developing nuclear weapons. Prime Ministers Kishi (1957), Ohira (1979) and Nakasone (1984) all stated that their country's non-nuclear status could be changed and that defensive nuclear weapons were not prohibited by the constitution. In 1969, an official report recommended that Japan build nuclear weapons. However, the Japanese government kept to a non-nuclear policy, relying on two American policies. The US undertook to use nuclear weapons to defend Japan and at the same time committed itself to the pursuit of global non-proliferation and disarmament through the NPT.

Japan has the resources to go nuclear if it chooses. Its nuclear-power industry has created a stockpile of more than five tonnes of plutonium, enough for hundreds of weapons. They are at present under the safeguard arrangements of the IAEA, in accordance with Japan's non-nuclear membership of the NPT. Japan also has its own rocket, the HA-2, which can lift a five-tonne payload into earth orbit, effectively giving it a prototype intercontinental ballistic missile. Submarines and warplanes could also be adapted to a nuclear role. For Japan to go nuclear, there would have to be a combination of internal and external influences to force a change of policy. A comparison can be made with India, which test-fired nuclear weapons in 1998 after years of warnings that it might do just that. By the late 1990s, the collapse of global nuclear disarmament talks, combined with a rise in Indian nationalism, triggered India's decision and Pakistan rapidly followed suit.

The prospect of a Korean bomb – whether in the north or the south – is one factor that Japanese analysts always mention as a trigger for their own decision. Now North Korea appears to have the bomb, this influence will become greater. Korean–Japanese relations have long been difficult, not least because of Japan's military occupation of Korea between 1905 and 1945.

The present Japanese government has already raised the nuclear issue, and the Prime Minister has gone out of his way to associate himself with Japan's leaders in the Second World War. He has on several occasions visited a shrine dedicated to the belief that Japan's leaders were wrongly accused of war crimes.

Until now, a combination of the US nuclear guarantee and the UN-backed process of proliferation control has been enough to dissuade Japan from developing nuclear weapons. But today these arguments look far weaker. The 'unequivocal' undertaking to abolish nuclear weapons given as recently as 2000 by the US, Britain, China, France and Russia is now forgotten. In an international environment where the UN is no longer relevant and where there are already Indian, Israeli, North Korean, Pakistani and possibly Iranian nuclear weapons, a Japanese bomb may seem more 'natural' for the country with the world's second largest economy.

The nature of Washington's nuclear guarantee has also changed. It was based on the idea of the deterrent – what President Bush now describes as nuclear blackmail. Today, US policy is to carry out political and, if necessary, military pre-emption against any threatening state. It is possible that the US could carry out a military strike on North Korea that would be short, sharp and effective. But the risks of a larger war, even one involving China, cannot be discounted.

In today's Washington, even some of those who do not want to confront North Korea are by no means anti-nuclear. The influential Cato Institute recently published a report favouring a Japanese nuclear programme. The author, Ted Galen Carpenter, wrote: 'The United States does not need to press Tokyo and Seoul to go nuclear. It is sufficient if Washington informs the South Korean and Japanese governments that the US would not object to their developing nuclear weapons.'

Few, if any, Japanese policy-makers are enthusiastic about the nuclear option. However, the crisis with North Korea may continue to push them in that direction. The Japanese nuclear card can certainly be used by Washington as a means to try to get Russia and China to persuade North Korea to give up its programme, for a Japanese nuclear programme would be very bad news for both countries. But it is by no means certain that Washington's hardline approach will either produce North Korean disarmament or resolve the issue through war. Even Donald Rumsfeld may recoil from the consequences of a another conventional war in Asia. The longer North Korea's nuclear status is allowed to remain though, the greater the pressures will become on all concerned, not least in Japan.

In the past, the UN offered a safety net for nations locked in crises. Today, that net has been set aside. There are no global or regional nuclear-disarmament negotiations that could bring in the Koreans. A UN-brokered economic assistance and security package, such as might have been negotiated by other US presidents, is not in George Bush's political playbook. So do not be surprised if, as happened with India, you wake up one day to the Japanese bomb.

Because of the prominent role in the world of the US, and its large number of well-maintained and ready nuclear weapons, it is worth paying special attention to the possible use of nuclear weapons by the US.

President Bush may have considered using nuclear weapons on 11 September and shortly afterwards. Some officials in his government have privately expressed that view. The National Security Council is thought to have considered the question in mid-September 2001 but ruled it out. It still remains unclear why President Bush flew to the Headquarters of Strategic Command on 11 September. This command post at Offutt Air Force base in Nebraska controls US nuclear weapons in peacetime. It has little other purpose. It was a priority target in Cold War scenarios with Russia and is consequently not a likely place to take the President as part of some long-standing emergency plan. On the other hand, he may have gone there precisely because it was an unlikely place to go to and has good communications.

Much has yet to be clarified about the US response in those first days. For example, why was Vice-President Dick Cheney apparently been removed from his position of prominence for months after mid-September 2001? Keeping him in apparent isolation for so long on security grounds is one explanation, but scarcely adequate for a person of such influence. Why was the Secretary of State, Colin Powell, unable to speak to the President for ten hours after the attacks? Was this because of major disagreements about the best way to retaliate? Nuclear options against terrorists have been discussed in official US publications of the Department of Defense since at least the mid-1990s (emphasis added):

Enemy combat forces and facilities that may be likely targets
for nuclear strikes are:

- *WMD and their delivery systems, as well as associated command and control, production, and logistical support units*
- *Ground combat units and their associated command and control and support units*
- *Air defense facilities and support installations*
- *Naval installations, combat vessels, and associated support facilities and command and control capabilities*
- **Nonstate actors (facilities and operation centers) that possess WMD**
- *Underground facilities.*[12]

In a speech at the Royal United Services Institute in December 2001, the Chief of the Defence Staff, Admiral Sir Michael Boyce (now Lord Boyce), warned of the danger that the US might respond to further attacks by giving in to 'the desire to use greater force with less constraints, less distinction and less proportionality – something that strikes at the acceptable laws of armed conflict, and exposes our centre of strategic gravity [our will] by radicalising the opinion of the Islamic world in favour of Al-Qaeda'. It is unclear if he was talking about a mass conventional attack such as Second World War-style bombing of cities or referring to nuclear weapons. This kind of language is often a deliberately ambiguous reference to nuclear weapons.

A detailed study of the policy of using conventional and nuclear weapons to counter proliferation has been made by Physicians for Social Responsibility,[13] a group of anti-nuclear doctors who won the Nobel Peace Prize. They conclude that nuclear use cannot be ruled out and that with such purposes in mind there are some US officials determined to build and test-fire new types of nuclear weapons. This would require the US to withdraw from the Test Ban Treaty, agreed only in 1996.

India and Pakistan have been working on building nuclear weapons, and ballistic missiles to carry them, for many years. Both states exploded several weapons in underground tests in 1998. One response by the US to the 11 September attacks was to lift a ban on military exports to the two countries imposed after the nuclear tests, in order to gain political support for its operations in Afghanistan. There is pressure from UK arms companies to increase exports to these states.

A nuclear war between India and Pakistan cannot be discounted despite the recent ceasefire in the long-standing border war in Kashmir. The Indian defence minister has even explained that he thinks India could survive a nuclear attack and go on and win a nuclear war. With several dozen nuclear weapons on each side and an Indian population of around one billion people, he may turn out to be right. Yet the horror induced by a 'victory' of this kind, with vast amounts of casualties and nuclear contamination, could lead to an effective ban on all such weapons. On the other hand, states could react in the traditional manner of building more weapons to win the next war.

Terrorism and weapons of mass destruction

The potential use of WMD by Al-Qaeda or other groups
The events of 11 September and the subsequent anthrax attacks turned the possibility of this type of action on the part of a non-governmental group into a source of real anxiety for many people.

Until then, the conventional wisdom in governments was that an attack of this nature was unlikely because terrorists did not wish totally to alienate public opinion. Today it is clear that these attackers are not worried about public opinion and would destroy the societies they oppose if they could. The concern is that they and other groups may have the means to do so. Indeed, as long ago as 1979, Howard Morland published how he had discovered the existing techniques for building a hydrogen bomb.[14] Far simpler technology for building a Hiroshima-type atomic weapon has been in the public domain for years. A modern machine-engineering shop and a supply of uranium 235 are the main requirements.

The US now has well-established programmes to provide Russia with financial assistance to prevent nuclear materials getting into the hands of other countries and terrorists. Parallel programmes pay Russian nuclear scientists to work in civil programmes as an incentive against working abroad for such interests. Leading US specialists argue that these programmes need to be reinforced and a leading US Senator, Dick Lugar, has argued for making the programme global.

Secret production of chemical and biological weapons is also a problem. However, it is important to take a cool look at it. Dr Amy Smithson of the Henry L. Stimson Center in Washington DC is a leading world expert on the topic and has an excellent online set of frequently asked questions. Her view is that there is much exaggeration of the problem.

Before 11 September there was already a considerable literature about the problem of independent groups and so-called 'rogue states' obtaining access to various types of WMD. There are potential sources all over the world. For example, the post-Soviet stocks of nuclear, chemical and biological weapons give rise to the most serious international concern. Military stocks and industrial facilities in many other states are also important sources.

There is much debate about how independent groups have in the past gained and may in the future gain access to these materials. Finding out this information has been a key objective of intelligence agencies as well as in the broader world of journalists and academics. But international intelligence can only be effective against an international threat in an environment of international cooperation. There are international inspections of civilian nuclear materials but none of military nuclear materials or of biological agents. The Chemical Weapons Convention can be used to look at government and private activities. Such checks could be useful in ensuring that states not in the Convention are isolated from the sources and in detecting whether or not guerrillas or individuals were acquiring them. These issues are discussed in the chapter on weapons control.

Traditional attacks by armed groups were sometimes part of a bigger war intended to bring down a government, but more often they were designed to attract attention. Thus the Provisional IRA used to have an elaborate set of warnings that bombs were going to go off, giving the authorities time to evacuate people but still creating damage, and all too often death as well. This approach has been described as one where the perpetrators wanted a few people dead and a lot of people watching. The attacks on America on 9/11 were of a different scale and caused a fundamental rethink amongst security and defence forces around the world. They came to be contrasted with the previous method as having the objective of wanting a lot of people dead and lot of people watching. This, and the suicidal behaviour of the attackers, created a greater threat. In this form of warfare escape for the attackers does not need to be built into the plan; in combination with attacking strategic targets a new form of warfare has been developed.

Even more serious is the problem that an attack carried out by a stateless group, or even by a team of special forces, could successfully cause crippling devastation to a whole society. The traditional word for this kind of attack is 'sabotage'. Some examples of previous attacks and the events of 9/11 themselves have made many people think that there could be attacks that cripple a whole society – that would, in the language of military and political affairs, have a strategic impact. The long-term threat posed by this type of warfare was put rather well by Robert Cooper, the EU's top foreign-policy official, who has written that the threat was that governments would no longer have a monopoly of the use of armed force.[15]

Prior to 9/11 two former US Senators, Gary Hart and Warren Rudman, called for the creation of a new US Department of Homeland Security to deal with these threats. Since then a whole homeland security industry has sprung up and it is possible to imagine an almost infinite number of attacks that might be carried out, from cyber war to bio-terror.

On the subject of biological weapons, it is interesting to consider a story that is now a hundred years old and to contemplate the lessons it has for today. Since 9/11 an enormous amount has been written on the topic, with the five deaths from anthrax that occurred just after 9/11 adding to the panic. But the idea of bio-terrorism is not that new. The first mention that I can find is in a 1905 sci-fi tale by H. G. Wells. Not content with imagining atomic weapons and men from Mars, Wells also conjured up the first bio-terrorist in 'The Stolen Bacillus: A Tale of Anarchy'.[16] His anarchist attempts to infect the whole of London with a stolen bottle of cholera and the story features a chase in hackney carriages down Camden High Street. The fear we feel today was encapsulated by Wells a century ago:

> *Only break such a little tube as this into a supply of drinking-water, say to these minute particles of life that one must needs strain and examine with the highest powers of the microscope even to see, and that one, can neither smell nor taste – say to them ... Go forth, increase and multiply, and replenish the cisterns ... and death mysterious, untraceable death, death swift and terrible, death full of pain and indignity – would be released upon this city, and go hither and thither seeking its victims. Here he would take husband from the wife, here the child from its mother, here the statesman from his duty, and here the toiler from his trouble. He would follow the water mains creeping along the streets, picking out and punishing a house here and a house there where they did not boil their drinking-water, creeping into wells of the mineral-water makers, getting washed into salad and lying dormant in ices. He would wait ready to be drunk in the horse-troughs, and by unwary children in the public fountains. He would soak into the soil, to reappear in springs and wells at a thousand unexpected places ... Once start him into the water supply and before we could ring him in and catch him again he would have decimated the metropolis ... the Anarchist waved a dramatic farewell and strode off towards Waterloo Bridge, carefully jostling his infected body against as many people as possible.*

Wells's nightmare scenario raises lots of interesting issues that are relevant today. First, he reminds us that the threat is at least a hundred years old. Second, if the idea of bio-terrorism has been popularised for that long, it presents a powerful case that there are very few people who have wanted to carry out such attacks and that such attacks are easier to imagine than to commit. For example, a Japanese group used sarin gas, which attacks the body's nervous system, to carry out an attack on the subway system in Tokyo. It caused massive concern around the world but killed very few people. The group had invested over $1 billion in researching ways of killing people, including setting up facilities in foreign countries. The next known bio-attack came in the US in the aftermath of 9/11. Unknown attackers put anthrax powder into a few letters to prominent political and media figures. Five people died and mass anxiety was created resulting in the examination of millions of letters and the closure of numerous offices. The attacks confirmed that the threat certainly creates a mass effect without there being mass casualties.

Wells's choice of cholera is also interesting. In the mid-nineteenth century cholera had been a major killer, but by the end of the century new public water supplies and sewage systems had eliminated it as a public health problem. So Wells was conjuring up the return of a natural killer by deliberate means, a disease whose devastating effect was a living memory to many of his readers. Today, killer epidemics are seen as a thing of the past in the industrialised world, although they are still a fact of life in many poor parts of the world. The issue raised by a biological attack is very similar to that caused by a sudden natural epidemic such as SARS and the most appropriate response seems to be to enhance the UN-based World Health Organisation's programmes for responding to such occurrences.

The tale of Wells's bacillus has not so far foretold the future, in happy contrast to his prediction about nuclear weapons. One obvious difference is that people do seem to shy away from the self-destructive option and choose a destructive option that may offer victory, even in the era of Hitler and Stalin.

Nevertheless, we cannot discount or underestimate bio-terrorism. The suicide bio-bomber remains a real concern. The management of this deliberate release of disease is very similar to the methods used by the WHO (an organisation not yet attacked by the US unilateralists). The WHO has a global monitoring system and response mechanism that interacts with national health agencies. The reaction to a terrorist attack would be similar to the reaction to the SARS outbreak and the fears of bird flu.

After the anthrax attack on Washington in September 2001, national health agencies introduced new procedures to detect and contain deliberate outbreaks of disease. Most if not all of the potential outbreaks are treatable. In conclusion, since the threat of disease carries so much fear compared to its probable impact and that fear and panic is itself a cause of casualties and of success for the attackers, it is tempting to recommend a policy of GAG: Get A Grip.

*

The words 'nuclear' and 'terrorism' are enough to keep anyone awake at night. The fear has a sound basis. A nuclear bomb in the hands of persons unknown is a prospect that has inspired Hollywood. A nuclear reactor was certainly, after Chernobyl, seen as merely building a weapon for the enemy. As one British air marshal explained in a conference paper, Chernobyl had shown you did not actually need to have a nuclear bomb, and that a conventional weapon could act as an initiator. Somewhere in my files I have a post-Chernobyl marketing leaflet from some US manufacturer of missile-targeting equipment. It had a tasty little drawing of the crossed lines of a gun-sight lined up on a nuclear-reactor dome. As long ago as 1976 the Royal Commission on Environmental Pollution pointed out that had nuclear reactors been around during the Second World War, their inevitable destruction in the mass bombing and blitzkriegs of that era would have left parts of Europe radioactive today, and for the foreseeable future. Since 9/11 there has been a renewed flurry of concern over the danger of attack on nuclear power plants and storage facilities.

Clearly, people who oppose nuclear power as being generally hazardous to people and the environment can make a good case that nuclear facilities of almost any kind could be attacked with disastrous results. Some forms of long-term storage such as fixing the waste in glass and burying it in deep caverns or mineshafts would be beyond the reach of small groups or individuals.

However, the transportation and storage of waste radioactive materials are open to attack in various possible ways. In considering the evidence it is interesting to look at the sources and motives of those issuing the warnings and some of the historical background on how the problem of dangers from the civil nuclear programme have been treated by government and the public.

Since 9/11, the UK government's public concern over the nuclear-terrorist connection has focused on the issue of a 'dirty bomb' in a city centre, although one cannot entirely rule out that a group may get hold of a complete nuclear weapon. A dirty bomb is a normal high explosive used to disperse a mix of radioactive material when it explodes. Except for some very special circumstances this type of weapon is most unlikely to kill in a mass way in the short or long term. This is partly because radioactive material is heavy and falls to the ground quite quickly, and also because radiation effects on health tend to impact over many years. However, the political and psychological effects of such a weapon would be huge. This is why the term 'weapons of mass effect' is used in preference to 'weapons of mass destruction' by many professionals working on the topic.

The low profile given by government to the problem of attacks on nuclear facilities may partly be explained by the desire to not put ideas into the minds of the enemy and perhaps from not wanting to scare the public. However, the comparative silence on this issue compared to other problems where the government clearly wanted to create a greater degree of public awareness makes me wonder whether some officials within the government are keen to assist the nuclear industry with its public profile. If so, this approach has not worked well so far. This was exemplified when Britain's Secretary of State for Trade and Industry, Margaret Beckett, announced the opening of the Thorpe reprocessing facility at the same time as a major speech by the Prime Minister on the dangers of terrorism.

More broadly, the lack of public information from the UK government left the debate open to others, notably the Irish government and anti-nuclear NGOs. Their case that nuclear facilities were a latent threat was somewhat strengthened by the decision of the French government to deploy surface-to-air missiles around the major nuclear plant near Cap de la Hague, and by statements from Al-Qaeda leaders that they had considered, but rejected on humanitarian grounds, attacks on US nuclear facilities.

If governments gave full and frank information, it would be easier to dismiss concerns from groups such as the World Information Service on Energy (WISE), Greenpeace, the Nuclear Control Institute and the Union of Concerned Scientists. As WISE puts it,

'We do not pretend to give a complete picture – we just want to show the problem is not new, not over and not properly dealt with.' Although good information is hard to come by, it is worth considering the conclusion of Mohammed ElBaradei, Director of the IAEA, who simply remarked after 9/11 that nuclear plants were not built to withstand crashes from large heavily fuelled airliners.

One of the best public studies of the problem posed by nuclear power plants and waste has been prepared by the engineer John Large, long an accurate critic of the nuclear industry. Looking at these and other studies on the topic, a number of fairly simple conclusions can be reached by the layperson when considering the issue of nuclear waste.

Nuclear waste is not kept in facilities designed to withstand 9/11 air attacks, or attacks with military force including hand-held anti-tank weapons. Commando-style raids using these types of weapons or truck bombs are most difficult to defend against given the potential for surprise. Prevention through counter-intelligence operations and political measures should be the first and second lines of defence.

If we look at the potential impact of attacks on waste facilities the greatest dangers come not from the immediate impact of a weapon but from the potential draining off of cooling liquid that permits fire to break out in the radioactive material. This in turn would tend to produce hot, rising clouds of radioactive particles. The quantities concerned in storage facilities are very considerable, including several generations of reactor cores. Some of the material is potentially highly flammable.

Some officials take a fairly relaxed view of the numerous 'ghost' stories of fanciful terrorist attacks and put attacks on nuclear facilities on a long list including the electrical grid, chemical plants and oil refineries. From this perspective, we have so many vulnerabilities and so much nuclear material lying about already that it does not make a whole lot of difference if we have some more. This is a fatalism more usually found in the Eastern religions than in the UK. The public takes a rather different view and, it seems, cannot stomach an expansion of the nuclear industry at a time when we are told we are in an indefinite war on terror. From this perspective national strategy must be to minimise risks wherever such a choice is possible. It is, I think, questionable to continue to devote scarce national resources to foreign military adventures when at home the national infrastructure is highly vulnerable.

The example of the vulnerability of nuclear-waste facilities highlights the risks to the arteries and organs of the industrial states and indicates that there should be a very strong national security imperative for adopting the dispersed and inert energy sources associated with renewable energy rather than the concentrated and explosive character of the nuclear electrical industry.

Consideration of the risks of attacks by stateless groups upon civil nuclear power plants highlights a key issue about modern industrialised society. Many of its vital components are highly vulnerable to attack. Like the use of judo to overcome a more muscular opponent, attacks with truck bombs or stolen planes have the potential to cause huge damage and have the advantage for the attacker of not requiring the specialist skills and resources needed to make a biological or nuclear weapon, let alone build up a conventional army.

The 'war on terror' could be a forty-year war according to Jim Woolsey, former Director of the CIA. If the threat is likely to last that long, then governments need to make sure that industrial strategy contains a strong element of civil defence, so that technology choices favour back-up systems and redundancy, decentralisation, and non-toxic options. In this respect, renewable energy has distinct advantages over centralised fossil fuel power stations and especially over nuclear power plants. Solar power and wind generation are decentralised and do not involve poisons. Where these choices cannot be made then additional physical security needs to be systematically upgraded.

The extensive public discussion of the threat from terrorists with WMD ignores the way modern industrial society has created weapons for the enemy. The use of trucks filled with explosives, and then on 9/11 of planes as flying bombs, indicates a historical practice of attackers using cheap and easy methods over the expensive and complicated. Detonation of the WMD that already exist, or attacks on latent WMD in nuclear and chemical civilian factories, are a far more tangible threat than Wells's bacillus on Waterloo Bridge.

Could Al-Qaeda win?

Al-Qaeda's objectives as expressed in statements by Osama bin Laden include getting Crusaders and Zionists out of Saudi Arabia, getting Crusaders and Zionists out of other Islamic areas and uniting and expanding the community of believers.

The initial statement from bin Laden of 23 August 1996 stated:

> Today your brothers and sons, the sons of the two Holy Places,
> have started their Jihad in the cause of Allah, to expel the
> occupying enemy out of the country of the two Holy places ...
> in order to re-establish the greatness of this Ummah and to
> liberate its occupied sanctities. ... Due to the imbalance of

power between our armed forces and the enemy forces, a suitable means of fighting must be adopted using fast-moving light forces that work under complete secrecy. In other words to initiate a guerrilla warfare, where the sons of the nation, and not the military forces, take part in it. ... It is wise, in the present circumstances, for the armed military forces not to be engaged in a conventional fighting with the forces of the crusader enemy ... unless a big advantage is likely to be achieved; and great losses induced on the enemy side ... that will help to expel the enemy defeated out of the country.

More recent statements are available on my website www.danplesch.net. Al-Qaeda acts on the widespread belief in the Islamic world that Islam is under attack and that the fighters are conducting a last-ditch defensive battle for the survival of Islam itself. With Western powers in direct or indirect occupation of Islamic states, the last straw was the US military presence in Saudi Arabia after 1991.

Al-Qaeda's origins are in a small Islamic sect within Saudi Arabia and the anti-soviet fight as in Afghanistan. However, its appeal has been crafted to be of far wider appeal to Islamists around the world, partly because its resources have acted as a bank or supermarket for would-be supporters of armed jihad. At present Al-Qaeda clearly does not have mass active support in the Islamic world. There are no mass street demonstrations in support of its actions, nor large-scale attacks involving thousands of people. At the same time the passive approval for people hitting back at perceived oppression appears high. It is worth noting that within Islam there are many who believe that the prophet taught that jihad is a solely spiritual quest, while others believe it to be the form of holy war that has become notorious.

We can think about Al-Qaeda as an organisation like a company with a board and middle managers, or a network or loose association. In traditional revolutionary Marxist ideology, Al-Qaeda would be the vanguard party leading the workers by example. Indeed Malise Ruthven makes this point in some detail in his insightful book *Fury for God*.[17] Another model is that of a football club like Manchester United and its supporters. In this model there are some professionals, some selling the scarves and badges, but many more supporters all around the world, backing the team, needing no instruction as to how to be a supporter, organising local associations and delighted if one of the stars asks for help. As the 'team' grabs the headlines so other supporters jump on the bandwagon, carrying out copy-cat attacks. The horrific attacks in Madrid appear, to have been an example of this kind of activity.

The Madrid bombings mark a change of another kind in the spate of attacks since 9/11. Until the bombers killed themselves to avoid capture on 4 April, the attacks in Spain had not been suicide bombings, or martyrdom operations. This change is at once worrying and encouraging. Worrying, because it indicates a broadening of the ideology and politics of the attackers, which had placed the example of martyrdom as a central part of the political act. Worrying, because this broadening opens up the possibility of far more attackers, since martyrdom or suicide is a weak tradition in Islam with little historical or cultural support, while the Madrid bombings fall within a far wider tradition of guerrilla or terrorist warfare. Encouraging, because difference between attackers implies splits, particularly for people for whom their own precise interpretation of Islam and its requirements is vital to sustaining the sect.

Whatever Al-Qaeda actually is, it is necessary to think about how it could achieve its goals as an essential part of defeating it. And this means having some understanding of its point of view. Looking at how things look from the other point of view is simply good practice, but it can seem incredible to think about, almost a disloyal question. On the other hand, some opponents of Western policy assume that the terrorist threat is deliberately exaggerated and that in any case the West and the US in particular are so strong that they are invulnerable. Critics of present Western policy should consider that incompetence more than aggression by Washington and London could be the biggest problem. In the Cold War, we heard a drumbeat of stories that the Soviet military could win unless America built a bigger armed force. There seems to be no such analysis of Al-Qaeda even though the US and UK governments talk about the severity of the new type of threat.

There are potentially disastrous implications of the failure to make worst-case analyses. Such complacency can lead to a blindness to the negative effect of actions such as the invasion of Iraq, the setting aside of international legal constraints and indicates a serious problem of organisational culture amongst security planners and the media, especially in the US. The static and homogeneous institutional thinking so evident over the assumptions over Iraq's WMD is also evident in considering the potential peril faced by the West.

It is not likely that Al-Qaeda would win, but present policies make it more likely.

The West, and especially the US, are now much more on guard. There has been considerable success in arresting Al-Qaeda leaders. The vast majority of Muslims reject Al-Qaeda's approach. There remain deep religious differences between the sect supporting the attacks and many others traditions of Islam, so I do not want to confuse considering a worst case with saying it is likely.

Today's extremists look to the past. In the distant past in the time of the prophet, Islam overcame Persia, Egypt, Baghdad and Syria within a few years and reached southern France within a century. The history of Islam is punctuated with the overthrow of decadent urban civilisations by religiously 'purer' rural insurrection and, in recent centuries, of isolated revolt against Western Christian attack. In some parts of the world, such as Chechnya, this pattern of conflict has a long history.

In the recent past, in Afghanistan Islamic guerrillas were credited by both Ronald Reagan and Margaret Thatcher with playing a vital role in the defeat of the Red Army, and the subsequent collapse of communism. For Islamic fighters, the defeat of the Soviet empire provides inspiration for the idea of defeating the US-led West. For Al-Qaeda, there is an attractive parallel with Mohammed and his successors in the seventh century. At that time the superpowers were Christian Byzantium and Persia. Within a few years, Islam overthrew Persia and permanently captured Egypt and Syria/Palestine from Byzantium, forcing it to retreat to the mountainous border of modern-day Turkey.

Building on their success against the Soviets and after carrying out the attacks of the last few years, Al-Qaeda could make some pretty encouraging cost-benefit analysis. They are clearly carrying out attacks designed to have a strategic impact on the country that is attacked. And they have succeeded. On 9/11 for the sacrifice of five teams they inflicted $600 billion damage, transformed the international political agenda and turned bin Laden from a figure with a small and enthusiastic following in the Arab world into a global charismatic leader. In my local community centre in London there was, I am told, like it or not, and I do not, cheering as the twin towers fell.

Some analysts say that Al-Qaeda has been prevented from carrying out more attacks on the scale of 9/11. This may well be true. But from another perspective, the attacks serve the function of puncturing the balloon of Western invincibility. There is little point in puncturing the balloon twice. Further attacks would create an even stronger and more unified backlash from the West, making it more difficult for Al-Qaeda to recruit and creating unity when it is better served by division.

In Turkey, Indonesia, Kenya, Morocco and Tunisia there were inhuman attacks on innocent people; but these attacks also show coordinated global reach that targets 'sell-out' Muslims and Christians, destroys decadent tourism in oceans of poverty, forces the withdrawal of Western flights, business and tourism, and applies further pressure to the Western-orientated economy of 'sell-out' or, as they are called, apostate Muslim governments. The attacks begin to destabilise societies in these countries and make them more open to support Al-Qaeda ideology. The idea of a heroic 'vanguard' taking actions that others will follow is not confined to Islam. In socialist revolutionary theory, Fidel Castro pioneered the idea that revolutionaries could create popular support by launching attacks, rather than waiting first to build up that support.

The US and the West's strategic position has got worse. In the run-up to the attack on Iraq, Washington failed to see that it would not have Turkish support and that Turkey would distance itself from US policy more than ever before, when the US has been accustomed to regarding Turkey as a loyal 'fortress' in the Middle East. For very different reasons, the US position in both Pakistan and Saudi Arabia is weaker than could have been imagined.

On 9/11 and now in Afghanistan and in Iraq the US has been shown to be vulnerable and its soldiers capable of being killed like those of any other army. The debunking of US might, is itself a political setback for the US.

In Spain the train bombings were timed to influence the elections, and they succeeded in making political change in this major European state. It is easy to say that Spanish people gave in to terrorism. Rather, most of them considered the Iraq war to be a very bad idea, and that, with the bombings, came home with a vengeance. Moreover, had the outgoing conservative government been prepared to accept an Arab – in this case Moroccan – aspect to the case from the start, the sense of being lied to over the war in Iraq and then over the bombings might not have been so great. Whatever the thinking actually was, the bombers achieved great political change with their actions and this will only encourage more of the same.

Far from defending their homelands, America and Britain may even have marched into traps, or created traps for themselves, in Afghanistan and Iraq. Even Donald Rumsfeld now says that Iraq and Afghanistan will be long, hard slogs. With US forces potentially in unwinnable wars, their opponent has more room for manoeuvre than could have been imagined a few years before. Richard Clarke, George W. Bush's counter-terrorism adviser, has observed that the attack on Iraq played to bin Laden's propaganda by fulfilling his prophecy that the US would attack an oil-rich Islamic state. This action, Clarke has argued, has done much to strengthen Al-Qaeda.

At the time of writing, the global guerrilla war associated with Al-Qaeda is going on in several states and Al-Qaeda has known connections in scores of countries in the Middle East, though several of the conflicts have yet to be joined up. Although Al-Qaeda appears to have drawn strength in Iraq from Saudi-sponsored Islamic activity, and there appears to be external input into the attacks on Americans, at present the continuing war in Iraq is not directly connected either with Saudi Arabia or with Palestine. Many in the Arab world see Israeli participation in US actions in Iraq, but as yet there has been no assertion or allegation that the suicide bombers in Palestine and in Iraq are part of the same organisations. Were such an allegation or claim ever made or substantiated the explosive content of such a combined battle would be extremely good news for Al-Qaeda and very worrying for everyone else.

In the broader Islamic world one form of political change may be the rise of a new generation of Islamic 'Colonel Nassers'. (Nasser was the nationalist leader of Egypt in the 1950s and 1960s.) In his era, military coups in the Arab world became common. In the coming period such leaders may have a strong religious motivation, born of the humiliation of the Muslim world. Such political change is a possibility in countries from the north African coast across the Middle East to Indonesia. Change in any one country could start a trend, and many of these countries are producers of scarce oil and gas.

As is discussed in the chapter on resource wars, the fall of the royal family in Saudi Arabia could have a catastrophic impact on the US and Western economies. While the situation in the country is very unclear, the level of violence is increasing and Al-Qaeda has apparent support from sections of Saudi society. US forces have apparently left Saudi Arabia. The blasphemy of their presence was a key reason for beginning the war. Is the US withdrawal a sign of victory and an indicator that more victories may come, or was it a prudent and conciliatory measure by the US and the Saudi leadership?

As Robert Baer, former Deputy Director of Operations at the CIA, has described it, the fall of the House of Saud and a disaster for the US is likely, even inevitable.

The United States' policies on Saudi Arabia, Baer argues, are built upon the delusion that Saudi Arabia is stable – that both the country and the flow of its most precious commodity can continue indefinitely. Sustaining that delusion is the immense amount of money (estimated at $19.3 billion in 2000) exchanged between the two partners: the US buys oil and sells weapons, Saudi Arabia buys weapons and sells oil. Oil and the defence contracts underpinning its protection bind these two countries together in such a way that when Saudi Arabia falls – a fate Baer feels is absolutely certain – the US will fall too. Perhaps not all the way down, but, if we don't curtail our dependence, he argues, a failure in Saudi Arabia could have catastrophic consequences for the US.[18] Any major economic impact on the US would also affect Europe and the rest of the world. A strategy for taking oil out of politics is discussed in chapter seven.

In addition to having the West over the oil barrel, there remains the problem of Islamic extremists acquiring nuclear arms. As discussed earlier, this is less likely than media hysteria might indicate. Nevertheless, any Islamist government in Pakistan, for example, having access to its nuclear weapons, or even supplying them to a new regime in Saudi Arabia to deter a US attack, would be a boon to Al-Qaeda and its allies and emulators.

In addition to the attacks on supposed apostate regimes in the Islamic world, to the oil threat, and to the acquisition of nuclear weapons can be added the continuation of large-scale attacks within the West of the type seen first on 9/11 and then in Madrid.

The 'Perfect Storm' for radical Islamists might be a combination of oil pressure, nuclear-weapons acquisition and large-scale civil disorder and repression around the Muslim populations of Western Europe. At present, the war waged by Al-Qaeda has not become a clash of the West with Islam. However, continued Western occupation and attacks in Islamic countries, coupled perhaps with new attacks in the West, and no resolution of the Israel–Palestine war may yet produce an escalation in violence globally. With political actions globalised by TV a revolution in one country may have a domino effect elsewhere. Some argue that this was feared after the Iranian revolution and no such chain reaction occurred. However, this view does not take into account the Sunni/Shia divide in Islam. The Shia are mostly Iranian and operate under a tight religious hierarchy, while Sunnis have a far more decentralised religious basis. Thus a major change in a Sunni-populated state would not have the self-contained character of the Iranian revolution.

Underlying all of these discontents is widespread poverty in a great arc of mostly Islamic countries from north Africa to Indonesia. It is argued that many supporters of Al-Qaeda are middle class and that therefore the poverty argument does not apply. This complacent view ignores the 'Robin Hood' model in which Robin – a nobleman – robs the rich to feed the poor. As Ruthven points out in *Islam in the World*:

> The Quran's attacks on social injustice and the abuse of wealth, combined with the prophet's activist example, can always be invoked to mobilize opposition to Muslim governments perceived as corrupt or unjust, especially those which fail to equip themselves with convincing Islamic credentials. To that extent Islam seems set to remain on the political agenda for many decades.[19]

However, while we remain understandably focused on violent expressions of fundamentalism it is worth dwelling on Ruthven's conclusion that

> *freed from the rigidity which makes so much Islamic activity*
> *seem culturally sterile ... Islam could prove a highly suitable*
> *faith for the next century of the common era, and one with*
> *an important message. ... It is a message which calls on men*
> *and women to show gratitude for the world's bounty, to use it*
> *wisely and distribute it equitably.*

However, with poverty unabated around the world, the wealthy getting wealthier and the powerful not inclined to moderation, the trends suit Al-Qaeda and friends.

The threat of destitution

> *We must act, not only because it is morally right, but because*
> *it is now essential for stability and security. Many of us grew*
> *up thinking there were two worlds – the haves and the have-*
> *nots – and that they were quite separate. That was wrong*
> *then. It is even more wrong now. We are linked now in so*
> *many ways: by economics and trade, migration, environ-*
> *ment, disease, drugs, conflict and – yes – terrorism.*
>
> Gordon Brown, Chancellor of the Exchequer
> and Jim Wolfensohn, President of the World Bank.[20]

The reality and the fear of having no food or home dominates the lives of the majority of people on earth. Their total number is increasing and so too is the wealth gap between this majority and the prosperous minority. Concentrations of wealth now mean that a few score individuals with wealth on the scale of Bill Gates, the billionaire founder of Microsoft, have more resources at their disposal than the poorest billion people put together. The details have been documented extensively in many places from the World Bank to the UN and in new processes such as the World Social Forum. There is disagreement about whether these trends are getting worse or stabilising. However, the World Bank estimates that around 2.8 billion people live on less than $2 a day:

> When estimating poverty world-wide, the same reference poverty line has to be used, and expressed in a common unit across countries. Therefore, for the purpose of global aggregation and comparison, the World Bank uses reference lines set at $1 and $2 per day in 1993 Purchasing Power Parity (PPP) terms (where PPPs measure the relative purchasing power of currencies across countries). It has been estimated that in 1999 1.2 billion people world-wide had consumption levels below $1 a day – 23 percent of the population of the developing world and 2.8 billion lived on less than $2 a day. These figures are lower than earlier estimates, indicating that some progress has taken place, but they still remain too high in terms of human suffering, and much more remains to be done.[21]

Global warming presents a huge threat of further destitution. In simple terms, a large percentage of the world's population, especially in the developing world, live in coastal cities around river estuaries that are at risk from rising sea levels resulting from melting icecaps. One example[22] of the studies highlighting this threat is the report of the German government's Advisory Panel on Global Change.

The report, written by eight leading German professors, says that 'dangerous climatic changes' will become 'highly probable' if the world's average temperature is allowed to increase to more than two degrees Celsius above what it was before the start of the Industrial Revolution. Beyond that level the West Antarctic ice sheet and the Greenland ice cap would begin gradually to melt away, eventually raising sea levels by up to thirty feet, submerging vast areas of land and key cities worldwide. London, New York, Miami, Bombay, Calcutta, Sydney, Shanghai, Lagos and Tokyo would be among those largely submerged by such a rise.

Above this mark too, other 'devastating' and 'irreversible' changes would be likely to take place. These include a cessation of the Indian monsoon and the ending of the Gulf Stream, which would dramatically worsen the climate in Britain and western Europe, even as the world warms. Another risk is the so-called 'runaway greenhouse', where rising temperatures lead to the release of huge reservoirs of methane stored in permafrost and the oceans, adding to global warming and starting a self-reinforcing cycle that would eventually make the earth uninhabitable.

There are a host of programmes being run by governments, charities, development agencies and other organisations to alleviate poverty around the world and assist in development. The huge UN conference on sustainable development in Johannesburg in 2003 was the latest major effort, but it is not working. Brown and Wolfensohn highlighted the continuing failure of the existing political and economic structure to solve global poverty and did so with the authority of their positions as the head of two major global financial organisations:

> *Five years ago, every world leader, every major international body and almost every single country signed up to*

eight millennium development goals. ... Instead of cutting child mortality by two-thirds by 2015, 30,000 children continue to die unnecessarily each day from avoidable diseases. Yet the promise we made on child health for sub-Saharan Africa was to be achieved in 2015, not – as it now looks – 2165. Without greatly increased growth, sub-Saharan Africa, the Middle East, North Africa, Latin America, the Caribbean and the transition economies of Europe and central Asia will all fail to see their poverty halved. Yet the promise made to sub-Saharan Africa was for 2015, not – as now seems likely – 2147.

It should be clear by now that the some of the negative effects of huge corporations and the economically powerful nations have a crucial role in the perpetuation of hardship for billions of people. In Chapter 4, I look at new ways of establishing fairness and equality that can reinforce existing campaigns for sustainable development and economic justice.

The impact of destitution on war, civil war and personal violence is not inevitable. In some societies religious and ethical systems teach the benefits of accepting a life of poverty. For example, Buddhism teaches that desire itself, even for food, shelter or wealth, is the source of suffering. A similar ascetic approach can be found in parts of other world religions. Nevertheless, fighting for resources plays an important part in many wars.

The role of poverty in creating a climate of social dislocation and general threat is well known to us all in the cities we live in. Deprivation is no excuse either for crime or for war, but equally it is idiotic to pretend that there is no connection. The issue of fighting over resources is discussed in the chapter on oil and gas dependency. For now I just want to establish that any strategy for world peace must include the issue of destitution around the world. The facts are clear and the advocates of change are authoritative. They do not get any clearer by writing more words.

Before leaving Part 1 and moving from the diagnosis to the treatment it is worth summing up. The problem of weapons of mass destruction and terrorism is a major issue for the twenty-first century. But it is not, as Tony Blair claims it to be, the only or even the most important threat we face. The existing threat of governments using WMD can still inflict more damage than any terrorist could dream of, and the means of managing this problem developed over half a century have now mostly been abandoned. Nor it is useful to try to manage the existing threat from weapons of mass – or we should say – self-destruction and the new issue of global guerrilla war by abandoning the international system so painfully established through two world wars and a cold war. As we will see in the following chapter, in the global village both guerrilla war and mass destruction need law, broad political consensus and the redress of grievances if the weapons are to be defused, the intelligence gathered and action successful.

Part two

A guide out
of the mess

Three

Strategy

Politicians have neither the time, the training nor the inclination for strategic thought.

General Jack D. Ripper
in Stanley Kubrick's *Dr Strangelove*

Strategy is one of those important-sounding words that's hard to pin down. We have media strategies, corporate strategies, military strategies and so on. The simplest way to think about strategy is that it is about how to get to where you want to be: how to get from A to B. It also depends on how much you want to do. If you only want to get from A to B then getting from A to B is strategy. If, on the other hand, you want to get from A to Z then getting from A to B is relatively smaller – or what is called a tactic. In strategy, the ideal is to apply energy to weak points in an adversary's position, or in business to develop opportunities at low cost. That is to say, to get from A to Z without working through the alphabet each letter at a time. The British government offers a useful guide about how to survive strategic discussions and reorganisations on its Cabinet Office website.[1] This is a useful starting point for anyone who wants to help develop the proposals in this book. The proposals I have selected are intended to attract a broad consensus of support by means of their novel ability to bring decisive change while remaining rooted in, indeed reviving, core values.

The revolutions in military affairs discussed in Part one make cooperation rather than war the key to success. The revolution caused by the industrialisation of warfare resulted in the strategic approach embodied in the UN. The second revolution caused by globalisation is the emergence of global guerrilla war. A strategy to tackle this challenge can be found in traditional British textbook approaches to war. To this end it may come as a surprise to find that cooperation is also a central part of the British Army's traditional approach to guerrilla or civil war, sometimes called 'insurgency'. In the British Army, General Frank Kitson is famous for developing a set of principles drawn from the many colonial and policing operations carried out since 1945.[2] He drew a good deal on the ideas of Sir Charles Gwynn in his 1939 book *Imperial Policing*.[3]

Kitson wrote: 'The first thing that must be apparent ... is that there can be no such thing as a purely military activity, because insurgency is not primarily a military activity. At the same time there can be no such thing as a purely political solution.' This is not of course the approach taken by the United States under George W. Bush. But what it tells us is that we need to be looking at overall non-military approaches to what is called terrorism.

Kitson then lays out five key areas of policy:

1   any overall plan which is made up of several different measures must be coordinated so that the different elements do not cut across each other.

2 Establish a favourable political atmosphere, particularly with respect to redressing grievances.

3 Have good intelligence on the potential attackers.

4 Everything done by any imperial government and its agents must be within the law, even in an emergency. If a government uses the law to regulate the lives of its citizens it loses any legitimacy when it flouts the law itself.

5 Secure the home base and deny the enemy a base of operations.

It is easy to be cynical about such principles. On the one hand, some Americans and French deride such wimpishness; on the other, people on the receiving end of British imperial policy may have a less generous view of British practice over the centuries. Its advocates would claim that its implementation permitted the operation of the Empire, outside of Ireland, with minimal force through the imperial period, including the withdrawal after 1945, and that even in Northern Ireland these principles have proved effective in the latter part of the twentieth century. The point, they argue, is to concentrate on the system rather than argue over the history.

It is useful to compare these strategic principles for tackling guerrilla war with the overall set of priorities agreed by the United Nations at the Millennium Summit in 2000; the full text is in contained in Appendix II.

The UN Millennium Goals

In September 2000 the nations of the world agreed a strategy for the coming millennium based on the UN organisation and Charter, which they agreed are 'indispensable foundations of a more peaceful, prosperous and just world'. They stated that 'the central challenge we face today is to ensure that globalisation becomes a positive force for all the world's people. For while globalisation offers great opportunities, at present its benefits are very unevenly shared, while its costs are unevenly distributed.'

The agreed core values of freedom, equality, solidarity, tolerance, respect for nature and shared responsibility were focused on a set of key objectives such as peace, security and disarmament based upon compliance with the International Court of Justice and the UN Charter and including:

- Increased national support for UN work on conflict prevention, peaceful resolution of disputes, peacekeeping, post-conflict peace-building and reconstruction;
- Concerted action against international terrorism, countering the world drug problem and transnational crime in all its dimensions;
- The elimination of weapons of mass destruction, particularly nuclear weapons and in the interim the reinforcement of arms control treaties.

In addition, the UN's development and poverty eradication objectives aimed to help the more than one billion people in extreme poverty attain through good governance an open, equitable, rule-based, predictable and non-discriminatory multilateral trading and financial system and an enhanced programme of debt relief for the heavily indebted poor countries. The nations set themselves the objective of halving by 2015 the proportion of the world's people whose income is less than one dollar a day, who are hungry and who have no clean water, and of creating universal primary education and improved health care.

They also agreed that protecting our common environment should be based on principles of sustainable development, including those set out in Agenda 21, agreed at the United Nations Conference on Environment and Development and included in the Kyoto protocol for the reduction in emissions of greenhouse gases. Other environmental strategies include support for the Convention on Biological Diversity, water management strategies and free access to information on the human genome sequence.

The Millennium agenda also sought to expand and strengthen the protection of civilians in emergencies, in conformity with international humanitarian law, and to support the Convention on the Rights of the Child and prevent the sale of children, child prostitution, child pornography and the involvement of children in armed conflict. Other work on human rights, democracy and good governance emphasised respect for the Universal Declaration of Human Rights and the Convention on the Elimination of All Forms of Discrimination against Women. Many of these goals were given prominence in a special set of priorities for Africa. This set of objectives laid out by the UN provides a useful benchmark for the coordinated effort needed to produce a favourable political climate and reinforce the rule of law.

Our strategic challenge is that it is progress in all of these millenium goals that is lacking rather than any shortage of military force.

Former British SAS officers at a conference at the Royal United Services Institute laid out the problem of meeting this challenge not long after 9/11.[4] Their approach may seem 'left wing' compared to stereotypical military attitudes, but in my experience it is normal in the military and intelligence services:

We all live in a 'Global Village' where economic interdependence knits us all together. There can be no isolationism. There can be no unilateralism.

The 'battlefield' has no front or rear. We all live in multi-ethnic societies. There is no safe base. The very complexity of the modern world makes it extremely vulnerable. The media reaches everywhere. Hence, one incident has sent the airline, financial and tourist industries reeling all over the world.

What, therefore, should we be doing about this threat in the future? Is it a war? I do not think so – it is a protracted campaign, perhaps – but it certainly is a struggle for hearts and minds, for perceptions and, therefore, for political power.

The mechanics are simple – the military and police forces exist – but the genius is putting them together in a coherent fashion to best effect. The guidelines for this are, to my mind, the same principles we have both mentioned earlier.

If, therefore, we return to the principles and look at them in this new context, they could perhaps guide us to what shape the future counter-terrorist effort might take. Obviously, all I can do here is make suggestions and highlight issues, rather than produce a blueprint:

Removing the underlying grievances. This is a contentious area where I am perhaps not qualified to talk. But I would mention among others, and in no particular order:

- The need for far greater involvement of the West in helping countries develop. If the West is to gain, it must put back.
- The resolution of the Middle East Peace Process.
- The need for the Muslim world to come up with a political doctrine which is compatible with the tenets of the faith.
- A new policy on Iraq.
- The distribution of more of the wealth and serious action against corruption.

All of these policies would assist in removing the potential grievances.

Stay with in the law and proportionate use of force. Inevitably there has to be some form of UN involvement. There has to be a legal framework to give legitimacy and therefore, there have to be definitions, etc. How will we resolve the issue of one man's terrorist being the other's freedom fighter? What will constitute a domestic or global terrorist threat? Who and how will we differentiate? Where does the sovereignty of states sit with these issues?

All military actions have political consequences. Do not play into the hands of the enemy. Do not reinforce enemy propaganda. Always seek legitimacy.

Although the global guerilla threat is new, there is much to be learned from old principles. Over time the principles of low-intensity conflict, counter-terrorism and counter-insurgency are lasting. The challenge is to apply them in the twenty first century.

I believe this requires a radical reorientation of the way we view ourselves. It requires understanding that there are no superpowers any more. Their might is irrelevant. It means that we must be involved and multilateral. The threat concerns us all; it is not 'them and us'.

Unfortunately, the most influential force in American and British policy follows neither the precepts of the UN nor the classic doctrine of the British Army.

A good deal of this book is critical of this dominant policy and I do not want to repeat myself. But before looking at a strategy that might meet the criteria and objectives set out above it is important to summarise quite how counterproductive present policy is.

The UN agenda is widely despised by US decision-makers and opinion-formers. In other countries too the UN is merely given lip service. Almost regardless of the rights and wrongs of the agenda, the reality is that by trashing the UN and its agenda, it has proved impossible to generate a good political atmosphere. On the specifics of disarmament, international law, environmental protection, sustainable development and above all on redressing the imbalance of power and wealth in the world, US and British policy is also materially making the world a more dangerous place for everyone. For many people, global warming can create far more mass destruction than terrorists could with a dozen nuclear bombs.

British policy is at various points somewhat more positive, but its overall support for the States provides the US with the illusion of speaking for the 'civilised' world. Other countries (Sweden, South Africa) attempt to lead a more positive course of action. But the other major powers, China, France, Germany, Japan and Russia, have not taken up a strong position of leadership, in the manner of, say, Mikhail Gorbachev in the 1980s or the German Chancellor Willy Brandt in the 1970s.

The explicit rejection of international law by some in the US, the illegal attack on Iraq, the legal limbo of Guantanamo Bay and the torture in American camps all violate the precept of keeping within the law and maintaining legitimacy. The people who espouse these policies do so in the name of anti-terrorism and freedom; in reality they are doing exactly what their enemies want them to.

The UN and international law are flawed. This is a fact. But since the overall strategic assessment is that they are essential, then more, not less, political will and bargaining must be devoted to their improvement. The present official approach is unable to look, as is necessary, at the world from the adversary's perspective or to develop the necessary self-consciousness. It is a normal part of good human communication to try to see how others see us. In war, gaining such insight is indispensable, unless one is utterly confident of victory. On 11 September the US suffered an unprecedented blow and there should now be no such confidence. Unfortunately, the debate in the US on 'why do people hate us?' is cut short by accusations of appeasement or weak-minded liberalism. This can only give comfort to the guerrillas. Seeking to understand the other point of view does not mean that we have to like it. We do not have to sympathise in order to empathise. Whatever the result of elections in the US, this naïve bravado will remain a powerful influence.

In terms of the TV series *Star Trek*, we in the West see ourselves as a 'Federation' of benevolent, globalising, free-market democracies. 'They' see us as the Borg, preaching that they must be assimilated, as we 'teach the world to sing in perfect harmony'. 'Suicide bombers' would, in Western fiction, be resistance heroes. 'Our' Christianity is a religion of compassion, which to others has its own horrors such as the idea that babies are born sinful, not to mention the apparently cannibalistic ceremony of eating and drinking the flesh and blood of the Messiah. Such an image may seem offensive, but it is indeed how many people see it.

What is especially interesting about Kitson's British Army approach to countering guerrilla warfare is that it is compatible with the strategy and strategic goals laid out in the document agreed by consensus at the UN. It is important also to be aware that there are other police and military approaches to internal security which are far more reliant on killing with little account for the law. One only has to think of the present war in Chechnya or the various continuing civil wars in Africa and South America. In a textbook analysis of war between guerrillas and the central government, a key guerrilla objective is to trap the government into overreacting and becoming repressive and illegal, so justifying in its actions the initial claims of the guerrillas. The invasion of Iraq is an example of how to walk into such a trap. From my perspective I think that people working in peace and justice organisations should take heart from the extent to which their concerns are shared by some of the military officers who have had to go to war in Iraq, and conversely that many who instinctively support an approach backed by British officers may be surprised at how liberal and 'force-lite' their approach actually is.

Existing conflict prevention and conflict resolution efforts

There is a lot of existing work around the world to build on and to take encouragement from. There was an enormous effort by many governments to control armaments although this has fallen out of fashion more recently. This effort is described in Chapter 8 along with ideas to build stronger controls out of the building blocks of established treaties covering particular types of weapons.

There is also rarely reported work on conflict prevention and resolution going on around the world. At local level there are many successful examples of people coming together. The Oxford Research Group has detailed more than fifty of these. In Washington, the Carnegie Endowment for International Peace's Commission on Deadly Conflict provides an overview of the local and regional problems around the world and of efforts to tackle them. In some governments, there has also been increased attention to peace and conflict prevention. The Norwegian government sponsored the Arab–Israeli Oslo Process and negotiations in Sri Lanka, and in Britain the Labour government has a conflict prevention budget focused on Africa. At the UN there have been countless reports and recommendations on improving peacekeeping – such as the Brahimi Report – and conflict prevention and early warning – Boutros Boutros-Ghali's Agenda for Peace.

Ideally, these skills should be brought together and refocused on areas of the world where grievances are most severe, including Palestine, Kashmir, Chechnya, Ache in Indonesia and Algeria. It is clear from Al-Qaeda's operating style that it is working with aggrieved people in Islamic parts of the world and seeking to unify them into a global civil war. An intelligent global counter-insurgency strategy would focus a legal, legitimate, UN-based effort on these regional and local issues.

All of these efforts are of vital importance, but they have major structural problems that the proposals in this book attempt to deal with. Conflict prevention studies and efforts usually just look at small areas or regions of the world and not at the so-called hard-security issues of the politics and rivalry between the big powers and the economic, political and military forces that affect the world as a whole. Even these efforts are poorly funded and supported. For example, at the UN there is still no group of peacekeepers ready immediately to be sent to a trouble spot. Peacekeepers always have to be brought together on a temporary basis. And this is despite many proposals from within the UN itself and from smaller states such as Sweden and Argentina to create such a rapid-reaction capability. Regional efforts do not tackle issues such as corporate power that are global in character.

Ready or not, the world and the UN will soon be considering whether military intervention should take place in some new part of the world. After Iraq how should we decide whether an intervention is justified? A report sponsored by the Canadian government[5] has laid out a useful checklist of issues to be considered, which I have briefly summarised. They provide for a strict legal framework for overriding the 'Westphalian principle' of non-intervention discussed earlier:

- *Principles*: The legal principle of state sovereignty assumes that the state has a general responsibility to look after its own people. A broader international duty to protect overrides state sovereignty when the state is engaging in the widespread murder or driving out of its own people. This principle, the report argues, is enshrined in the general duty that the UN Charter lays on the UN organisation to maintain peace in the world (Article 24), and on various treaties, such as the genocide acts, which place an obligation on states to prevent abuse.
- *Responsibilities*: The international community has three responsibilities in this situation, which can be summarised simply as Prevent, React and Rebuild. Prevention is clearly the most important, and reaction must not be overreaction.
- *Just Cause*: Any military action must be to prevent large-scale loss of life or ethnic cleansing. Military action must:
    - be the right intention, i.e. not be just an excuse;
    - be a last resort;

- use proportional means;
- have a chance of success.

The legal authority must come from the UN Security Council or the UN General Assembly or in extreme circumstances from a UN-recognised regional organisation.

There is room for a lengthy discussion of these and other approaches to the issue of intervention, but my purpose in this book is to look primarily at structural changes that can provide the political will for the UN and its approach that is so sorely lacking, rather than to discuss ideal procedures. Nevertheless, personally, I am very cautious about military intervention on humanitarian grounds. In many cases the real issue was to have carried out timely prevention, and above all there is a grave danger of starting moral crusades, a point where, to my alarm, I find myself lining up with Henry Kissinger in defence of national sovereignty. How long before we are back in the nineteenth century, taking over countries to civilise the barbaric natives?

Efforts at reform of UN systems deserve stronger support. It is clear that what is lacking at present is policies capable of changing the overall climate and helping reinforce, unify and focus existing efforts.

Priorities for a progressive strategy

The following policy strategies are designed to meet the requirements of the millennium goals, and the following challenges:

- Respond to the two Revolutions in Military Affairs: self-destructive war – WMD – and the advent of civil war in the global village.

- Respond to the challenges of both fundamentalist violent ideology and the US trend to set aside international law, each of which compounds rather than solves the challenges of the Revolutions in Military Affairs.

In making strategic choices it is inevitable that some important issues have not been included. The Israeli–Palestinian issue is an example. The Oslo accords still provide a way out of the present warfare and there seems little that I can add, except to say that reducing conflict in the surrounding region and reducing corporate power, will tend to have a positive impact in this bitter dispute.

I have also only touched on the question of whether there is a clash of civilisations. As Fred Halliday has demonstrated in *Islam and the Myth of Confrontation*,[6] there are those both within Islam and within the West who seek such a confrontation, but neither present societies nor past history show such confrontation to be inevitable. Nor should we think that Islam has a monopoly on fundamentalist extremism. I have heard British officers tell how they squirmed with embarrassment as their US Air Force commander led them in prayer prior to bombing missions over Afghanistan to carry on the Lord's work. I was myself present in the US Senate when the Chair of the Foreign Relations Committee explained that he was happy to confirm John Bolton as an official in President Bush's government because he was the sort of man he wanted at his side when the Book of Revelations became reality and that those days were indeed coming.

Against this context of irrationality it is essential to reassert rational ideas for the real world. The policy choices I have selected may seem far-reaching and over-ambitious but they are designed to have a decisive long-term effect in the following areas:

- *The power and economic disparity between the rich and the rest.* The problem of economic injustice and the unaccountable actions of corporations is both a crucial long-standing issue in the world and, as a result, one of the key grievances that must be addressed in order to establish a good political atmosphere both within our own home base and in the wider world.

- *The lack of democracy at an international level.* The issue of lack of democracy at an international level is one that cannot be set aside for later. With every other aspect of life having a global dimension, our democratic institutions also have to have a global dimension.

- *The critical global resource struggle over oil and gas.* In order to remove the vast military and political competition and investment over control of oil and gas supplies we need a wholesale shift to renewable energy supplies such as wind or solar and new engines and fuels for road vehicles.

- *The uncontrolled machinery of warfare.* We need a comprehensive approach to the management and elimination of WMD and other armaments and military organisation.

Who can use this strategy? Ideally, I would hope that this strategy has wide appeal to individuals, organisations and national governments. If any of the ideas in this book are of use they will be taken up by many of those in what has become called global civil society: the world of pressure groups, academics, political parties, development agencies and relief groups. I hope these proposals meet some of their needs. I write from London and in the aftermath of the decision to go to war in Iraq there seems to be a new desire for a way to fit ideals to practical policies.

The proposals are designed both to be useful in the short term and to enable a major shift internationally. They may strike no chord and soon be forgotten. However, clearly my hope is that they will be found to be useful in many places. For these reasons it is overly presumptuous to specify who might do what. Nevertheless, I hope it is clear that these policies can suit both a progressive agenda in the developing world, and the European Union and US.

In previous campaigns on issues such as global warming, leading to the UN Kyoto protocol, the international campaign to ban landmines and the banning of nuclear testing, success has been achieved through a combination of efforts from governments in Europe and around the world working in combination with international pressure groups, public opinion and demonstrations. These and other campaigns provide powerful examples that give encouragement for the future.

Four

Money

Curbing corporate power

People are ripped off, day in, day out, by the easy availability
of limited liability for off-the-shelf companies and the protec-
tions provided for them, and with no real remedies.

Andrew Phillips,
legal advisor on the BBC *Jimmy Young Show*

According to the Atlantic Charter, international economic cooperation after the Second World War was to include 'the object of securing,
for all, improved labour standards, economic adjustment and social
security'. This objective was a clear attempt to offer the removal of
economic grievances as a source of political conflict and to rally
support for a better postwar world. Popular discontent over economic
conditions and the widespread popularity of both socialism and
communism at that time have been mostly forgotten today. The
public provision of health care, education, unemployment benefit and
old-age pensions was improved by governments in Britain and the rest
of Europe immediately after the Second World War. Today, fair

working standards and social security are under strong attack from neo-conservatives and neo-liberals alike who see them as impediments to the free market and the operation of corporations.

But the acceptance of world poverty, economic injustice and the strengthening of a hugely wealthy elite is a recipe for conflict and war. Battles for access to wealth have been one of the greatest causes of international and civil war since earliest times. On the other hand, shared prosperity is a powerful force for peaceful conditions. William Cobbett, the English eighteenth-century radical, remarked that he defied anyone to agitate a man with a full stomach, a double-edged remark conjuring up both the image of after-dinner bloat and the desperation of those with empty stomachs.

This chapter reviews the great grievance felt around the world over the uncontrollable power of corporations and the continuation of poverty for the many. It recommends that the power of big businesses can be balanced and controlled by removing the special-interest protection that enables the shareholders who own corporations to avoid legal responsibility for the consequences of their actions. This protection is called limited liability.

Corporate power

It is easy to believe that corporations run the world. Their power is often greater than governments'; sometimes we seem to exist only in order to consume their products and boost their profits. What's good for General Motors is good for America and the rest of the world too. And if you don't like it ... it doesn't matter because you are irrelevant, and in any case look at all the wealth being created. Free markets work, despite their problems, and there is simply no alternative – or so we are told.

This attitude – triumphal from the supporters of big business, wearily defeatist from those who try to restrain them – pretty much describes the present corporate domination of societies around the world. In the advanced democracies, corporations are sweeping aside government controls and socially owned organisations; in the rest of the world the protections given to the wealthy through the limited-liability laws provide a blank cheque for old and corrupt elites in supposedly reformed and democratic societies.

There is widespread public concern over the power of corporations. The needs of business have come to define politics today. The Anglo-American 'Third Way' and Britain's New Labour have been attempts to fit public demands for a fair and just society with the needs of business. At a global level the strength and diversity of resistance to a political agenda driven by the needs of major corporations has been made evident by protests at the world trade talks in Seattle and Cancun. Meanwhile, Enron, WorldCom and similar scandals have produced a feeling in the general public, and even amongst shareholders, that they are being ripped off.

Attempts to make businesses behave better by campaigns for what is called good corporate governance have had little effect. Today, corporations usually follow the legal advice that it is unlawful to pursue any other goal than delivering profit to shareholders. Other social or environmental objectives can be pursued, but they must contribute to this primary goal. The enormous political energy poured into corporate governance by so many people can achieve very little because of this legal imperative. A new strategy is needed to help corporations reinforce rather than undermine the fabric of society. The reforms I suggest would hold the major investors accountable in law and give small investors more confidence that companies were being run responsibly.

A close examination of the core of the common structure of corporations reveals a fundamental injustice. Focusing on the reform of this injustice should be the basis of controlling corporations.

The key idea in the modern corporation is the concept of limited liability. This concept provides the owners, the shareholders, with complete power, but with no responsibility for the consequences of their actions. Their liability is limited to the sum of money they invest. This power without responsibility is driving the whole structure of global civilisation and yet it violates fundamental principles of justice and human rights in a free society. Limited liability creates inequality before the law by allowing the most powerful to be above the law, when in a free society all should be equal before the law.

Attempts to find voluntary means of controlling corporate power have not had sufficient impact. There now needs to be a debate about the need for legal reforms to make shareholders and directors accountable for the actions of the companies they own. A movement for this reform should be the economic centrepiece of a global strategy for stability and prosperity. Such reform is necessary because existing attempts to obtain voluntary agreements from corporations to behave well are not working. Many people are unaware of the injustice created by limited liability, and consequently it is necessary to make the argument plainly and strongly. This does not mean that I believe that there are millions of people out there going to work every day saying to themselves, 'Goody, I'm off to operate an unjust system.' The dominance of limited liability has crept up on us over the years; people are rarely if at all deliberately operating a system that they are aware is unjust and violating the human rights of their fellow citizens.

The existing debate on corporate power

Corporate power has grown considerably since the collapse of communism and the widespread discrediting of state socialist approaches to running society. Will Hutton has argued with great clarity that the world as a whole has to face the damaging consequences of the triumph of Anglo-American business practice.[1] Agreements in the World Trade Organisation and the Organisation for Economic Co-operation and Development (OECD) have extended and entrenched an agenda that favours international corporations in the name of free trade and free markets.

Hutton's argument is echoed by many of those supporting this approach. Two leading US academic economists, Henry Hansmann and Reinier Kraakman, provide a typical example of this analysis in their paper 'The End of History for Corporate Law'.[2] They argue:

> Despite the apparent divergence in institutions of governance, share ownership, capital markets, and business culture across developed economies, the basic law of the corporate form has already achieved a high degree of uniformity, and continued convergence is likely. A principal reason for convergence is a widespread normative consensus that corporate managers should act exclusively in the economic interests of shareholders, including noncontrolling shareholders. This consensus on a shareholder-oriented model of the corporation results in part from the failure of alternative models of the corporation, including the manager-oriented model that

evolved in the US in the 1950's and 60's, the labor-oriented model that reached its apogee in German co-determination, and the state-oriented model that until recently was dominant in France and much of Asia. Other reasons for the new consensus include the competitive success of contemporary British and American firms, the growing influence worldwide of the academic disciplines of economics and finance, the diffusion of share ownership in developed countries, and the emergence of active shareholder representatives and interest groups in major jurisdictions. Since the dominant corporate ideology of shareholder primacy is unlikely to be undone, its success represents the end of history for corporate law. The ideology of shareholder primacy is likely to press all major jurisdictions toward similar rules of corporate law and practice.

The notion of organising the world around the needs of shareholders has been questioned across the political spectrum, from the World Social Forum at Porto Alegre to the billionaire George Soros.[3] Noam Chomsky,[4] Naomi Klein and George Monbiot are authors whose work provides insights into the problems of corporate power and who begin to suggest alternatives.

I do not wish to take time here to go over the familiar arguments about the problems presented by uncontrolled corporations beholden to their shareholders. But to summarise the argument: corporations are accused of ignoring the interests of those communities they hurt; of polluting the air, land and water; and of forcing nations and communities to give up nationalised and community-based businesses and services. These problems are compounded by a tendency for national and global markets to become dominated by a handful of huge corporations. Their resources are often larger than those of the countries in which they operate and they are able to use structures of linked corporations in many countries to avoid being held to account by the governments of the countries in which they operate.

Think about cars, oil, accounting or pharmaceuticals, for example. In each of these industries only a handful of companies control the market. The problems caused by these corporations have come to dominate the proceedings of elite international gatherings such as the World Economic Forum at Davos.

The opponents of corporate power suggest two main types of strategy for opposing it: local initiatives and corporate governance. Supporters of local initiatives, for example Colin Hines in *Localization: A Global Manifesto*,[5] propose strengthening networks of local non-corporate economies and cultures, such as cooperatives and schemes to promote local produce. These networks include resistance to the idea of third-world farmers being driven into producing cash crops at the expense of existing, more integrated and sustainable economies. An example in the developed world is the network of Italian cities supporting local produce and using local-authority regulations to keep out global chains on the basis that they lack local content. These initiatives appear to work well, but they are by definition small scale, working at the edges of the economy. They can provide a safe place to hide from the trampling feet of the megacorps, but they are neither an effective defence nor an effective means of control. They are, however, a potential base from which such efforts at control can be built.

In parallel with the growth of localism, there has also been a movement to reach voluntary agreements with corporations to persuade them to act with more consideration towards the people and the environment that they affect. Often termed 'corporate governance', this strategy aims to persuade business to become more socially and environmentally responsible. According to John Wolfensohn, then President of the World Bank, 'Corporate governance is about promoting corporate fairness, transparency and accountability.'[6]

The rebranding of British Petroleum as 'Beyond Petroleum' is an example of the effects of campaigns for corporate responsibility. The company has, at least in its advertising, engaged in social and environmental issues. Corporate governance has led to a less confrontational and more constructive relationship between pressure groups such as Oxfam or Greenpeace and the business community, but it has not led to much change.

Christian Aid's case studies of corporate social responsibility make a powerful case

'The image of companies working hard to make the world a better place is too often just that – a carefully manufactured image,' – says 'Behind the Mask: The Real Face of Corporate Social Responsibility', a new report from Christian Aid. Its target is the burgeoning industry known as corporate social responsibility – or CSR – which is now seen as a vital tool in promoting and improving the public image of some of the world's largest companies and corporations.

But, as the case studies in this report – featuring Shell, British American Tobacco and Coca-Cola – demonstrate, the rhetoric can also mask corporate activity that makes things worse for the communities in which they work.

'Some of those shouting the loudest about their corporate virtues are also among those inflicting continuing damage on communities where they work – particularly poor communities,' says Andrew Pendleton, senior policy officer at Christian Aid and author of the report. 'Legally binding regulation is now needed to lessen the devastating impact that companies can have in an ever-more globalised world.'

Christian Aid, January 2004

Stock market scandals at the end of the twentieth century revived a different type of call for reform. This time it was not from those who had bad experiences from the direct operations of corporations, but from shareholders who lost money when the businesses failed. Corporate misdeeds have produced periodic reforms back into the nineteenth century. These reactions were at times especially strong in the US. At the time of Presidents Taft and Theodore Roosevelt in the late nineteenth and early twentieth centuries, regulations against monopolies and price-fixing were introduced and monopolies such as that in the oil industry were broken up. The notorious stock market crash of 1929 produced some useful regulation of stock market activity and, under President Franklin D. Roosevelt, a host of union-friendly legislation protecting workers' rights.

The latest scandals had two notable characteristics. Accountants had themselves cooked the books on a massive scale as their role morphed from being independent auditors to becoming integrated into company operations as 'consultants'. Secondly, on the stock market, the corruption of independent financial advisers into sales staff for particular companies' shares destroyed their hard-won reputation for impartiality.

The effort at reform after the excesses of the 1990s has been weak and is already failing. The *Financial Times* reported in August 2003 that William Donaldson, the new chairman of the Securities and Exchange Commission, had 'voiced worries that entrepreneurial zeal was being stifled by regulations and new legal advice'. And Alan Greenspan, the guru chairing the US Central Bank, said that 'such concerns might be one reason why corporate investment was being held back'.[7]

In Britain, the chairman of Unilever, Niall FitzGerald, has elegantly described how demands for stronger corporate governance have been deflected:

> *On corporate governance, the trade and industry department should be congratulated for having resisted knee-jerk legislation or regulation in the wake of the Enron and WorldCom scandals. Initially it appeared too quick to accept recommendations in the Higgs report on corporate governance, but effective and extensive consultation has led to an outcome acceptable to all parties. In future such consultation will help head off a growing sense that Britain is no longer as friendly a place for business.*[8]

The final remark is interesting for its implied threat that business might move elsewhere, not because Britain may become unfriendly to business, but because it may just not remain friendly enough. That this hostility to better governance comes not from some dodgy speculator but from a company which sells soap powder indicates that the problem of improving corporate behaviour is deep-rooted.

As Andrew Phillips, Lord Phillips of Sudbury, explained,[9] once a private company becomes a limited-liability company, any thought that wider interests may be served is apt to be set aside and even government studies on governance pay little attention to broader issues:

> As the chairman of a large family business [Cadbury] put it when they finally went public, 'once we became a quoted company, we were answerable to our shareholders in the same way as any other company and subject to the same external disciplines. We are, therefore, not in a position to make any special claims about the way in which the business is run and the values which lie behind its management, nor would it be right for us to do so.' How sad, and how diminishing for our society.
>
> The fact of the matter is that the only stakeholders of the modern limited company recognised by law, beyond a sidelong glance at employees, are the shareholders. Indeed, the government report last month [January 2003] by a business luminary, Derek Higgs, on the role of non-executive directors, reinforces that narrow focus. In over one hundred pages there is scarcely a nod in the direction of the wider public interest, or of corporate citizenship. He repeatedly asserts that the required attributes of such directors are those of 'skills, knowledge and experience' without reference to their character, judgement or wisdom. This reflects the reality, namely that most such businesses operate within exceedingly introspective, two-dimensional parameters.

One of Higgs's key recommendation to improve corporate governance is to widen the role of what are called non-executive directors. These are people who sit on boards but are not involved in the day-to-day running of the business. Their purpose is mainly to protect the rights of investors from managers and directors seeking to feather their own nests.

One form of developing corporate responsibility is the idea of stakeholding, which has been made popular by Will Hutton. His approach focuses on the question of the distortions caused by the requirement to maximise profits for shareholders. He attempts to redress this distortion by suggesting a change to company law that would require companies also to take into account a broader range of people with an interest in the company's activities. Such people with an interest, or stake, in the company are termed 'stakeholders'. Key stakeholders, such as insurance companies, pension funds and other large institutional investors, could be made to control companies. Tony Blair had a brief flirtation with stakeholding shortly before coming to power in 1997. However, the negative reaction from business led to his dropping the idea.

Stakeholding is an attractive idea because it offers the prospect of involving a broader range of people in a company's activities. But this also creates significant problems of defining who does and does not have a stake in the company, and precisely what companies would have to do to meet these somewhat ill-defined demands. Hutton recommends that stakeholding be introduced by revisions to company law. This would be welcome, but as he recognises, it has so far failed to gather enough support. More fundamentally, although it adds some rights to people who are not shareholders, the stakeholding concept does not emphasise restoring natural responsibilities on shareholders for the consequences of their actions.

A number of economists and business leaders have always rejected the idea that business should have a conscience and so far this view prevails. Milton Friedman[10] consistently argued that anything that reduces the priority of delivering financial returns to shareholders is wrong. This view predominates today, as is indicated by the definition of corporate governance given by the OECD. The OECD is a club of the world's richest nations. Its view of corporate governance is quite different from Wolfensohn's. According to the OECD,

> *Corporate governance is the system by which business corporations are directed and controlled. The corporate governance structure specifies the distribution of rights and responsibilities among different participants in the corporation, such as the board, managers, shareholders and other stakeholders, and spells out the rules and procedures for making decisions on corporate affairs. By doing this, it also provides the structure through which the company objectives are set, and the means of attaining those objectives and monitoring performance.*[11]

There is nothing here about fairness, transparency and accountability. This definition is concerned with the rights and responsibilities of corporate decision-making.

The application of this narrow definition of corporate responsibility is intended to ensure that business plays by the rules and minimises corruption. An example of this approach is a speech to key Chinese business leaders by Britain's top financial regulator, Howard Davies.[12] His topic was 'Corporate Governance and the Development of Global Capital Markets'. That is to say, he was discussing the ways in which corporate governance matters to the development of global capitalism. His key point is that corruption in business makes doing business more expensive and so less attractive to investors coming from outside a particular culture:

> *Another, harder piece of evidence comes from some American research on the cost of capital. US academic researchers have found that in countries where the policing of insider trading is regarded as weak, or where the legal framework is poor, the cost of capital for firms is typically some 3 percentage points higher than in countries where insider dealing is policed effectively.*
>
> *So good corporate governance, and effective regulation, contribute both to the attractiveness of a country in terms of inward investment and business development, and also to the efficiency of its capital markets, and their effectiveness in the service of the real economy. It is always as well to remember these points when considering what can sometimes be a rather dry topic. And it is important to make these arguments robustly to those who argue that efforts devoted to upgrading corporate governance are costly and bureaucratic, and add little value to the economy. In my view, investment in good corporate governance arrangements, and good regulation of those arrangements, is among the most effective and rewarding investments a developing market can make, and there are figures to prove it.*

These are important objectives as far as they go but they ignore the broader question of the relationship of the corporation to society.

The concept of corporate governance contains no financial or legal power to correct business behaviour beyond improving returns to shareholders. It is an ill-defined approach that absorbs enormous energy from NGOs, academics, unions, government departments and businesses. After more than a decade of political activity, attempts to control businesses through this approach have failed to produce results that even keep up with the problems.

Another approach to controlling corporations has centred on the idea of increasing the power of shareholders. In large modern corporations, the directors and managers of the business have come to assume a very large degree of power. Shareholders often own too few shares, are too ill-informed, or are simply too uninterested to get a grip on company operations. The scandals of the 1990s referred to earlier, produced new calls for accountability to shareholders as a means of preventing financial mismanagement. It is this type of concern that the Higgs report in Britain and new regulations from the US Securities and Exchange Commission were meant to address. But, unfortunately, it is these very same constraints that the leading business figures quoted earlier were so keen to cast aside. The push for shareholder accountability is thus proving as ineffective as the governance and stakeholding efforts to control corporations.

Pressure groups have often used purchasing shares as a means of putting corporate behaviour in the spotlight. The idea is that as share-owners, protestors can gain access to the annual general meetings of corporations and then ask questions and make points during the meeting. A typical example comes from Greenpeace in New Zealand, where it was seeking to stop pollution:

Greenpeace campaigns don't always end up in inflatable boats or with activists locked on to smokestacks. We took the Auckland International Airport Ltd (AIAL) incineration campaign straight to the boardroom challenging AIAL to live up to its vision through a shareholder resolution at their AGM.

Greenpeace purchased the minimum number of shares to allow it to take the resolution forward. Greenpeace board chair Gordon Duncan and campaigner Sue Connor presented the argument for a clean alternative to a packed AGM in Auckland. Residents of Mangere community, located downwind of the incinerator, also attended to convey their concerns.

The resolution was not formally passed but there was a lot of support for its spirit. AIAL can be left in no doubt that this is an important issue for many individual and corporate shareholders.

AIAL agreed to fulfil the demand of Manukau City Council, the third largest shareholder, that the company urgently investigate alternative ways of treating their waste. However, they have yet to make any real change.

Greenpeace will continue to put pressure on AIAL to ensure that the investigation is robust and that the true social and environmental costs of incineration are taken in to account. Any thorough investigation will show the only viable option is to move to a cleaner alternative such as steam sterilisation.

This type of activity can be used to forward the public interest, but it is rare that these activist shareholders have the money and numbers to win at the end of the day. Nevertheless, the tactic serves to highlight the privileged immunity that shareholders enjoy. Greenpeace had rights to debate with the company because it became a part-owner in it. Had Greenpeace members just been citizens standing choking in the fumes, the company would have had no automatic duty to engage with them.

Unlimiting limited liability

Most businesses are organised as companies with a legal structure in which the shareholders hold limited liability. This means that if the company fails or causes damage, the shareholders only lose the sum of money they invested. The company is designed to provide them with money, while protecting them from the responsibility for their actions or inactions in relation to it. A company can be prosecuted or sued if it sells defective products, destroys the environment or sells weapons to the enemy, but its shareholders are immune. Shareholders have regulated protection, at a time when other regulation is being swept away in their favour. Company directors also escape personal liability, seemingly because they are agents of shareholders, who are not liable. Nowadays, directors seem to exist in a privileged twilight zone beyond the reach of shareholders and public alike.

Shareholders' power without responsibility is central to the problem of corporate globalisation. Shareholders are the greatest beneficiaries of government regulation, yet demand that only they enjoy the protection of such regulation. As corporate power has grown, shareholders together have exercised vast powers over the world economy without having to take responsibility for the consequences of their actions. Some of the worst examples of abuse in fact come from undemocratic societies, or societies with elites that have recently moved from communism to democracy. All too often these cliques have neatly grabbed a nation's assets during privatisation and find that the protected existence of a United States-style economic aristocracy provides them with an even more special status than they enjoyed so recently as members of the Communist Party elites.

To restore the balance in society, shareholders' limited liability must be deregulated so that they no longer hold a special status. The very phrase 'free market' is a nonsense because the special interests of shareholders are protected from free-market forces.

The economist Adam Smith was one of the first to identify the problems of limited liability companies, or joint-stock companies, as they were originally called (and are so still in some parts of the world, such as Russia). Joint-stock companies had first been developed by the Dutch and were quickly taken up in London when the Dutchman William of Orange became King William III of England in 1689. The first stock market speculations and crashes came soon afterwards, the crashes following on from scams involving Dutch tulips and the famous 'South Sea Bubble'. This was not, as I fondly imagined as a child, some gigantic soap bubble – perhaps blown by a whale – but an investment con selling the idea of luxury imports from newly discovered territories in the oceans of the Southern hemisphere.

It was against this background that Smith considered limited-liability companies in *The Wealth of Nations*, his great book on free-market economics, published in 1776. In it he generally opposes the development of limited-liability companies, though he saw a limited value for them in the construction of some public works.[13]

Adam Smith denounces limited liability in
The Wealth of Nations (emphasis added)

Joint stock companies, established either by royal charter or by act of parliament, differ in several respects, not only from regulated companies, but from private copartneries.

First, in a private copartnery, no partner, without the consent of the company, can transfer his share to another person, or introduce a new member into the company. Each member, however, may, upon proper warning, withdraw from the copartnery, and demand payment from them of his share of the common stock. In a joint stock company, on the contrary, no member can demand payment of his share from the company; but each person can, without their consent, transfer his share to another person, and thereby introduce a new member. The value of a share in a joint stock is always the price which it will bring in the market; and this may be either greater or less, in any proportion, than the sum which its owner stands credited for in the stock of the company.

Secondly, in a private copartnery, each partner is bound for the debts contracted by the company to the whole extent of his fortune. In a joint stock company, on the contrary, each partner is bound only to the extent of his share.

The Trade of a joint stock company is always managed by a court of directors. The court, indeed, is frequently subject, in many respects, to the control of a general court of proprietors. But the greater part of those proprietors seldom pretend to understand anything of the business of the company; and when the spirit of faction happens not to prevail among them, give themselves no trouble about it, but receive contentedly such half yearly or yearly dividend, as the directors think proper to make to them. This total exemption from trouble and from risk, beyond a limited sum, encourages many people to become adventurers in joint stock companies, who would, upon no account, hazard their fortunes in any private copartnery ... The directors of such companies, however, being the managers rather of other people's money than their own, it cannot well be expected that they should watch over it with the same anxious vigilance with which the partners in a private copartnery frequently watch over their own. Like the stewards of a rich man, they are apt to consider attention to small matters as not for their master's honour, and very easily give themselves dispensation from having it. Negligence and profusion, therefore, must always prevail, more or less, in the management of the affairs of such a company.

* * *

To establish a joint stock company, however, for any undertaking, merely because such a company might be capable of managing it successfully; **or to exempt a particular set of dealers from some of the general laws which take place with regard to all their neighbours, merely because they might be capable of thriving if they had such an exemption, would certainly not be reasonable**. To render such an establishment perfectly reasonable ... it ought to appear with the clearest evidence that the undertaking is of greater and more general utility than the greater part of common trades. ... The joint stock companies, which are established for the public-spirited purpose of promoting some particular manufacture, over and above managing their own affairs ill, to the diminution of the general stock of the society, can in other respects scarce ever fail to do more harm than good.

Notwithstanding the most upright intentions, the unavoidable partiality of their directors to particular branches of the manufacture, of which the undertakers mislead and impose upon them, is a real discouragement to the rest, and necessarily breaks, more or less, that natural proportion which would otherwise establish itself between judicious industry and profit, and which, to the general industry of the country, is of all encouragements the greatest and the most effectual.

So, the man held up as the ancestral guru of the business world disapproved of the legal structure of most modern businesses. He also provided an analysis that accurately describes the concerns many feel about company mismanagement today. Company directors act as the 'stewards' of the rich absentee landlords – the shareholders. However, in the contemporary world the annual general meeting has minimal power. Perhaps it needs to be reinvigorated as the 'general court of proprietors' mentioned by Smith.

Smith's condemnation of limited liability is omitted from the way his views are handed down by free-market advocates. Britain's Adam Smith Institute is a bastion of corporate rights. Fans of globalisation such as Philippe Legrain find it useful to cite Smith's wisdom in support of their arguments, but omit his critique of the structure of modern capitalism. Even Arnold Schwarzenegger cited *The Wealth of Nations* as one of the most important books in his life, though he is scarcely an advocate of repealing limited liability.

Smith's concerns over limited liability are discussed by John Micklethwait and Adrian Wooldridge in their recent hymn to corporations, *The Company: A Short History of a Revolutionary Idea*.[14] They state that Smith had two objections to limited liability: that such companies were inefficient and tended in his day to be monopolies. Whatever the merits of these objections, Micklethwait and Wooldridge fail to consider at all Smith's main objection, namely that society should not exempt some people from general laws simply because they may thrive as a result.

It may seem a startling idea to reform or remove limited liability. We look back at past ages and think, how could people have put up with an obvious injustice like feudal serfdom or the slave trade? Perhaps when you are born and brought up in such a system it seems natural and it would be dangerous to tamper with it. 'Squire knows best,' mutters the peasant in many a period drama. A similar fear exists around business: 'It has always been like this and the economy will collapse if we challenge the basis of corporate organisation.'

Blindness to the issue of shareholder responsibility is illustrated in the recent *Progressive Manifesto* edited by Anthony Giddens, which offers new ideas for the centre-left. He argues that citizens need to take much greater responsibility, rather than relying so much on state provisions, but the key powerful class of shareholders is not even mentioned. The focus is on the mostly economically weak recipients of government money: they are the ones who have to change their ways. Nevertheless, there are some outright critics of limited liability, such as the Australian academic John Quiggen, who points out that many economists criticised the proposals for limited-liability laws in the nineteenth century. In the US, David Korten has written power-fully against the problem of limited liability.[15]

Equality before the law is often cited as one of the fundamental rights of a free society. It is enshrined in Article 7 of the 1948 United Nations Universal Declaration of Human Rights, which states: 'All are equal before the law and are entitled without any discrimination to equal protection of the law. All are entitled to equal protection against any discrimination in violation of this Declaration and against any incitement to such discrimination.' But, as Smith pointed out so succinctly two hundred years ago, 'to exempt a particular set of dealers from some of the general laws which take place with regard to all their neighbours, merely because they might be capable of thriving if they had such an exemption, would certainly not be reasonable.'

Does this exemption amount to inequality? Well, that is what exemption means. Some people may argue that the limited-liability laws have been created democratically. This is true but also irrelevant since they can also be repealed democratically. The debate should be about changing the law which provides for this inequality, and it is clear that those who cling to the way things are believe that this inequality is a good thing, helping make society as a whole better off, and that to threaten this inequality is merely destructive nihilism.

It is also true that shareholding was entrenched in the Western democracies long before the Universal Declaration on Human Rights. So, again I can hear an argument coming: 'Since shareholding existed before modern human-rights law, then surely it cannot be affected by it.' This argument is similar to an infamous argument over the US Constitution. It is based on the assumption made in the Declaration of Independence: 'We hold these truths to be self-evident, that all men are created equal, that they are endowed by their Creator with certain unalienable Rights, that among these are Life, Liberty and the pursuit of Happiness.' However, when it was written, few of the men who approved it would admit that black people were people at all. They were merely property. The point of relevance to the limited-liability debate is that it is possible to re-examine how definitions are applied as circumstances change.

It is especially helpful to reopening the debate over limited liability that there is a history of clear criticism from leading public figures all the way back to the time when limited liability was first introduced. Today the social damage created by limited-liability companies has become the major focus of political concern about the global economy and is overdue for reform.

In theory such reform should be a concern of American conservative and libertarian lawyers such as the Federalist Society, who aim to roll back laws that they construe as going beyond the statements of the Founding Fathers. Limited liability is the most damaging and glaring example of going beyond the intent of the Founding Fathers by creating a whole class of people exempt from the law.

To summarise, limited liability can be seen as removing the human right of the vast majority of people on the planet to equality before the law, the core value of a free society.

Limited liability protects corruption

When I started considering the reform of company law I stumbled over a legal idea that seems to come from *Lord of the Rings* or *Buffy the Vampire Slayer* – 'piercing the corporate veil'.

In the imposing terminology of the legal profession, there is a 'veil' that protects shareholders from liability. Now, I am sure that legal historians will be able to find all sorts of explanations for the evolution of this term. The veil is worn by women to hide their sexuality or grief, customary in Muslim societies and made erotic in the dance of the seven veils; this is the legal concept upon which corporate globalisation rests, a veil through which shareholders can see but not be seen, a one-way mirror, a one-way street of power where they can act but not be acted upon. I would have thought that both Freudian psychoanalysis and feminist theory would have generated a few dozen PhD theses on the imagery invoked by this idea, but sadly I have not found any.

The concept of 'piercing the veil' describes some barely known circumstances in which under certain states' laws shareholders can be held liable for their actions. According to one British specialist discussing a case relating to claims for asbestos-related injuries that were thwarted by layers of Russian-doll-like limited-liability companies with one hiding inside another:

> Any modern consideration of lifting the corporate veil must almost certainly begin with the decision of the Court of Appeal in Adams v Cape Industries [1991] 1 All ER 929. The case saw the most detailed judicial review of this aspect of company law ever undertaken in the UK. Justice Scott, and then the Court of Appeal, refused to allow the veil to be lifted on an English parent company whose American subsidiary had been successfully sued by American litigants but which had insufficient assets to satisfy judgement. Lord Justice Slade said: 'Our law, for better or worse, recognises the creation of subsidiary companies, which though in one sense the creatures of their parent companies, will nevertheless under the general law fall to be treated as separate legal entities with all the rights and liabilities which would normally attach to separate legal entities.' The law will not permit the lifting of the corporate veil just because the interests of justice would be better served by doing so.[16]

This specialist went on to say that the veil of incorporation may be lifted where a company is a sham and no third party has an involvement with it. It may also be lifted where the company is a party to a fraud. It will not be lifted just because justice demands it. A director can escape personal liability to a third party in negligence by acting through his company and ensuring that he is perceived as accepting no personal liability for what he is doing. He cannot escape personal liability where he acts fraudulently on behalf of his company. A similar legal protection exists in the US.[17]

Even in a key organ of corporate globalisation, the OECD, there is a recognition that this type of activity, especially when hidden behind the seven veils of subsidiary companies, does represent an obstacle to shareholders turning an honest profit. The 2001 OECD study 'Behind the Corporate Veil: Using Corporate Entities for Illicit Purposes' concludes:

> *Corporate entities – corporations, trusts, foundations and partnerships – are often misused for money laundering, bribery and corruption, shielding assets from creditors, tax evasion, self-dealing, market fraud and other illicit activities. The veil of secrecy they provide in some jurisdictions may also facilitate the flow of funds to terrorist organisations.*

'Behind the Corporate Veil' concludes that the types of corporate entities that are most frequently misused are those that provide the greatest degree of anonymity to their beneficial owners. In response, the OECD calls on governments and other relevant authorities to ensure they are able to obtain information on the beneficial ownership and control of corporate entities and, where appropriate, to share this information with law enforcement authorities domesti-

cally and internationally. Specifically, the OECD recommends that
governments should consider taking action to:

- Require up front disclosure of beneficial ownership and control
  information to the authorities upon the formation of the
  corporate vehicle;
- Oblige intermediaries involved in the formation and management
  of corporate vehicles (such as company formation agents, trust
  companies, lawyers, trustees, and other professionals) to maintain
  such information;
- Develop the appropriate law enforcement infrastructure to enable
  them to launch investigations into beneficial ownership and
  control when illicit activity is suspected.

As should now be clear, it is now the company that gets sued; even
though the company is not actually a person, just an idea, the law
says that a company is treated as a person. A limited-liability
company can simply be the expendable fall guy that can be declared
bankrupt or shut down while the shareholders are long gone.
Companies have additional structures to protect themselves even
further. This is through the creation of subsidiary companies. In this
case the subsidiary may be sued but its parent company cannot
because it is the shareholder. In this way a further incentive to irre-
sponsible behaviour has been created.

The argument for shareholders' privilege

John Micklethwait and Adrian Wooldridge uphold a tradition of
enthusiastic supporters of limited liability. They assert that 'the most

important organisation in the world is the company: the basis of the prosperity of the West and the best hope of the rest of the world.' This is the main idea used to defend the special-interest protection enjoyed by shareholders. It is at least odd to hear the argument that limited liability provides a unique public benefit from those who argue at the same time that there must be no public duty at all placed upon shareholders and companies. They seem to be saying, 'Look, we are making the whole world work, don't mess it up.' In addition, there is the argument that there is no real privilege because anyone can buy shares or, as Marie Antoinette might have said, 'anyone can buy cake.'

Limited liability is credited with creating the vast increase in wealth since the Industrial Revolution. Any attempt to tamper with it will meet great resistance. Even calls for a minimum wage and for social security have been thought to have the potential to cause lasting damage to business. The first time I raised the issue of deregulating shareholder immunity, I came across the vehement objection of a group of venture capitalists. They argued that even raising the prospect of suing shareholders would damage investor confidence and was therefore a dangerous idea. It is certainly true that a market in stocks and shares has been an effective means of raising capital for businesses for more than two hundred years. Some people believe that raising money in this way is essential to the organisation of the economy.

The Industrial Revolution was well under way before the limited liability became the norm.[18] The joint-stock company with tradable shares was not made generally available for business activities in England until 1844, and limited liability was not added to the form until 1855. While some American states developed the form for general use a few years earlier, all general business corporation statutes appear to date from well after 1800. By around 1900, however, every major commercial jurisdiction appears to have provided for at least one joint-stock company. As the BBC's History Timeline explains,

> this allowed companies to limit the liability of their individual investors to the value of their shares. Prior to this, investors in a company stood to lose all their wealth if economic circumstances forced the company they had invested in out of business. The curtailing of risk as a result of the act is credited with being the basis for the increased investment in trade and industry, although most of the evidence for this is apocryphal.[19]

Until the 1930s in the US there were two major exceptions to limited liability. California not only had no limited-liability law, but it insisted that companies based in other parts of the US did not have limited liability in California. The US banking system did not operate under limited liability either.

Different approaches to liability were used in these instances. In California there was a system called pro-rata liability.[20] Pro-rata liability means that in addition to risking their investment, shareholders are responsible for the debts of the company in proportion to the amount of the company they own. Own one per cent of the shares and be responsible for one per cent of the debt. In the US banking sector it was common until the 1930s for shareholders to be responsible for the debts of the company to the extent of two or three times the face value of the shares that they owned. The face value is the value of the shares when they were sold to the public. For example, a company might offer 1,000,000 £1 shares for sale on the stock market, they might then be traded at a value of 10p or £10, but the liability would be based on the issued share price of £1.

There have been a few studies that attempt to provide evidence that unlimited liability can work as well as or better than limited.[21] Lewis Evans and Neil Quigley studied the legal structure of shareholding in the banking industry of nineteenth-century Scotland. At this time some banks used the system of limited liability that we know so well today, while others used a system of unlimited liability. This was at a time when Scottish capital was playing a crucial role in the financial development of the British Empire. They found that in some special circumstances, unlimited liability might even be more effective. A study by Mark Weinstein[22] of the introduction of limited liability in California found that it had no discernible effect on the stock market price of companies' shares, although at that time Californians had not developed the art of suing corporations, still less their shareholders. This form of company law, which I will call 'traditional Californian capitalism', has much to offer the twenty-first century.

In the modern age, perhaps the most famous and largest example of unlimited, rather than limited, liability is the practice in the London insurance market run by Lloyd's. Lloyd's of London has for many years been the major insurer of businesses in the world. Under this system people known as 'names' agree to put their entire wealth at risk to guarantee the insurance market. As a result of their willingness to accept an unlimited risk they receive high returns on their investments. For many years, the insurance industry was regarded as a source of great wealth for those already wealthy. Regardless of its recent problems where some insurers have gone bankrupt, Lloyd's of

London provides an example of a key part of the structure of international business that is not run on the basis of limited liability. The existence of such a key, world-leading industry, not reliant on a limited-liability structure, is of great importance. It provides a substantial example to counter those who argue that limited liability is the only way global markets can operate.

Professions such as law, accountancy and architecture have all operated as successful businesses for many years without the protection of limited liability. However, starting in the US, a new concept of limited liability has been introduced to allow these professionals to escape liability for their actions. When new laws were proposed in Britain to extend limited liability to the professions, Phillips made a vain attempt to at least force companies to advertise any previous names they had used to conduct business. In debate, the government minister makes a crack at Phillips's own profession of law:[25]

> *Lord McIntosh of Haringey: 'But was it not Adam Smith who also said that all professions were a conspiracy against the laity?'*

> *Lord Phillips of Sudbury: 'That is precisely why I have opposed this Bill stock, root and branch. I am a great admirer of my own profession. But I am afraid that this measure is apt to be a conspiracy against the public interest from start to finish. However, I am more concerned with the small traders who will take advantage of the special privileges of this Bill. Let us make no bones about it; this will provide your two-man cowboy building outfit with a*

> *uniquely flexible and light framed means of screwing the*
> *public, to put it in Anglo-Saxon terms ... One of my jobs is*
> *that of legal adviser on the* Jimmy Young Show. *Over 25*
> *years I have heard of hundreds of thousands of cases of abuse*
> *in relation to small, local companies that get nowhere near*
> *the attention of the DTI and get nowhere near being*
> *addressed by the various provisions to which the Minister*
> *refers. It depresses me that in this House we are so far out of*
> *touch with public opinion, if I may put it this way, at the*
> *bottom end of the social spectrum. People are ripped off, day*
> *in, day out, by the easy availability of limited liability for*
> *off-the-shelf companies and the protections provided for*
> *them, and with no real remedies.'*

Supporters of the expansion of limited liability as the dominant form of social organisation downplay other economic models, including European social democracy and various forms of Japanese and south-east Asian economies that have all produced significant and sustained economic growth in the contemporary world. In much of the world and indeed in much of US history, shareholder privilege was balanced by other laws and powers in society. At present these balanced and socialised forms of business are under attack. This may be because they are less effective, or simply because they provide fewer benefits to those with power.

Today corporations and their political allies are seeking to sweep all of these protections away. Rather than resist this by defending the more socially integrated forms of business, it will be more effective to attack the injustice fundamental to unfettered share-holder power.

The idea that the economy can only function when property-owners are protected from having any responsibility for their actions is not historically accurate. It is easy to forget that an international economy had existed and prospered for thousands of years before the invention of limited liability. Business and trade are ancient practices that have been helped and hindered by the social practices of the times. In England for example, Cornish tin-miners were trading successfully as far away as the Mediterranean even before the Roman Empire. Trade and business are as old as civilisation.

One of the reasons most often given on behalf of business and shareholders for the continuation of limited liability is that anyone can freely choose to go into business or invest through buying shares. Millions of people own shares through their pension schemes or through investment companies that manage the money of many small investors. There is no doubt that this has benefited many millions of people, myself included; however, even in the US only one-half of all households participate in the stock market through pension plans, and of these households very few have more than a tiny proportion of the shares of any one company. It will be simple to if necessary, make a cut-off point for liability for small shareholders – just so long as that does not provide a loophole for large institutional investors. In any case, the major corporations, institutions and the super-rich are the groups that own significant parts of major companies. As has been demonstrated in the studies by Professor Edward N. Wolff of New York University in 1989,[24] ten per cent of US families owned eighty-nine per cent of stocks and bonds traded on the stock exchange. Since then these concentrations have increased. Similar concentrations of wealth protected by limited-liability laws now exist around the world.

US families are classified into wealth class by Wolff on the basis of their net worth. In the top one per cent of the wealth distribution (the 'Super Rich') are families with a net worth of $2.35 million or more in 1989; in the next nine per cent (the 'Rich') are families with a net worth greater than or equal to $346,400 but less than $2.35 million; in the bottom ninety per cent ('Everybody Else') are families with a net worth less than $346,400:

	Stocks	Bonds
Super Rich	46.2%	54.2%
Rich	43.1%	34.3%
Everybody Else	10.7%	11.5%

Supporters of mass shareholding often make exaggerated claims that a few years down the road result in great disappointment. In the 1980s Margaret Thatcher's government had TV advertising campaigns trying to persuade members of the public to buy shares in the newly privatised utilities. A few years later large corporations were buying out these small shareholders – few had ever bought more shares and the cost of providing them with information was very uneconomic for the privatised companies. During the stock market boom of the 1990s conservative politicians in the US and Britain began to campaign to privatise social-security holdings. This would have meant that this money was no longer held by the government bank but could be invested in companies. This idea was becoming fashionable until there was a sudden dramatic fall in the stock market, after which little more was heard of the idea.

Strategies for restoring freedom

As I have discussed, the idea of freeing the market from special-interest protections and distortions should have special appeal in the US. Conservative and libertarian lawyers and activists are keen to remove regulations of all kinds. In their key network the Federalist Society they argue for some particular views of what they see as the original US Constitution and oppose laws that seek to develop and change policy with time. From this perspective, limited liability is a classic example of a distortion of the clear constitutional principle of equality before the law.

For Americans, restoring equal rights may be an especially important argument for creating a more equal society. This is because it destroys the myth that the rich are rich by dint of hard work or inheritance and that any tax to help the less well off is simply theft to assist the lazy. Exposing limited liability for what it is, explodes this delusion once and for all.

From the left, Professor Harry Glasbeek has argued: 'There is an entirely plausible argument to be made that criminal law should hold major shareholders responsible for the many evils done by the corporation on their behalf. And many social and environmental campaigners are now focusing their attentions on the laws that allow shareholders and investors the protection of their "invisible friend" – the legal fiction that is the corporation.'[25]

'Sue the shareholders' may look good on a protest banner. But to be effective, a campaign to restore equal freedoms to the economic market needs to have some practical intermediate stages. In general terms a clear understanding of the special status enjoyed by shareholders should make it easier to argue for balancing rights for community groups, elected governments and trade unions. More specifically, there need to be some adjustments to the laws that govern corporations. Fortunately, there are useful historical examples. Two mentioned earlier should be considered. These are the ideas of having a liability two or three times the price of the share and of pro-rata liability.

The insurance system could be employed to help manage the risk. Apart from shareholders, almost every person in the industrialised world ends up needing insurance. Our car insurance protects us if we damage someone else or another car; every business needs public-liability insurance. Rent a civic centre to throw a party and you will find that, before you can, you will have to buy a public-liability insurance policy. This is because if someone is blinded by a party popper you could get sued. Even your house insurance is likely to provide cover in case a roof tile lands on someone's head.

The contrast between what does and does not need to be insured is easy to illustrate. Oxford University has a service for its academics looking to spin off limited-liability companies. It provides a fairly typical list of the types of insurance that will be needed: 'The spin-out will need to obtain a number of insurance policies including: directors, and officers, insurance; building and contents insurance; employer's liability insurance; public liability insurance and product liability insurance.' No sign of shareholder insurance.

The creation of insurance for shareholders could be a relatively simple way of re-establishing equality before the law and placing shareholders as normal citizens with responsibility for their actions equivalent to everyone else in society.

Some people may argue that the insurance industry is already too powerful and has introduced too much nannying in society. If the insurance industry is itself behaving badly this is perhaps because it too has to provide maximum returns to shareholders, something a reform of limited liability would help solve. Insurance is an industry quite well suited to nationalisation or to non-profit status. Social insurance for health and old age are two of the best-known examples of the nation taking responsibility for insurance provision. Another less well-known example is where the nation underwrites mass damage from a terrorist attack, an innovation made in the UK after the Provisional IRA attacks on the City of London in the mid-1990s.

Restoring equality before the law will help many social, economic and environmental campaigns. The removal or reduction of limited liability would ensure that power does not come without responsibility. This would do much to redress the imbalance between the powerful and the powerless. The accelerating power of the business interest would be likely to come to an abrupt halt if it were faced with such a direct challenge to its privilege. Such a challenge would affect the organisation of thousands of companies all over the world. The mere threat of having their privilege exposed may encourage better behaviour.

The argument that the regulations protecting shareholders should be removed can be used as a direct reply to corporate demands for deregulation of other aspects of the market. Opponents of increasing corporate power can argue that the deregulation agenda pursued by corporations had better begin with the regulation that prevents citizens from suing shareholders. This argument is a much more effective lever than socialist demands for the abolition of capitalism or the idea that companies should start behaving like charities.

The removal or reduction of limited liability is consistent with the universal values that power should be matched with responsibility and that we all should be equal before the law.

Within the US, the restoration of the right to sue is a core American value that can be expressed in simple language. In the developing world and in the new European democracies, making shareholders liable can be a means of bringing within the law the rampant corruption that is aided and abetted by the immunity of limited liability. Campaigning to be able to sue shareholders in the same way as anyone else is a clear political demand that can reinforce and complement existing efforts to limit the damage caused by corporations. In recent years, attempts by the public and pressure groups to tackle corporate power have had several public campaigns. These include debt, fair trade, privatisation and climate change. Each of these has produced important and imaginative proposals, gained considerable public support, but in the end made insufficient progress.

When corporations destroy the environment, as for example in the case of the tanker *Exxon Valdez*, which was wrecked on the Alaskan coast, releasing vast quantities of oil that devastated marine life in the region, massive lawsuits can sometimes be brought against the company. All too often, the corporation is found to have been driven by the need to provide maximum returns to shareholders. But these shareholders are immune from any normal duty of care in carrying out their actions. Were it possible to sue the shareholders, one can be sure that they or their insurers would make much stronger demands upon the company to be certain that it was not cutting corners to maximise profit. Quite rightly, the environmental movement is concerned to introduce stronger legislation requiring corporations to act in an environmentally friendly manner. However, if environmentalists include the proposal that shareholders should no longer be above the law, then they are likely to find that corporations might well begin to make concessions to pre-empt demands on shareholders. In similar fashion, corporate demands to remove regulations protecting the environment should be met with a counterbalancing proposal to make their stockholders environmentally responsible in law.

Another area where removing special-interest protection can help existing campaigns is in the area of deregulation of public services. The demands for compulsory privatisation of public services and nationalised industries have been gaining ground continuously around the world since their inception in the early days of Margaret Thatcher's government in the 1980s. The debate in Britain has seen service after service put into private hands for the benefit of shareholders. Most recently, the issue that has come to the forefront of public attention is the use of private medical concerns to supplement the NHS.

The issue of shareholder liability, or lack of it, is especially interesting in the case of medical issues, not least because most of us are now familiar with the idea of suing incompetent doctors, administrators and hospitals. But consider the difference. Let us suppose that the same serious problem occurs in both an NHS and a private hospital. In the NHS any compensation claim will have to be met by the hospital and, if it runs out of money, by the government in London. A private hospital is in a very different situation. If it runs out of money its directors can declare it bankrupt and simply walk away from it. In the meantime, the shareholders could have sold up, taking their earlier profits with them. Even if their profits were made at the time that the medical negligence occurred, no one can touch them.

These imaginary examples are designed to show how much more powerful a campaign can be if it is reinforced with the issue of making shareholders equal before the law. The power of the argument can become mutually reinforced if it is taken up simultaneously on a wide range of issues and in a wide range of countries. The issue of making shareholders behave like normal people has the potential to focus the efforts of a lot of different campaigns. Paul Kingsnorth has shown the diversity and also lack of focus of the anti-globalisation movement in *One No, Many Yeses*.[26] I hope that reform of limited liability can serve as a unifying interest.

Reforming limited liability should improve the overall quality of business activity by providing a legal basis on which to build the social responsibility that so many people are working for from inside and outside corporations. The proportional liability used in conservative Californian capitalism can provide the basis of reform and should be able to attract support from across the political spectrum, including those who believe that governments should not provide any protection to interest groups. These reforms have the potential to help develop fairer societies less open to exploitation by extremism.

This key economic reform will be most effective if it is accompanied by improvements to the way we organise democracy. Money and political power are the vital elements of the way society is organised and reforms in each area should support each other.

Five

Power

Taking democracy global and reinforcing it at home

Democracy is a vital part of building world peace because it keeps governments accountable to their people and because democratic states have a good record of staying at peace with one another. Globalisation, and the revolutions in military affairs discussed earlier, mean that democracy is also a necessary part of the reform of global institutions. This chapter diagnoses our failure to modernise democracy to keep up with globalisation and prescribes a range of reforms to the way international institutions carry out their business. When parliaments were first created back in the Middle Ages, representatives were chosen by each county – now hundreds of years later we need to make our whole country the constituency and have people elected to world institutions directly by the nation as a whole. Business operates globally and so too do pressure groups like Greenpeace and Oxfam. It is only democracy that is being left behind. This upgrade will plug our democratic power into the places that matter. The chapter ends by looking at weaknesses in democracy in Britain and proposes that more key public offices be elected.

It is too easy to be cynical about democracy, especially when with Iraq we have seen a cynical manipulation of public opinion by the UK and US governments to obtain support for the war. It is too easy to forget that democratic pressure has had a continued and strong effect on government policies about war. Indeed in the UK, in the run-up to the Iraq War the Labour government established two constitutional precedents that transferred the power to make war from the Crown – effectively the Prime Minister – to an affirmative vote in the House of Commons. The first occasion was to authorise the Desert Fox attacks on Iraq in 1998, and the second was to authorise the invasion in March 2003.

Without democratic pressure, there would be no incentive to use so-called smart weapons and civilian casualties would be counted in the tens and hundreds of thousands and not 'just' in thousands. Without democratic rights there would be no discussion of so-called friendly-fire casualties; non-voting soldiers would indeed be just cannon fodder. In the non-democratic era, the idea that a sergeant's wife would get to meet a secretary of state because she believed her husband had been given the wrong kit would be unthinkable. The problem of failing to appreciate and to use our democratic rights is discussed in the next chapter, but do not fall into the trap of believing democracy to be useless.

Democracy and peace

We are asked to fight to defend democracy but somehow the campaigns we are asked to support involve tanks, planes and anti-terror laws but never increased democratic control over our government or international institutions. The preservation of peace and the defence of democracy require that democracy itself be strengthened in order to build political strength at home to support any attacks that may come. This democratic reform is needed both at home and in our international representation if we are to meet the challenges of rogue states, a rogue superpower and global terror.

There is strong evidence that democracies do not go to war with each other, although historians are still arguing the point. The main argument is that the major democracies in Europe, the Americas, Asia and Australasia have not fought each other for a century. However, the US and European states have supported anti-democratic regimes in many parts of the world and carried out interventions themselves – particularly the United States in Latin America – that overturned democratic movements and governments. As recently as February 2004 the US supported the overthrow of the democratically elected government of Haiti and supported the brief coup in Venezuela. Both indicate that at least the Bush administration retains traditional US double standards on democracy. We should also remember that electoral success was a key part in Hitler's rise to power.

Some writers, notably the historian Michael Howard,[1] have gone as far as to argue that the idea of peace as a political concept is an invention of modern liberal democratic society. However, he does not consider the contribution of the European medieval philosophers in encouraging a peace policy amongst the princes of the day. Terry Jones and his colleagues provide an interesting insight into peace politics in western Europe over six hundred years ago in their book *Who Murdered Chaucer?*.[2]

From the moment Richard [II] took over personal control of the government in 1389, the pursuit of peace with France became a priority. On a theoretical level, this shouldn't have come as a shock. Peace was seen by many influential thinkers of the day as an ideal of kingship and the desire for peace as the mark of a just ruler. For example, the Italian theologian and philosopher Giles of Rime (1245–1316) taught that a true king desires peace and is not tempted to conquest ... He was supported by Dante ... Chaucer, too, notes that it is the mark of a tyrant to delight in war and that it is always preferable to pursue policies of peace.

The idea that war must be just is found in the Christian tradition as long ago as St Thomas Aquinas. In other philosophies, notably in Buddhism, pacificism and the idea of unjust conflict have a history that is both older and more geographically widespread than in the Western world. So we should not assume either that democracies have a monopoly on peace or that Western democracy is the only legitimate form of government. Nevertheless, I write as a person educated and working mostly within liberal democracies such as the UK and the US, and consequently I am most concerned with improving the effectiveness of democracy in my own culture.

Democracy is neither a cure for all problems, nor a good reason for attacking other countries so as to make them democratic. Nevertheless, it is hard to imagine that a world without democracy would be more peaceful, or indeed that democracy is not a value that in extreme conditions is worth fighting for.

Western, especially US, leaders demand that other states become democratic. We are told that we are fighting for democracy from Iraq to Afghanistan. But it does not feel that way. Power is beyond democratic control. We don't feel relevant.

Fewer people vote; we feel that our opinions, even when there are millions of us on the street, do not count. One reason is that politics seems to be about less and less. The supposed triumph of business has tended to take money – economics – out of politics. This, in combination with decisions being made at international rather than national level, adds to the feeling of irrelevance. However, restoring our human rights with respect to corporations should bring financial issues back on to the table and electing the key officials will create a far more direct and relevant relationship between representatives and people.

The weakness and obsolescence
of existing democratic controls

More and more people around the world can vote. But electoral power is not plugged into the places where important decisions are now made. We feel strongly about the principles of democracy, freedom and the rule of law. In practice, it feels that democracy doesn't make a difference and that we are free just so long as we can pay for our freedoms.

Global bodies such as the United Nations and the World Trade Organisation (WTO) lack both the authority and accountability that comes from being elected. At present the connection between national electorates and the officials who represent them overseas is so remote that these bodies might as well be on Mars; indeed even local decision-making is too remote for comfort. A point made with delightful elegance by Douglas Adams in the opening of *The Hitch-Hiker's Guide to the Galaxy*.[3] The point of this chapter is, in Adams terms, to elect a person to sit in the planning department at Alpha Centauri:

As you will no doubt be aware, the plans for the outlying regions of the galaxy require the building of a hyperspatial express route through your star system, and regrettably your planet is one of those scheduled for demolition. The process will take slightly less than two of your earth minutes. Thank you. ... There's no point in acting all surprised about it. All the planning charts and demolition orders have been on display in your local planning department in Alpha Centauri for fifty of your earth years, it's far too late to start making a fuss about it now.

Tony Blair or Jacques Chirac have the power to give instructions to civil servants at the UN in New York because they have been elected, but unlike domestic issues such as housing there is no politician on the spot required to answer to the public, let alone one we have elected directly.

The Green Room Process

In practice, the WTO and its predecessor, GATT [General Agreement on Tariffs and Trade], have been dominated by a handful of industrial countries. Often, these countries negotiate and take decisions among themselves. Then, in informal meetings, they embark on an exercise of winning over (sometimes through intense pressure) a selected number of developing countries deemed to be more important or influential. Most WTO members may not be invited to these meetings and may not even know that they take place, or what happens there. When agreement is reached among a relatively small group, the decisions are rather easier to pass through the larger body. This process of decision-making by a limited number of countries is known in WTO jargon as the 'Green Room process', so named after the color of the room of the Director General in which many such meetings took place.

From *The World Guide 2003/2004*, Instituto Tercer del Mundo, *New Internationalist*[4]

At home and abroad the world has grown ever more complex. Business, sport and the media have created sophisticated operations at global and local level. But democracy has not been upgraded to keep pace with social change. The last major reforms in the West were concluded in the mid-twentieth century with the extension of full democratic rights to women. In the US, the extension of effective voting rights to African Americans is also now an achievement nearly half a century old.

In looking towards 2020, 2050 and beyond, it is clear that the issues that concern us all will be decided more and more at a global level. We may see one of several models developing: a system of one overwhelming superpower; an oligarchy of the most powerful corporations; or democratic global governance. The alternative is an anarchic system of competing states and corporations. As global institutions develop, we should apply the core democratic values of our society to them. Extending representative democracy directly into these bodies is likely to have a number of positive effects.

In the UK we may now be able to use our sovereign power as citizens to elect the government but we do so in a very antiquated manner. We do not elect many other officials, often just one local councillor and a member of the weak European Parliament. Other nations with different systems, including Australia, Germany and the

US, elect a broader range of local and regional officials and regulators. But so far no nation has caught up with globalisation by directly electing the nation's representatives to global bodies such as the UN.

The election of members of Parliament for geographical areas, or constituencies, remains the main form of democratic organisation in the UK. This structure of organising our voting power has not changed much since the Middle Ages. In the Great Hall in Winchester, in southern England, there is a wall painting listing all the people elected to represent the city in the House of Commons since 1283. Today, the entire adult population of Winchester has the vote, rather than a just few wealthy men as in the past, but the form of organisation has not changed: one person from the local area to the national centre of government.

This pattern of electing local representatives to a central, national, decision-making body has become the model for liberal representative democracy. Its form has remained largely unchanged for more than two hundred years. In those days it took months to send a message around the world and horse and sail were the fastest means of transport, as they had been for thousands of years. Since then, technology has enabled the huge growth of populations and a vast increase in the size, complexity and speed of change in business, government and other social organisations. But we still choose to exercise our sovereignty just with an MP at Westminster. No wonder we feel left behind and left out.

Plugging democratic power into the places that matter

Expanding the connections between citizens' democratic power and the political organisations that act in their name is the key to making democracy more relevant again. We shouldn't remain content to have our democratic power plugged into society only via a councillor, an MP and an MEP; the democratic power of the people needs to directly control more of the key decision-makers at home and abroad. This can be done by electing officials to the key offices of the political process, and these people could then supervise the bureaucrats who now operate without immediate day-to-day supervision.

The present situation in foreign affairs and in much of non-central government is that top officials are left to themselves with instructions sent back and forth by what are still called telegrams. It's a bit like having the country run by Whitehall without Westminster. In terms of the sitcom *Yes, Minister* international institutions are all Sir Humphrey and no Jim Hacker. In London the civil servants have to work with ministers every day, and the ministers are in and out of TV studios and each other's offices. In contrast, at the UN, the WTO or NATO, the civil servants only work with each other on a day-to-day basis, never – or hardly ever – talk to the media unless in a secret 'background' discussion, and have to deal with elected MPs and ministers when they pop in for a visit or some formal meeting or ceremonial occasion. It's a bit like having MPs who only ever turn up at Parliament for the State Opening, when the Queen comes along in her carriage, and spend the rest of the time in their constituencies, occasionally trying to get Sir Humphrey on the phone.

We can transform the way international politics is conducted by sending elected people to supervise the daily work of officials representing us at the UN, the WTO and other institutions. These representatives would supervise the diplomats who currently do the job. Previous attempts to improve democratic input to international institutions by constitutional reform and consultative arrangements have lacked leverage to redistribute power. Democratising our representation would give us new leverage. Parallel reforms at home should be applied to the public services and regulation of the private utilities.

Politicians would get a far better understanding of the issues and paperwork that they deal with. At present ministers, however capable, are overwhelmed with material. The norm is that they turn up at an international meeting, sign documents and fly home. They may pay close attention to new material, but there is a mass of material that officials present to ministers as routine and which only a few ministers ever become familiar with, although it frequently contains important issues. The BBC sitcom *Yes Minister* showed how this was done. When politicians are part of the daily work of international organisations they would also start to build relationships with colleagues in other countries.

With elected representatives on the scene, secret discussions would be forced into the public domain. There would be much more news and information in the papers and on TV from places where the organisational culture favours keeping everything private. Ambassadors and other officials rarely talk to the media, and if they do they are always quoted as some mysterious unaccountable 'source'. At present, if diplomats are asked for an interview, they will reply: 'You have to ask the minister's office back in London.' In this way, international institutions continue for decades with barely anything they do seeing the light of day. There is much more media, and therefore public attention, if politicians are present at meetings. Journalists and television crews will wait into the small hours of the morning for an interview with a politician, but meetings of officials receive little or no coverage. A politician in residence in New York, Washington or Geneva would want to, and indeed have to, give interviews. The secrecy of institutions would start to crumble. There is only so long that a politician would be able to maintain the line that everything is confidential, especially if an MP from another country such as Canada or South Africa was giving a briefing down the hall.

Democratising our international institutions would also help correct the cultural weakness of British and European diplomacy in negotiating with the US. European official representatives abroad are career diplomats whereas their US counterparts tend to be trained in a business culture. The business culture is far more assertive and result-focused than the more conciliatory style of traditional diplomacy. Other nations can be outmatched, not simply by US power, but by the negotiating approach of its officials. If countries that use the traditional European diplomatic model sent elected representatives to reinforce their diplomats, this would help address this weakness in their representation.

As the culture of foreign policy changes and becomes more open, we will find a new generation of people who understand how to run global affairs. Today, even most politicians see foreign affairs as a hidden and mysterious process. Outside the diplomatic service there is a serious shortage of people with experience in how the world of international politics works. To my surprise I found this argument being put to me by a serving British minister who was concerned about how long it had taken him to find out what was going on, and more concerned that a younger generation was even worse equipped to follow him.

It can be argued that party politicians cannot match the professionalism of ambassadors trained in foreign ministries. However, as in any Whitehall ministry today, the officials would continue to provide a vital support and implementation role to the policy direction given by politicians. I am not suggesting that officials are done away with, that would be stupid; the point is to introduce democratic representation and a political culture. Political culture is messy, noisy and at times corrupt, but without it we would be far worse off, for the bureaucratic culture is all of these things and it is invisible and unreachable as well.

Fast-track reform

To achieve change, we need to plug our democratic power into key points in government structures, not just through two or three people remote from the places where key decisions are made.

We can start by sending elected people to official positions in international institutions. In Britain, there is no constitutional or legal obstacle to posting MPs serving as government ministers to be our permanent representatives at the institutions that govern global issues in Brussels, New York or Washington. There is a historical precedent in Britain for this: in the Second World War, Winston Churchill did not simply rely on ambassadors from the Foreign Office; he posted Harold Macmillan, an MP, to Cairo as his minister for the Middle East.

Posting MPs abroad to represent us is a relatively easy way of introducing democracy into our global institutions, but it should only be regarded as an interim step on the way to direct election of our international representatives. Countries with proportional representation (PR) could introduce this change to elected international representatives in one step. In these countries, voters choose between national lists from each party. The more votes the party attracts, the more people on its list get elected. Particular individuals on the list could be designated as the party's nominee to represent the country at each international institution.

In nations with PR national lists, such as the Netherlands, even a single party could begin this process. This would, by itself, trigger debate in an election campaign and might bring other parties to follow suit. Of course, the party might not, at first, end up in the new government, or it might be in coalition, with no overseas representatives. On the other hand, it might be elected, and its sibling parties in other nations might take up the idea as well.

In one or two elections' time, we might find more and more countries sending elected representatives to key institutions. Experience shows that actions in other countries can speed up reform in Britain. During the late 1980s my colleagues and I revealed NATO and Pentagon plans to deliver thousands of new hydrogen bombs to NATO forces. In Britain, under the tight grip of the Thatcher government, campaigns involving Labour MPs and articles in the *Observer* had no effect. However, when German journalists took up the topic, it soon became a major national and international issue because the German government and public had a different attitude to battlefield nuclear weapons. The delivery programmes were cancelled, despite Margaret Thatcher's objections, because of action on the Continent. This type of multinational collaboration has become routine for non-governmental organisations (NGOs) working on international issues.

Posting ministers abroad should be the first step for Britain. There may be an opportunity to move on to the next stage, by introducing PR, when the present government loses its majority, which is likely to happen in the next decade. A domestic and international strategy for directly elected representatives should be prepared in advance to take advantage of future political changes. There would not need to be more elections or a ballot paper the size of a book. The election to the new posts could occur at the same time as the general election and involve parties much as at present. It would, however, start to bring the global institutions down to earth.

PR is only one route to electing our representatives abroad. In addition to listing prospective MPs, ballot papers could include a list of representatives to global institutions elected by the whole nation. This would mean a change from our present system, where the Cabinet is chosen by the Prime Minister, to one where members of the Cabinet, including the Prime Minister, are directly elected.

It can be argued that having many politicians away from home could lead to difficulties with communication and policy coordination. Would there be conflicting mandates between a Prime Minister and directly elected representatives? How would we manage the possibility that financial policy may be developed by several different people: one at the European Union, one at the World Bank and one at the International Monetary Fund (IMF)?

This problem came up in a panel discussion I took part in with Tony Benn and Mike O'Brien, the Foreign Office minister. Both Benn and O'Brien had some sympathy with the idea of posting ministers abroad, but had grave doubts about direct elections. Benn saw a potential conflict of interest between several directly elected ministers competing for influence with the Prime Minister, each claiming the authority of being elected directly.

This argument appears powerful, until one considers other potentially comparable situations. For example, some countries, such as Ireland and Austria, combine a parliamentary system with an elected President. In theory this creates a situation where the President, who is elected directly by the people, could claim to have authority to rival the Prime Minister. In reality, each has a job description laid down in the country's constitution and it is clear to everyone what they are or are not authorised to do.

Resolving coordination problems between competing interests is the normal business of government but tends to be hidden from public view. For example, policy on weapons exports involves the Foreign Office, the Ministry of Defence, the Department of Trade and Industry and the Prime Minister, as well as, on occasion, the Department for International Development. The need to coordinate policy across departments is the rule rather than the exception and is one of the main functions of Cabinet committees.

In a future system of elected international representation, ministries of national governments would have several ministers posted abroad. The Treasury would have ministers of state reporting to the Chancellor of the Exchequer from the EU, the WTO, the IMF and the World Bank. The Ministry of Defence would have a minister at NATO and the EU. The Foreign Office would have ministers in the EU, at NATO, the Organisation for Security and Co-operation in Europe (OSCE) and the UN. Other departments would also have elected ministers stationed in the EU Council of Ministers. They and their colleagues from other nations would be accountable and on the spot – a great advantage over the present position.

Connecting American democracy with the world

In countries such as the US, which have a separation of powers between an elected legislature (Parliament) and an elected executive (President), different procedures for increasing democratic engagement of the people with global decision-making would be needed. A number of options come to mind, both long term and short term.

It is worth bearing in mind that the US has adapted its system of internal government over time by, for example, changing the Senate from an indirectly elected to a directly elected body. And while at national level only two executive offices are elected – the President and Vice President – at state level other offices such as treasurer and secretary of state are also elected, providing a precedent for constitutional change at national level.

Whilst it is hard to see such a constitutional change being passed in the medium term, other incremental changes would be far easier to introduce. First, individual states could use referenda to elect state representatives as observers to international bodies. Strong supporters of the federal government and the uncontrolled power of the President in foreign affairs might be opposed to states acting in this way. However, it is often American conservatives who argue for states' rights. People in Montana, a state with some scepticism of the UN, might welcome the chance to send a representative to New York to see what the UN was really up to. Another adaptation of US practices would be for the House of Representatives and the Senate to create standing observer missions at the UN and the WTO. This would merely be a development of the past practice of having visiting observer groups at key negotiations.

NGOs, especially the strong ones, need to embrace the idea of extending representative democracy. As unelected bodies, they are coming under attack from conservatives for their undemocratic interference in government decision-making. They also face considerable criticism from political traditionalists on the left who believe that organisations not focused on the formal democratic process serve to drain and not enhance the centre of political life in some countries. But conservative critics of NGOs cannot be found challenging the undemocratic power of one key non-governmental sector: corporations.

The best way to respond to these critics is to raise the political demand for formal representation at international bodies for non-governmental groups such as Amnesty International. This point has been well argued by Michael Edwards of the Ford Foundation. However, in the present political climate NGOs need to go further and argue for national elections of the public offices in the international institutions. Such an approach will renew and focus the outrage about the illegitimate and ineffective nature of international decision-making that led people to create international NGOs in the first place.

It is easy to think of reasons not to extend representative democracy to the international level. For a start there is the fear that world government means world tyranny. Indeed, Immanuel Kant, the father of the idea of world peace through world government, thought that it would need to be enforced with tyranny. As we discussed in Part 1, world peace is in fact rather popular, the problem is trying to make it stick. Moreover, world government and tyranny are thought by many of those protesting at the WTO to have come about already, in the form of huge unaccountable corporations and secret agreements between governments. The proposals in this chapter would mean merely that people's representatives got a more direct input than they do now. In an interconnected world, leaving only accountable government and law unconnected will not keep tyranny at bay.

People tend not to vote if they think it will make no difference. In the last British general election turnout was low. It was clear that Labour was going to win because there was no reasonable alternative. In places with a massive majority for one party, people do not bother to vote. In the US, only about ten per cent of the Congressional districts are at all competitive. The party in power, be it Democrat or Republican, will get in almost regardless. People do not vote either if they see the institution as powerless, as in many local elections and in elections for the European Parliament. On the other hand, people do vote when it matters to them and when they think it can make a difference. In local elections in Britain about the transfer of council housing to housing associations the vote can be over eighty per cent. People are also more likely to vote if the process is easy.

We should place the organisations people are most bothered about under democratic control. The rail regulator, the IMF and NHS trusts might well top the list. We should continue to make voting easier, following of the policy of the current UK government, putting polling stations in supermarkets and holding elections at the weekend, for example.

People often say 'the last thing we need is more politicians' and it is easy to sympathise with this view, until you look at the alternative, which is to have people in charge over whom we have no control at all. But compared with the vast armies of unaccountable bureaucrats there are very few politicians. Politicians are no more perfect or corrupt than anyone else and it is easy to fall into the trap of thinking that they should not exist at all. Listen hard to those who criticise them loudest and you may find that their agenda is really about removing political control as much as possible. At present, we have countless silent and unaccountable bureaucrats who may be readier to meet the needs of business than those of the country as a whole. If they received the media attention given to politicians, we would soon be complaining far more about their conduct.

Electing representatives to fill official positions will not solve all the world's problems. What it will do is give us a chance to influence and make decisions. At present they are out of reach in a world of initials – GATS, EU, UN, NATO – that we have a hard time even understanding. Having more politicians to abuse or even applaud brings matters down to earth and under our control. In the end, the argument that 'they' know best is against all democracy. We might as well leave it to the Queen and the hereditary peers.

What is GATS?[5]

The General Agreement on Trade in Services (GATS) is an international trade agreement that came into effect in 1995 and operates under the umbrella of the World Trade Organisation (WTO).

The aim of the GATS is to gradually remove all barriers to trade in services. The agreement covers services as diverse as banking, education, healthcare, rubbish collection, tourism or transport.

The idea is to open up these services to international competition, allowing the way for huge, for-profit, multinational firms: 'The GATS is not just something that exists between Governments. It is first and foremost an instrument for the benefit of business.'(European Commission, 1999)

Since February 2000, negotiations are underway in the WTO to expand and 'fine-tune' the GATS. These negotiations have aroused concern worldwide. A growing number of local governments, trade unions, NGOs, parliaments and developing country governments are criticising the GATS negotiations and call for a halt on the negotiations.

Their main points of critique:

• Negative impacts on universal access to basic services such as healthcare, education, water and transport.

- Fundamental conflict between freeing up trade in services and the right of governments and communities to regulate companies in areas such as tourism, retail, telecommunications and broadcasting.
- Absence of a comprehensive assessment of the impacts of GATS-style liberalisation before further negotiations continue.
- A one-sided deal. GATS is primarily about expanding opportunities for large multinational companies.

We may worry about wasting public money with lots of new elected representatives. However, the salaries and expenses of our representatives are cheap at the price when you consider the benefits of being able to control how the policies that affect our lives are made. They are also cheaper than any comparable example in the business world. In any case, people who don't want to see more democratic control of the powerful often make these arguments.

Improving democracy in international institutions and the European Union

Many member states, non-governmental organisations and academics believe the UN to be weak and undemocratic. The UN Commission discussed this issue in the 1995 report on global governance, *Our Global Neighbourhood*.[6] It recommended that we grasp the opportunity provided by the end of the Cold War to reform international institutions, improve global security and achieve a more equitable economic system. Five years later, at the Millennium, the authors revisited these issues, concluding that little progress had been made on any part of the agenda and that a number of events had reduced the authority of the UN, notably NATO action in Kosovo.

By 2004 the UN was in the crisis described in more detail previously. The Bush administration, supported by the UK, has set aside traditional methods of crisis management and war prevention, taking international law into its own hands and, according to its critics, destroying it.

It is worth recapping the earlier and continuing debates on UN reform to see how poor were the chances of reform even before the US's recent actions. Among other things, discussion has focused on making the Security Council and the General Assembly more representative.[7] There have been suggestions for including as new permanent members of the Security Council states with large populations such as India and Brazil and incorporating the former imperial powers, France and the UK, into an EU seat.

There is also an argument that states' voting power in the General Assembly should be proportionate to their population and that this should form the basis of an elected General Assembly. The idea of world elections has been discussed ever since the UN was created.[8] At that time, Labour's Foreign Secretary, Ernest Bevin, told the House of Commons: 'I would merge that power [of the House of Commons] into the greater power of a directly elected world assembly ... I am willing to sit with any body, or any party, or any nation to try to devise a franchise or a constitution for a world assembly...'[9]

All of these proposals have at least one problem in common. They can make no progress until there is a consensus amongst all states to make change. As there are considerable vested interests and rivalries, no progress has occurred or is likely in the foreseeable future. The UK and

France are unlikely to give up their power on the Security Council. The rivalry between India and Pakistan is an important obstacle to giving India more prominence. Robin Cook, the first Foreign Secretary in the Labour government of 1997, has expressed his great regret at being unable to secure reform of the Security Council during his time in office. Discussion on the reform of the Security Council continues in the permanent (and luxuriantly named) UN Working Group on the Question of Equitable Representation On, and Increased Representation In, the Membership of the Security Council and Other Matters Relevant to the Security Council, but no change has happened yet or looks possible for the future on the basis of present proposals.

Making the UN more democratic does not have to wait for every country to agree. There is nothing in the regulations of the UN, or indeed any other international body, that determines how countries choose their representatives. Countries could send political representatives to join the career diplomats that represent them at present. Once a few nations began this new practice, it is likely that more would follow.

Getting politicians into the UN would bring its activities into the open. At present, business is conducted by professional diplomats used to a culture of secrecy. I have spent years reporting and lobbying on military and disarmament issues at the UN, perhaps the most secretive area of international politics. Most documents that are, in theory, public, are only seen by officials. The role of myself and my colleagues was to get these documents into the light of day and to brief politicians in national capitals about what their own ambassadors and those of other countries were saying. The debates got much livelier and more pointed when the politicians got involved.

If existing global trends continue the UN will have less and less authority. A few powerful states and global corporations will dominate. However, in five or ten years, the UN could be evolving into an elected General Assembly. It would have renewed legitimacy and power to tackle global problems. It would be far more difficult for the international news media to ignore and disparage the UN and far harder for the major powers to ignore the majority when more and more of their representatives were elected.

The arguments for introducing representative democracy into the UN apply just as well to the other major international institutions. There has been little recent debate on the democratic nature of NATO and the OSCE but there has been an active discussion about the democratic deficit in the financial institutions: the WTO, the World Bank and the IMF. It is argued that these bodies only act on behalf of the rich and powerful nations and corporations. The conservative response is that the decisions of these bodies are taken by states, many of which are democratic and which are implementing policies designed to encourage free trade and free enterprise. However, this argument has done nothing to reduce the concerns of the anti-globalisation movement.

The response from these institutions to public protest about the democratic deficit has been retrenchment and cosmetic change rather than reform. In some cases, meetings are no longer held at all. Instead, delegates now can meet virtually, using a videoconference link, so there is no longer any physical place to attract protest. The IMF has recognised public concerns to an extent. It has made arrangements for occasional meetings of consultative groups of members of Parliament from various countries, but it is not changing its power structure.

The major security institutions, NATO and the OSCE, each have consultative assemblies of representatives from the parliaments of more than forty nations of the Euro-Atlantic region. However, the central functions of these organisations are conducted by officials, not elected representatives, drawn from the foreign and defence ministries of member states. Military issues are so clouded in secrecy that democratic control is hard to achieve. Few politicians have military experience and since the decline of the great peace movements of the 1980s there are fewer people outside government concerned with strategic issues. There has been a growth of academic and NGO involvement in the issue of intervention but this has generally been from the humanitarian perspective rather than from the perspective of geopolitical strategy.

In the US, the Freedom of Information Act has created a more open culture on security issues than anywhere in Europe except Sweden. This is indicated by the high technical quality of US studies on strategic issues. Applying US standards of freedom in the US-led alliance should be the minimal acceptable standard in NATO and amongst other US allies. If allies are to go along with US military policy, then they should have the same level of democratic control as in the US without jeopardising national security.

Joseph Stiglitz was chief economist at the World Bank and resigned to campaign against its negative impact on the international economy. He was consequently awarded the Nobel Prize for economics. He has pointed out a similar problem in the IMF, which operates with great secrecy. The US does not use its influence to export its own home-grown standards of free speech and freedom of information. Democratic representation at these bodies is the next crucial step to apply acceptable democratic standards. It is unfortunate that there is as yet little connection between US and overseas pressure groups seeking to insist that the US apply its own democratic standards to the internal operation of the international bodies that the US leads.

The direct election of international bodies may seem to be an over-reaction to present problems, but the transformation of the world into a global village requires that democracy keep up. It might be better to look at these changes as a natural evolution of representative democracy to meet changing circumstances

The nations of the EU are engaged in a negotiation aimed at creating a European constitution. These negotiations have centred on the issue of sovereignty. This sovereignty discussion consists of a debate between those who favour a Europe of nation states and those who favour creating a federal state. Whatever the result of the nego-tiations on the new constitution it is clear that none of proposals will produce a major change in the relationship between national elec-torates and the EU institutions. There may be a President elected on an EU-wide franchise – but most likely the President will be elected indirectly. However, the EU Council will not have democratic repre-sentation from national capitals on a day-to-day basis, and the members of the Commission will still be appointed through the patronage of national Prime Ministers and Presidents. Improved democratic representation throughout its institutions should be the test of acceptability of the new EU constitution, whatever new powers and political structures are created

The debate on the EU constitution engages both those who favour the EU becoming a new federal state and those who prefer a Europe of nation states. In either case as many as possible of the institutions of the EU should be elected, including its overseas representation. The EU should take the lead in creating a new era of global repre-sentative democracy.

The European constitution should create institutions where national representatives to them all are elected, and some may be elected by the EU as a whole. We should create an EU where all the commissioners are directly elected by national populations rather than nominated by the Prime Minister of the country concerned. The Council of Ministers consists of representatives of each member state and is broken down into many committees covering all the issues of government, such as the environment and health. At present, the day-to-day work is conducted by officials with ministers arriving only for key meetings. Democracy would be better served if there were elected representatives present all the time so that the Council of Ministers would actually be made up of ministers on a day-to-day basis and not just at summit time. A newly democratic Commission and Council would work with the proposed elected EU President.

The EU convention on a constitution is mostly concerned with the EU's internal structures. This is understandable as these are themselves huge issues. The discussions of how the EU engages the world as a whole have so far centred on military issues and on the EU's development partnerships in several regions of the world. There has been little attention to the question of how the people of the EU are represented in the wider world. It is important to set the reforms we want for the EU in the context of the reforms we want at home and in the governance of the world as a whole. It is essential that ideas for enhanced democracy at the global level flow through the EU and are neither diverted nor blocked by the changes made in Brussels.

Another reason for considering how Europe relates to the wider world is that changes within the EU may have bad consequences for the way the EU operates on the world stage. For example, one result of creating a federal state is that nations would have reduced representation internationally. It has been argued already that France and the UK should give up their seats on the Security Council in favour of a representative from the EU. Applying this argument to the other EU countries would mean that ultimately all would lose their representation at the UN in favour of an EU representative. If this were ever to happen the new representative should be elected by the Union as a whole.

Those who argue for a common EU position in foreign and military affairs need to think more clearly about the way the present Europe of nation states is represented abroad. It is not satisfactory that national representation should wither away until it is all vested in a single EU diplomat representing an EU President.

In reality, at present the EU acts as a group in all international bodies, including NATO and the UN. EU member states, informed by the Commission and led by the 'troika' of present, past and future EU presidencies, develop a collective view that is then carried forward. As is well known, there is an informal arrangement that where a member state has a particular interest, for example France's and the UK's nuclear weapons, then their views are deferred to in reaching collective decisions. More importantly, member states' regional interests and colonial histories give the EU a global reach that would be much weakened if member states no longer had international representation.

EU member states are most unlikely to give up their national representation abroad. Whatever the view might be in old-established states such as the UK or the Netherlands, it is inconceivable that nations such as Croatia, in the first flush of national pride, would agree to cease to be represented abroad.

The importance of national ambassadors will decline as the power of the centralised EU institutions continues to grow. As a result, even if they are retained in present form, these national ambassadors may become merely ceremonial. But rather than see these representatives dwindle into insignificance, we should take the opportunity to revitalise their role. The EU should take the lead in helping create a new era of global democracy. This can be done by encouraging member states to send elected representatives as the permanent representatives to the EU Council of Ministers for such key topics as finance, defence, environment and transport. In a few years' time the EU should be sending a delegation of twenty-five directly elected representatives to each of the major global institutions. Such a democratically elected delegation would act as a coordinated group, much as it does at present. It would grow beyond being a delegation of officials to being a mature and self-confident political group able to speak for and to its citizens. Such a delegation would do a great deal to transform the climate in all the global bodies and help encourage other nations to also elect their representatives. It would also help set an example, encouraging non-democratic states to become democratic as it would reinforce a norm in favour of democracy.

This form of overseas representation could fit into most of the options for a European constitution regardless of the outcome of the debate between federalists and states-righters in Brussels. Moreover, as the type of representation nations choose is decided by them and not at the EU level, the election of overseas representatives could be introduced separately from the agreement of the EU constitution.

Without such reforms, the Union will fall more and more into the hands of a self-serving elite, and European politics will see extremist parties benefiting from public revulsion at the collusion of the mainstream parties in robbing the people of their rights. A key test for whatever new institutions are created is that they should be elected.

Electing the regulators: UK local and regional democracy

At local level, other countries already elect many more officials than occurs in the UK. For example, in some US states, the police chief, some judges and the regulatory commissioners for electricity, water and gas supplies are all elected. In the UK, the regulators of the public utilities, Ofrail, Ofwat, Oftel, could all be elected accountable officials, rather than people appointed by Tony Blair, or one of the ministers in Whitehall. The chairs of the NHS trusts should be added to the ballot paper to give a direct and influential voice to the community in a service we all care about.

Elected public offices

	Elected by Londoners	Elected by New Yorkers
2004	MEP	US President and Vice-President
	MP	US Congressl Representative
	Mayor of London	US Senators
	Members of London Assembly	Governor and Lieutenant Governor
	Borough councillors	State Attorney General
		State Comptroller
		State Senators
		Mayor of New York City
		Public Advocate cont'd

Elected by Londoners	Elected by New Yorkers
	City Comptroller
	Borough Presidents
	City council members
	District Attorneys
	Surrogate judges
	State Supreme Court judges
	Civil Court judges
	School Board members

Proposed additional offices for 2020?

Elected by Londoners	Elected by New Yorkers
British representative to the UN	Federal Secretary of State
British representatives to the EU	Federal Assistant Secretary of State/UN
British representative to the IMF/WTO	Federal Secretary of Defense
British representative to NATO	State observer to the UN
Members of the House of Lords	State observer to the IMF/WTO
National Rail Regulator	
National Financial Services Regulator	
Chairs of NHS Trust	
Borough Education Committee	

The Labour government has introduced valuable constitutional reforms. Nevertheless, there are considerable strains on the constitutional structure of the UK and we still have few opportunities to exercise democratic choices over the policies that are made and how our taxes are spent. These decisions are often made by unaccountable bodies that need to be brought under more direct democratic control.

The domestic constitutional reforms carried out by Labour have completed much of the constitutional reform agenda of the twentieth century. The hereditary peers are being phased out and there has been devolution in Scotland and Wales, but it has yet to complete the reform of the House of Lords by making it a democratic body. At local level a system of mayors who select a cabinet from among the elected councillors has been introduced. This has had the positive effect of allowing people with no party allegiance to become elected as mayor, overturning long-entrenched party systems. Partnership working in local government has been promoted and extended.

The strain on the UK's constitutional structure as a centralised nation state comes from devolution, from Europe and from globalisation. Power in the central government in Whitehall is being pulled away, both upwards and downwards. This in itself may not be a bad thing and in any case the recommendations described above on global and EU reform should go a long way towards re-engaging the people with the powerful institutions in the world.

Within Britain, the main constitutional problem is that power is not being devolved evenly. Scotland and Wales have devolved powers but England does not. This leads to the problem of Scottish and Welsh MPs having a vote on English matters decided at Westminster, but their English counterparts having no say in the assemblies in Cardiff and Edinburgh. The English, especially the southern English, may not be content to see Westminster reduced to an English assembly, let alone a regional assembly for south-east England, with wider decisions mostly taken in Brussels.

Labour now has a large majority in England, Scotland and Wales so the problem of uneven devolution can be controlled by its overall power. But this problem will come to the fore when Labour loses its majority in England and is maintained in power by Scottish and Welsh Labour MPs. Then there will be a crisis unless the relationship has been thought through.

The government's next step in devolution is to consider creating new elected regional assemblies in England. It is unclear whether their proposals will have a positive or negative effect on the underlying problems. There is support for regional government, especially in the north of England, where decisions taken in London are felt to be remote. The experiences of the German *Länder*, Spanish regions and US state governments all encourage a similar process in the UK. English politicians and business leaders are also seeing the benefits to be gained by regions from EU funds that only regions can apply for.

In some parts of Europe, such as Catalonia and Brittany, there has never been much affinity with their national capitals in Madrid and Paris. The idea of a federal Europe providing a renaissance for regions with a strong historical identity appears to be gaining ground. Since Maastricht, there is even provision for representatives from regions to take the place of national ministers at the Council of Ministers, and a Committee of Regions is now functioning. Under the principle of subsidiarity applied at a regional level, regional government can take on functions historically associated in the UK with central government. Catalonia, for example, has thrived under this new dispensation and become a serious player in national and even

European politics. This positive context is encouraging the government to considering introducing regional government in Britain.

The demand for regional bodies varies around England. People in some parts of England may be enthusiastic for regional government. But in large parts of central and southern England regional government could appear to be a bureaucratic irrelevance, particularly in parts of England that see London as their centre. The creation of regional government could well fuel English nationalist concern about the break-up of the country into bite-sized chunks to be managed by the Brussels superstate. This could become more serious if the demand in the south is to stop paying subsidies to the north. This financial issue ignited conflict in the regions of the then Yugoslavia, and is a divisive feature of the north/south split in Italy, though in each of these cases it is the north that has the money.

There are no cost-free political or procedural answers to these issues. However, introducing elections for offices controlling matters that genuinely concern the public might do a lot to energise the entire process of elected government below the level of the national government in London.

High up the list of public concerns are the management of health care and the regulation of privatised railways and utilities. The election of supervisors is commonplace in the US and should be introduced here. Jonathan Freedland has made a powerful argument for introducing far greater numbers of elected officials in the UK, and cites US practice.[10] In the UK, where utilities are regionalised, as with water and electricity, some of the regulatory functions could be carried out by regional regulatory bodies that may be very popular and could become a vital part of regional government. Elected regulators would have greater legitimacy than the present appointees, however professional they are. A relatively short term of two or three years would keep the mandate fresh.

People might see another set of elections as creating yet more red tape. The best way around this is to begin with services that people feel most strongly about. The railways continue to be a huge public concern, especially in the south-east of England. At present the director of Ofrail is a government appointee. The chance of having a say in electing this person may be seized upon by the frustrated travelling public. A single regulator might be elected. Another option would be to create a combination of elected regional and national regulators as many of the issues are regional.

A similar process should be considered for the electricity, gas and water utilities. National issues such as pricing would be managed by a national regulator while issues of more local concern such as rural connection charges could be handled regionally. Regulation in California and the Pacific north-west provides a successful example of a good service to the public resulting from regulation with strong democratic legitimacy. Elections might be conducted by mail using the promotional services of the companies that at present just swamp us with junk mail. In California, temporary deregulation resulted in major disruptions to electricity services.

The chairs (but not the chief executives) of NHS hospital and primary-care trusts should be elected. This measure would address the continuing media and public concern over the quality of health service management. At present there is no clear elected office to which people can turn with concerns over their local health services.

The introduction of elected officers would provide a more effective method for channelling public concern and improving the service to the public than the present system, which relies on appointees.

It may be argued that the country has had enough constitutional change already. However, it is clear that the 'English question' is only just beginning to emerge in UK politics, and that regional government will not provide a sufficient answer in central and southern England. It is essential for the healthy development of our democracy that people have a chance to elect public officials who have responsibility for matters high up most people's list of day-to-day concerns.

Democracy need not decline. Upgrading representative democracy to catch up with globalisation is necessary, practical and can be begun by any party in any country. Such institutional reforms can go hand in hand with new policy reforms, both will be enhanced by a stronger democratic culture informed by a proper celebration of those who won the freedoms we enjoy today.

Six

Strengthening democratic culture

*Have we not an equal interest with the men of this nation,
in those liberties and securities contained in the Petition of
Right and the other good laws of the land.*
                              Women's Petition to Parliament 1649

Hanging on to our democratic freedoms is going to be tough in the years ahead. They are under attack from extremist fundamentalists and from governments that talk about democracy but in practice abuse it. It will be even harder to use democracy to build peace and limit war. When soldiers prepare for battle they are often inspired by their regiment's historic victories. We need to draw similar inspiration from those who won the political battles for the freedoms we now enjoy. Unfortunately, we know too little about them to be encouraged, and that is why this chapter will take us back, briefly, to the eras of Charles I, Napoleon and Victoria.

My arguments in this chapter focus on English history and democracy. I think, though, that in many other cultures there must be examples, all too often lost rather than celebrated, of people who have done the most to win the freedoms we enjoy today, or who, having lost, have been pushed out of the history books altogether.

Achieving peace with freedom is made more difficult in Britain because people have little historical knowledge about how our existing democratic rights were established. Fighting for democracy is made far harder today, when we know so little of those who fought to establish our democratic rights in the first place. The history we are taught in British schools talks all about kings and queens and hardly at all about the people who made our democracy. The British government keeps going on about how people are apathetic about democracy, but it is like asking people to support a football team when they are told nothing about its past glories. We hear more than enough about 'The Royals' but nothing about 'The Democrats'.

Without this cultural memory, we cannot draw strength from the successes of previous generations in preparing for future challenges. In other areas of national life, past events such as the Battle of Britain strongly influence the way we think about what we should do today. Today we need to defend democracy, but it should come as no surprise that we have difficulty rallying a unified team spirit when we lack a sense of our democratic heritage. This lack of democratic history amounts to a loss of memory. We need to rebuild our memories to better understand and tackle the future. We should create a variety of activities to celebrate our democratic heritage as much as we do our military and regal history.

The heritage deficit

Britain is a nation that celebrates its heritage like no other. The country's museums, memorials and historic events are a matter of pride, and rightly so. They form an important part of the nation's sense of identity. They are also a prominent part of a tourist industry generating billions in income for the country and projecting an image of Britain around the world. Our democratic heritage is hard to find amongst the plethora of historical attractions even though the country is world famous for its democracy. The House of Commons is often referred to as the Mother of Parliaments. Its offspring can be found in the United States constitution and in parliaments around the world. But visitors and immigrants to Britain are surprised how little there is on show to celebrate these achievements. There are notable exceptions such as the People's History Museum in Manchester and there are statues of Oliver Cromwell and Winston Churchill outside Parliament. But London is mostly populated with statues of dukes and generals. The celebration of Churchill's defence of democracy leaves him unjustly isolated as the main champion of the democratic cause in Britain's heritage.

There are no prominent memorials to the Chartists, the Suffragettes or even Simon de Montfort, the man credited with assembling the first House of Commons in the thirteenth century. There is no national museum of democracy. There is no British equivalent of America's 4 July or France's Bastille Day, which celebrate the people's liberation from tyranny. Even the memorial to Magna Carta at Runnymede was built by the Americans.

Television and the cinema provide a procession of royal and imperial histories but ignore the people who gave us the freedoms we enjoy today. And they gloss over the tyranny that underpinned the reigns of so many monarchs and of the Empire itself. It seems almost in bad taste to mention how badly the poor and political and religious dissenters were treated in times past. Their role in overcoming oppression and creating the democratic values we cherish has been ignored.

In France, by way of contrast, the revolution is celebrated and the tyranny of the Bourbon kings made clear. In Britain we learn much of the savage use of the guillotine in the Terror of the French Revolution. Books like Baroness Orczy's *The Scarlet Pimpernel* and Charles Dickens's *A Tale of Two Cities* have been turned into films showing the awful fate of the French aristocracy at the hands of the revolutionaries. But in Britain we hear little of the tyrannical behaviour of these self-same aristocrats towards the people, and nothing of the massacres perpetrated by the aristocrats to crush previous rebellions in France. For many years there had been revolts against arbitrary laws and taxes imposed by France's Bourbon kings. These had always been suppressed with great savagery by whichever Louis happened to be absolute ruler at the time.

This amnesia about the brutality of the pre-democratic era is even more marked when we look at British history. As well as celebrating what the Tudors, Victorians and other monarchs did for us, we might look at what the Tudors and Victorians did to us. For wealthy men who went to the Church of England, life was fine and they enjoyed political rights. But if you were female, Catholic or Methodist, for much of Britain's history you had few rights at all. Women could not own property after marriage until the mid-nineteenth century or vote as of natural right until 1928, two inhuman restrictions that seem unimaginable today. Right up to the middle of the nineteenth century people were executed for minor offences such as stealing bread. Until 1948 businessmen had two votes in local elections, one in their own right and another for owning a business.

The changes, when they did come, did not come easily. A history of the Chartist movement written in 1854 by the Sunderland doctor R. C. Gammage is punctuated with accounts of arrests, imprisonment and deaths in gaol. And this was at a time when the idea of one man, one vote was supported by only a handful of MPs.

Unsung heroes

I have chosen examples of unsung heroes from the time of Charles I, from the era of the Napoleonic wars, and from Victorian Britain. My examples are not intended to be a comprehensive history of democracy, or even a comprehensive list from British history, there are none of the barons who forced the Magna Carta of 1215 from King John, nor any of the Prime Ministers who in the end put voting rights into the law in the later nineteenth and early twentieth centuries. I have either not described those figures who are allowed a brief mention in our history, but are never accorded the prominence they deserve as trail-blazers: Wat Tyler and John Ball and their revolutionary rhyme, 'When Adam delved and Eve span, Who was then the gentleman?'. Nor do I discuss the early trade unionists or the Suffragettes. I have selected people who are, I think, virtually unknown outside small groups of enthusiasts and academics, but whose achievements were great.

Equal rights: the Leveller men and women: Thomas Rainsborough, John Lilburne and Katherine Chidley

The English revolution of the 1640s created the first republic in a major European state. The Civil War arose as a result of a confrontation between King Charles I and Parliament. Charles was seeking to abolish Parliament's right to control direct taxation of the people and establish the sort of absolute monarchy that the kings of France and other Continental monarchs were in the process of creating. In

Parliament itself a strong Protestant – Puritan – element pressed in turn for greater rights for Parliament. The Civil War produced many deaths and a radicalisation of the people and especially of soldiers who wanted to have equal political rights with the wealthy.

The republic was led by Oliver Cromwell, but shortly after his death, the monarchy was restored under Charles II in a settlement that limited the power of the King and gave taxation and other key powers to Parliament, but the deal also denied political rights to most people.

There had been a strong popular movement for equal political rights not just for men but also for women. The high point of the new democratic movement came in the late 1640s and was associated with the Leveller party. At the same time there was a myriad of religious and political groups arguing for and publishing many different points of view. The Levellers had strong support within the Parliamentary Army and thus were able ensure that their ideas were given serious attention by the parliamentary leadership. One key debate between their leaders, Cromwell, and other members of the Council who governed the Parliamentary Army happened in 1647. This took place that October at Putney, outside London, at a crucial point in the Civil War. The King had been defeated and the victorious Parliamentarians began to debate both how he should be treated and what the new political framework for the country should look like.

Thomas Rainsborough, a Leveller MP, argued:

> *I think that the poorest he that is in England hath a life to live as the greatest he; and therefore truly, Sir, I think it's clear that every man that is to live under a Government ought first by his own consent to put himself under that*

Government; and I do think that the poorest man in England is not at all bound in a strict sense to that Government that he hath not had a voice to put himself under.

The reply he received from General Ireton, the leading general after Cromwell in the Parliamentary Army, was scathing. Ireton argued that only people with property mattered and, as for the rest, the fact that they were born in England gave them no standing. People had no innate or natural rights in England simply because they were English. His view won for the next two hundred years in England, though for a shorter time in America, France and a few other countries.

The Leveller manifesto, *An Agreement of the People*, is the first clear statement of democratic principles in the English language. It calls for votes for all adult males, the supremacy of Parliament, freedom of religion and the abolition of church taxes. Their work was accompanied by a strong movement for female emancipation, led by some of the wives of the leading male Levellers.

One leader, Katherine Chidley, was a successful businesswoman in her own right. She and a reported ten thousand other Leveller women delivered a petition to Parliament in 1649 which declared: 'Have we not an equal interest with the men of this nation, in those liberties and securities contained in the Petition of Right [this was Parliament's statement against the King], and the other good laws of the land.'[1]

In political terms, the achievements of these people eclipse those of the King who came after them – Charles II, whose principal claim to fame is not getting executed and shagging anything in a skirt.

However, if you punch 'Tourism, London, Putney Debates' into the internet you will be lucky to find half a dozen entries, and most take you to the local museum of the borough of Wandsworth, where the debates struggle to be noticed alongside such epoch-shattering matters as the Surrey Iron Railway and Building the Suburbs. So I set out for St Mary's church in Putney with my wife and nephew to see how this great moment in world history is remembered.

And there on the gates of the church is a sign where the parish priest, the Reverend Dr Giles Fraser, states: 'Famously, St. Mary's was the venue for the Putney debates where Cromwell and his army laid the foundations for modern democratic politics,' though the battered A3 laminated notice and the rather small type do not quite seem to rise to the occasion. There is no Leveller museum featuring a re-enactment of the debates between Cromwell and the troops, no 'world hero' figurines of John Lilburne and Chidley, no 'Democracy Started Here' neon signs along the High Street, not even a 'The Leveller' pub opposite the church.

Extract from *An Agreement of the People*, 1647

Having by our late labours and hazards made it appear to the world at how high a rate we value our just freedom, and God having so far owned our cause as to deliver the enemies thereof into our hands, we do now hold ourselves bound in mutual duty to each other to take the best care we can for the future to avoid both the danger of returning into a slavish condition and the chargeable remedy of another war. For as it cannot be imagined that so many of our countrymen would have opposed us in this quarrel if they had understood their own good, so may we safely promise to ourselves that when our common rights and liberties shall be cleared, their endeavours will be disappointed that seek to make themselves our masters. Since therefore our former oppressions, and scarce yet ended troubles have been occasioned, either by want of frequent National meetings in Councell, or by rendering those meetings ineffectual; We are fully agreed and resolved, to provide that hereafter our Representatives be neither left to an uncertainty for the time, nor made useless to the ends for which they are intended: In order whereunto we declare,

1. That the People of England being at this day very unequally distributed by counties, cities and boroughs for the election of their Deputies in Parliament, ought to be more indifferently proportioned, according to the number of the Inhabitants: the circumstances whereof, for number, place, and manner, are to be set down before the end of this present Parliament.
2. That to prevent the many inconveniences apparently arising, from the long continuance of the same persons in authority, this present Parliament be dissolved upon the last day of September, which shall be in the year of our Lord, 1648.
3. That the people do of course choose themselves a Parliament once in two yeares, viz. upon the first Thursday in every second March, after the manner as shall be prescribed before the end of this Parliament, to begin to sit upon the first Thursday in Aprill following at Westminster, or such other place as shall bee appointed from time to time by the preceding Representatives; and to continue till the last day of September, then next ensuing, and no longer.
4. That the power of this, and all future Representatives of this Nation, is inferiour only to theirs who chuse them, and doth

extend, without the consent or concurrence of any other person or persons; to the enacting, altering, and repealing of laws; to the erecting and abolishing of Offices and Courts; to the appointing, removing, and calling to account Magistrates and Officers of all degrees; to the making War and peace, to the treating with forraigne States: And generally, to whatsoever is not expressly or impliedly reserved by the represented to themselves.

Which are as followeth,

1. That matters of religion, and the wayes of God's Worship, are not at all entrusted by us to any humane power, because therein wee cannot remit or exceed a tittle of what our Consceiences dictate to be the mind of God, without wilful sinne: nevertheless the publike way of instructing the nation (so it be not compulsive) is referred to their discretion.
2. That the matter of impressing and constraining any of us to serve in the warres, is against our freedome; and therefore we do not allow it in our Representatives; the rather, because money (the sinews of war) being always at their disposall, they can never want numbers of men, apt enough to engage in any just cause.
3. That after the dissolution of this present Parliament, no person be at any time questioned for anything said or done in reference to the late publike differences, otherwise than in execution of the Judgments of the present Representatives, or House of Commons.
4. That in all laws made, or to be made, every person may be bound alike, and that no Tenure, Estate, Charter, Degree, Birth, or place, do confer any exemption from the ordinary Course of Legall proceedings, whereunto others are subjected.

5. That as the Laws ought to be equall, so they must be good, and not evidently destructive to the safety and well-being of the people.

These things we declare to be our native Rights; and therefore are agreed and resolved to maintain them with our utmost possibilities, against all opposition whatsoever, being compelled thereunto, not only by the examples of our Ancestors, whose bloud was often spent in vain for the recovery of their Freedomes, suffering themselves, through fraudulent accommodations, to be still deluded of the fruit of their Victories, but also by our own woefull experience, who having long expected, and dearly earned the establishment of these certain rules of Government, are yet made to depend for the settlement of our Peace and Freedome upon him that intended our bondage, and brought a cruell Warre upon us.

In the evolution of democracy the Leveller formulations of democratic structures are as significant as the work of Nicholas Copernicus, Galileo Galilei or Isaac Newton were in science. In English history it is common to simply see the Levellers as an out-of-time irrelevance, but no one would think of denying scientific ideas their place in history because their ideas were not taken up immediately. Unfortunately, the sayings of Chidley, Lilburne, Rainsborough are not thought worth recording in the *Oxford Dictionary of Quotations*. And it is not true that the Leveller effort simply sank without trace. British emigrants to America took democratic ideas as well as their Protestant religion with them to the New World, as described in Alexis de Tocqueville's *Democracy in America*. There remained an active connection between English and American radicals.

When I travelled to America on an anti-nuclear speakers' tour in 1983, my first stop was to be the Wesleyan University in Middletown, Connecticut. To prime myself for the New World, I picked up Thomas Paine's eighteenth-century work *Common Sense* to read on the plane, and found in the introduction that there had been a centre of Anglo-American radical communication at the time of American Revolution in ... Middletown, Connecticut. So the original special relationship was a relationship about democracy, not about missiles and war and it is these values that we need to continue to reaffirm. And one way to do that is to create a more international celebration of our democratic history, not just with the US but with many other peoples.

Overthrowing imperial slavery: Toussaint L'Ouverture

My next choice of unsung heroes comes from the era of the French Revolution, Wellington and Napoleon. My hero is Toussaint L'Ouverture, the successful leader of a slave revolt on the Caribbean island of Santo Domingo, now Haiti.

We hear much about Spartacus, the slave leader who fought the Roman Empire in Italy 2,000 years ago, and whose revolt was crushed, leading to crucifixion for him and his followers. But although Toussaint also died at the hands of his enemies, he had already won the greatest victory ever achieved by slaves and made himself into one of the great generals of the Napoleonic era. His country has been independent ever since.

To understand his achievement you have to consider the place and times he lived in. The sugar trade from the Caribbean to Europe was hugely profitable. England, France and Spain repeatedly fought for control of the islands during the eighteenth century, and the trade itself was of comparable importance to the economies of Europe as is the importation of oil from the Middle East today. The sugar was produced on slave plantations in conditions of savagery that are hard to comprehend.

The slave revolt led by Toussaint broke out in the aftermath and in imitation of the French Revolution of 1789. Initially welcomed by the revolutionary leaders in Paris, the slave armies had to fight off attacks by the Spanish and British Empires and then, after an attempt to reintroduce slavery by France, an army sent by Napoleon himself. The most readable account of Toussaint's success is to be found in *The Black Jacobins*, a very political biography written by C. L. R. James in 1963.

In the middle of the wars freeing Haiti, Toussaint evicted the British General Maitland, but concluded a treaty favourable to both sides. The *London Gazette* of 12 November 1798 noted: 'No event has happened in the history of the present war of more interest to Great Britain than the treaty which General Maitland has made with the black general Toussaint upon the evacuation of Santo Domingo.'

His military achievement is described in J. W. Fortescue's *History of the British Army*, written between 1899 and 1906. Fortescue tersely comments that: 'England's soldiers had been sacrificed, her treasure squandered, her influence in Europe weakened ... The secret of England's impotence for the first six years of the war may be said to lie in two fateful words, St Domingo.'[2] The importance of this part of the war is neglected in most modern histories, airbrushed out of history. To be polite, the omission is a simple self-absorption of European historians with the familiar battles of the Peninsular War and Waterloo; to be blunt, it is simple racism to deny the achievement of black slaves in defeating every army the European empires could find to send against them. Fortescue's explanation for the fact that this episode – and Maitland's agreement to withdraw from the island – had been forgotten, is clear:

> *The bare notion of an agreement with a negro, much more with a chief of insurgent negroes, was an abhorrence to every white man in the West Indies. The proceeding therefore was bound to gain him the enmity of every planter in the British tropical possessions, of every West Indian proprietor or agent in England or elsewhere, of every naval and military commander, of every Emigrant and every royalist.*

Much is made of the role that disease played in defeating the Spanish, British and French forces sent to suppress the revolt, but Fortescue makes clear that the successful Spartacists won with military skill. His account is punctuated with such phrases as 'Toussaint bore down with sudden swiftness and overwhelming strength'; Rigaud, 'the mulatto chief, with astonishing industry and labour, had constructed military roads on every side, so that the natural defences of the place had been broken down.'

After the British defeat came the French Empire of Napoleon, bent on restoring French ownership and slavery where possible. They too wasted men and treasure, and as a result Napoleon abandoned all his plans in the Americas, agreeing to sell the Mississippi valley to the US. Toussaint and the revolutionaries in Haiti had first been greeted as comrades by the revolutionaries in Paris, but Napoleon had other ideas and sent a force of over twenty thousand troops to the island, either to trick the free blacks back into servitude or if necessary to conquer them. Napoleon's general succeeded in capturing Toussaint through a trick, but this only increased the determination of Toussaint's colleagues and soldiers. Napoleon's order for the campaign is attached as Appendix III as it is quite broadly instructive as to how 'realist' politics can be conducted.

As a society we should pay attention to the heroism of a general of the Napoleonic era who was fighting for freedom as we already do to Wellington, Nelson and Napoleon himself, who were all fighting for political systems that denied human rights to the subjects of their empires.

Freedom of the press: James Watson, Henry Hetherington and Richard Moore

Two hundred years after the Levellers, British men and women were still having to demand the natural rights that we now take for granted. Momentum for political reform had gathered pace in England in the aftermath of the American and French Revolutions and in 1832 a Reform Act was passed. The history of the campaign for this reform has been eloquently described by Edward Pearce in his recent book *Reform!*.[3] But the 1832 Act still kept the vast majority of men and all women from voting. In response the Chartist movement was created at the end of the 1830s, with millions of people signing the petitions to Parliament.

A free press is a vital part of a free society. And yet until the middle of the Victorian era, the press was not free in England. It was heavily taxed with the express purpose of preventing people without money from reading. Reading would produce knowledge and knowledge a population that made political demands. Such repressive instincts still exist in the world. Much to my surprise I heard exactly this view expressed recently by a young Mexican lawyer as we sat on the sidelines of a football match. Having politely enquired how things were in his country, he blurted out that 'democracy sucks' and went into a diatribe as to how for years the government had kept people ignorant, but now, stupidly, they had been given education and were making political demands.

In England, hundreds went to prison for flouting the tax on printing. The same group were also responsible for producing the People's Charter.

But I should declare my interest. Richard Moore and James Watson were ancestors of mine. Both worked for decades for democratic rights in England, but even within the family their efforts had almost been forgotten. One Chartist turned historian of the movement wrote of Moore: 'His name is not prominent in histories, yet to him, with Hetherington and Watson, more than to any other men, we are indebted for a free press in England.'[4] He was also amongst the first few signatories of the Charter in 1838.

Perhaps the Newspaper Publishers' Association could hold an annual event in conjunction with the BBC and other broadcasters to celebrate those who established the free press.

The impact of ignorance about our democratic history

As a result of the neglect of this part of our heritage, most British people have little understanding of how democracy developed. The British people have a great sense of some national events, particularly those in the Second World War but, in contrast, few people know about such landmark events as when we got the vote, free speech, political organisation and equality before the law. We should develop activities which would give a proper place in our national life to the history of democracy.

Government and other organisations should work together to create a range of connected and mutually reinforcing initiatives. Bank holidays should be designated to celebrate the story of how we won our freedom before the law, our right to free speech and the right to elect our government. They might be called Magna Carta Day, Leveller Day or Suffragette Day. Each should become a focus for educational and civic activity.

An annual series of special stamps should be created featuring leading democratic campaigners. There is no shortage of candidates. Several could be chosen each year.

The citizenship component of the new national curriculum should place a greater emphasis on historic events including the Magna Carta and the special importance of the fact that in England men were free before the law, when for centuries the norm in most of Europe was that men were serfs. British education should also do more to show the emergence of the Commons in the seventeenth century as a source of resistance to absolute monarchy; the Leveller call for universal suffrage; the growing pressure for reform in the eighteenth century; the successful export of democratic ideas to North America and later to the Dominions; the Chartist movement and the rise of the trade unions in the nineteenth century; and women's suffrage and the final removal of property qualifications in 1928. In further and higher education prominence should be given to the history of democracy, both academically and by celebrating the contribution to democracy made by past graduates. It is possible to take a degree in sports science or philosophy but I know of no degrees in democracy.

There is a great opportunity for the arts to make a contribution. National museums and galleries should stage special exhibitions and new permanent features. These should highlight the revolutionary politics of poets such as Samuel Taylor Coleridge, John Keats, John Milton and Percy Bysshe Shelley and of writers such as Mary Wollstonecraft and Thomas Paine. The National Portrait Gallery could give greater emphasis to democrats. The Public Record Office's exhibition of police files on radicals from the eighteenth century is a good example of neglected but exciting material that could be turned into popular historical drama.

We should build an international museum of democracy that would feature how Britain's democratic heritage influenced and was influenced by events in other countries. It could have much of the grisly appeal of existing museums such as the London Dungeon, because execution, beating, imprisonment and transportation were all meted out as punishments to early democrats. Schoolchildren could engage in games in which they could see what would have been done to them in previous times for speaking and acting as they do today – whether in criticising the Queen, having to pay an exorbitant sum to buy anything printed or even shoplifting.

Local museums, government and associations should make more of people from their area who made a contribution to this part of our history. These have often been forgotten. For example, Ware in Hertfordshire hosted a key Leveller convention in the 1640s, other gatherings sought equality for women. The demands of these conventions were rejected by those in power for nearly three hundred years, and advocating what was on the Leveller agenda was a criminal offence until the nineteenth century.

It may be said that the British are already too immersed in their history and should spend their energies looking forwards rather than forever backwards. It may be said that public money should not be spent on celebrating obscure malcontents who had little respect for law and order. But so long as public money is spent on history we should rescue from obscurity those who created today's laws and order. How can we nurture a sense of democracy in a country which celebrates its kings and ignores the first people who wished to be citizens rather than subjects?

It will be important to provide a non-party political approach and recall ancient rights of freedom as well as the more recent advent of universal suffrage. 'People do not appreciate what they are given, only what they have gained through their own efforts.' This adage has a lot of value, and it certainly informs much of contemporary government policies. It may even be true of democracy: deprived of knowing the achievements of their great-grandparents in winning democracy, people can much more easily see it as something of a handout rather than a precious jewel dearly won. A remedy presents itself.

More than three million Britons signed the People's Charter of 1849 and, although the Charter failed, its core programme became adopted by the Liberal and Radical parties and passed into law as male suffrage for middle and lower-middle classes in 1867 and 1884 respectively. In the early 1900s the movement for votes for women – the Suffragettes – attracted similar support.

Following the natural course of events, the descendants of the millions of Suffragettes and of the Chartists of 1848 now make up most of the population. It would make a wonderful national project for schools and colleges in conjunction with the government departments of education, culture and constitutional affairs to search out all our ancestors, to whom we owe our rights today. Tragically, until 1950 Parliament burnt all the petitions that it received, so finding out about our democratic ancestors will entail a rather more complicated search through the archives of national and local associations and newspapers than simply examining the petitions of the time.

In the coming years there are a number of anniversaries that can focus the creation of a national celebration of our democratic heritage. The year 2005 marks the centenary of the Reform Acts of 1905, which deserve rather more celebration than the bicentenary of the Battle of Trafalgar. And 2015 is the eight hundredth anniversary of Magna Carta – a suitable date to open an international museum of democracy.

The imaginative celebration of our democracy will help us strengthen our freedoms and provide the basis upon which we can renew our democracy for the future. Participating in running the country should seem as normal as placing a bet. Both need good judgement and luck and can soak up as much study as you want to put in.

The ideas of making shareholders equal before the law, globalising democracy and restoring pride in our democratic achievements are all intended to be mutually supportive ideas that can reverse some of the fundamentally negative trends in society that fuel grievances, weaken democracy and enable both oppression and extremist insurrection. These economic and political reforms can implement the values of the Atlantic Charter, the UN Millennium Goals and the global requirements of effective counter-terrorism principles. Our leaders never tire of telling us that the new war on terrorism will last years if not indefinitely; consequently a positive agenda must be at least as far-reaching in time and in the breadth of issues it can resolve.

Having set a context that can improve our confidence and morale, and offer short- and long-term financial and political benefits, the next step is to provide a more focused approach on removing the causes, indeed what some may even see as the need for war. The two most important of these are the struggle for resources and the weapons of war themselves.

Seven

Defusing resource wars
Removing oil and gas dependency
(while reducing global warming
and aiding development)

General Motors has invested about $1 billion in developing
fuel cells to power electric motors in vehicles, and wants to be
the first auto maker to sell a million FCVs. It hopes to
commercialize FCVs by 2010 — one of the most optimistic
targets in the industry.

Reuters

Fighting over resources is nothing new. For centuries, resources have been the prizes over which wars have been fought. Today this continues. Some notorious civil wars in Africa are about diamonds and precious metals. Water is another example of a critical resource in short supply that is adding to conflict around the world, not least in the Middle East and Africa. For example, Turkey's plans to dam the upper reaches of the Tigris and Euphrates may seriously affect the amount of water available for agriculture in Iraq and Syria. In the

Jordan valley, Israel's illegal settlements in the West Bank are often directed at controlling water supplies.

People have fought wars over resources for centuries. In the eighteenth century, Frederick the Great of Prussia seized the Silesian coalfields from Poland and used them to build Prussia's industrial and military might. A century and a half later, the Soviet leader, Joseph Stalin, called this same region simply 'Gold' as his armies advanced into Nazi Germany. He redrew the map and transferred the region back to Poland, then under his control.

The greatest conflict over scarce resources in the modern age is over oil. The reliance of the industrialised world on this single resource would not matter if oil was found all over the place as easily as coal or even trees. The fact that sixty per cent of world reserves are located in the Persian Gulf has resulted in intense and growing competition between states for access to it. In addition to dependence on oil imports, the UK, and Europe as a whole, is becoming dependent on the importation of natural gas to run electric power generation. As Britain's Institution of Civil Engineers (ICE) put it:

> *This country has been self-sufficient in electricity generation for the past 100 years. This is about to change dramatically. The (domestic) generation shortfall (80 per cent of current capacity) will be taken up by gas, 90 per cent of which will be delivered to this country through a very small number of pipelines.*

The mainstream view of the problem of energy security is summarised in *Strategic Trends*, a study by the Ministry of Defence's think tank, the Joint Doctrine and Concepts Centre:

*Global demand for energy resources will increase signifi-
cantly due primarily to development and industrialisation
in South and East Asia. There is little prospect of revolutionary breakthroughs in alternative supplies. Renewable
and nuclear energy sources will remain of moderate importance but fossil fuels, and particularly oil and gas, will
remain dominant. These will stay the key strategic resources
as the main areas of supply and demand are separate. Their
location and transport routes will therefore be security
drivers for the developed and developing nations alike.*

The argument of this chapter is that it is both necessary and possible
to make a revolutionary breakthrough in alternative supplies. Such a
strategic shift in technology towards renewable sources for transport,
business and home use is possible and should be made a national
security priority in the UK, the European Union and in the world as
a whole. This economic-security argument for shifting to renewables
complements the compelling evidence for renewable energy as a
means to limit global warming.

For those interested in a detailed technical analysis of global energy
issues, the United Nations Development Programme's World Energy
Assessment is one-stop shopping. It includes discussion of the well-
established issues of global warming and sustainable –
environmentally friendly – development.

Most people are familiar with renewable energy as an environmental
issue. Renewables are rightly preferred to nuclear power on grounds of
safety and to coal and gas as a means of reducing the creation of the
gases that create global warming. These are powerful arguments for
renewable energy. There is also a debate on when we will need to shift

to renewable energy as the fossil fuels, mainly oil and gas, run out. Some experts argue that oil and gas production in the world will soon go into decline, others that we have another half-century. What is also clear is that economic development around the world based on current industrial practices will increase demand. So oil and to a lesser extent gas are already at the centre of international competition for their control and a combination of declining resources and increasing demand will only increase the conflict unless something is done.

This chapter explores the existing security and economic costs and conflicts over oil and gas. I argue that it is not only essential to national and international security to make a rapid change, but that ending oil and gas dependency within twenty years is practical, financially and technically. If this seems over-ambitious it is worth remembering that twenty years ago coal was a dominant source of supply and has now been phased out, while the idea that sports cars would run on diesel engines would have been treated as laughable.

A historical example indicates that a revolutionary transition is practical. In the early 1970s France drew less than ten per cent of its energy from nuclear reactors; today it is around seventy-five per cent.[1] The shift required massive investment by the French government and was implemented to free France from dependence on oil-fired electric power plants and from the problem of the decline in its own and German supplies of coal. The technical challenges presented by windmills and solar panels are far less than those of creating nuclear reactors. So, if the French were able to increase the role of nuclear power in their electricity production in such a rapid and dramatic manner, we should be able to achieve the same scale of change with renewables.

The main study on the costs of the French transition was carried out for the French Prime Minister, Lionel Jospin, in 2000. One of the authors of Jospin's study wrote to me that 'in total, France spent about 1,189 billion FF – or roughly 180 billion euros – in the first 21 years of operation of its nuclear fleet, corresponding to an average of 8.6 billion euros by year.'[2] This does not include decommissioning costs. By way of comparison, the UK is seeking funding of some £6 billion to achieve around ten per cent electricity production from wind by the end of the decade. Just for the sake of argument, suppose we wanted to create 150 per cent of present UK electricity supply from renewable energy over twenty years; the cost at these rates would be £90 billion or just over £4 billion a year. A huge sum to you or me, but quite manageable for the government or industrial investors.

Renewable energy, including shifting to new engines and fuels for cars, presents significant technical problems. But the problems are mainly concerned with driving down costs and, as we shall see, can be accomplished by economies of scale achieved by large-scale production and from increasing research and development. Securing oil supplies has a large ongoing cost to the industrialised world and to oil producers themselves and this is rarely included when traditional energy strategies are evaluated or when an assessment is made of the benefits of shifting to renewables. The security cost of oil – and in the future of gas – is counted in the cash required to support military forces, and in putting the concern to secure oil ahead of other priorities such as democracy and human rights in some of the countries concerned. These costs form what we can call a human-rights and military subsidy required to secure oil and gas. In addition, the crises threatening to interrupt supplies from the Middle East cause the oil price to go up and down with a consequent huge negative impact on the international economy amounting to hundreds of billions of dollars every year.

It may seem odd to include these costs, because it is not normal to find them included in analysis in the media, although the potential extra costs of developing renewables are often dismissed because it is said that they will need a 'green subsidy' or 'green tax'. As Shimon Awerbuch of Sussex University has observed, 'the mystery about all this is why policymakers have not exploited the obvious connection between the enormous costs imposed by fossil [fuel] volatility and the potential for mitigating these costs offered by renewables.'[3] Once the costs of price volatility and security are considered the economics of a shift to renewables are even more attractive.

Officials in Western governments assume that any major disruptions to supply will be short-lived. If they prove to be wrong in this assumption the economic and political consequences would be severe and could be catastrophic. Fortunately, using wind and solar power for electric generation and new fuels and engines for vehicles can reduce and eliminate these costs and risks. New fuels and engines include petrol substitutes from plants and electricity-generating fuel cells drawing electric power from wind and solar energy as well as traditional sources. Major corporations and governments around the world are already pursuing some of these options.

These new options should be implemented rapidly. Doing so makes sense in terms of the realist politics that are supposedly being pursued by hawkish governments in Washington and London. Indeed a shift out of oil and gas would be a strategic move that tackles one of the worst-case scenarios that may be inflicted upon the country and the industrialised world in general. However, getting out of oil and gas and into renewable energy is an elegant sidestep compared to the bull-in-a-china-shop approach preferred by Washington at present, and indeed for some time past. In the jargon of strategic studies it is asymmetric grand strategy. The result of the shift would be to remove a major strategic weakness, a major cause of conflict, and to create a stronger strategic position.

This chapter is concerned primarily about oil dependency. However, as the ICE has pointed out, dependency on natural gas is also a problem. So before discussing the oil security problem in detail I want to explain why there is a comparable, but less urgent, need to reduce dependence on gas. For environmentalists natural gas is a relatively good fuel, producing less greenhouse gas (carbon dioxide) than coal or oil. In addition world gas supplies are less highly concentrated in the Middle East than are oil supplies. Nevertheless, the major regions of gas supply outside the Middle East are north Africa and Russia, both areas of some political tension. Russia in particular is using its oil and gas reserves to rebuild its economy and its political influence. It is noticeable that Western criticism of the decay of Russian democracy under President Putin has been muted, not least because Europe and the US are competing with Japan and China for access to Russian oil and gas. As usual, ignoring human-rights issues is a short-sighted approach to international policy and at variance with the overall strategy outlined in Chapter 3.

A short history of oil dependency

In the nineteenth century, the Industrial Revolution created massive new demands for energy. This was met through coal production and, from the early twentieth century, more often by oil and most recently by gas as well.

Oil first became a strategic issue at the beginning of the twentieth century when Winston Churchill, then in charge of Britain's navy, decided to shift the fleet from coal-fired to oil-fired propulsion. Ships were then able to sail far further on a single load of fuel, reducing the navy's dependence on a global network of coaling stations. Churchill's shift to oil to fuel the navy required the use of imported supplies, mostly from the Persian Gulf.

By the Second World War, oil had become a necessity for powering tanks, planes and other vehicles necessary in modern battle. But crucially, neither Germany nor Japan had supplies under their control. In Germany's case this was part of the reason for Adolf Hitler's desire to conquer the Soviet Union and the specific reason for the disastrous Stalingrad campaign, which was intended to capture the oilfields of the Caucasus. In Japan's case it provided the incentive for the invasions of Indo-China and Indonesia. Both nations' war efforts were weakened by the need for oil and in the end they literally ran out of petrol.

After the Second World War there were successive global economic crises over oil supplies arising out of war in the Middle East. In 1956 the Suez canal, linking the Gulf to the Mediterranean, was blocked after an attack on Egypt by Britain, France and Israel. Until then oil had been shipped to Europe in tankers small enough to go through the canal. Its blockage meant that ships had to travel all the way around Africa and there were simply not enough tankers to sustain supplies. In the short term, the British had to issue ration cards for petrol, and in the longer term the oil industry invented the now well-known supertankers to sustain supplies.

During the 1967 Arab–Israeli war several Arab oil producers refused to sell to the US and some of its allies. In 1973 there was a much greater crisis resulting from Egypt's failed attack on Israel. Partly as a means of applying political pressure on the West and to increase their own incomes, the Arab oil producers gave renewed political power to a sellers' club called the Organisation of Petroleum Exporting Countries (OPEC). With the creation of OPEC oil prices jumped from around $4 per barrel to $17 before stabilising around $11. This oil shock was enough to trigger an economic recession in the US and Europe. The crisis was contained with OPEC established as a powerful grouping of states in international affairs.

Continuing pressure from OPEC gradually pushed prices higher until they reached $42.75 at the end of 1980, after Saddam Hussein's unsuccessful blitzkrieg against the new Islamic republic in Iran. Then the introduction of new supplies from the North Sea and other areas together with a more moderate approach led by Saudi Arabia saw a fall in prices again. But the short-lived impact of the now declining North Sea production makes an important point. The Gulf remains the key source of supply and new smaller finds do not change this long-term dependence. In fact two-thirds of the world's oil resources are located in the nations around the Persian Gulf, one-quarter in Saudi Arabia alone.

Proven oil reserves 2002

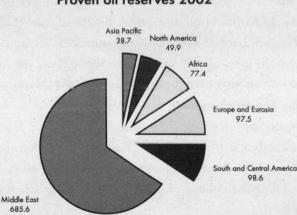

Asia Pacific 38.7

North America 49.9

Africa 77.4

Europe and Eurasia 97.5

South and Central America 98.6

Middle East 685.6

Other sources are far smaller. For example, there is a great deal of media debate over oil resources in Russia, central Asia and the Caucasus, but so far these reserves make up altogether around six per cent of known world supplies, or just a tenth of the supplies around the Persian Gulf.

The vast majority of oil production is used to fuel vehicles, with a small amount used in plastics and other industries. In addition, gas, found alongside oil, is being burned to produce electricity as a cheaper, cleaner option to both coal and nuclear power stations. The EU as a whole used oil and gas to meet more than half of its total energy needs in 2000, importing seventy-five per cent of the oil and forty per cent of the gas. The EU predicts that these proportions will rise to ninety per cent for oil and seventy per cent for gas by 2020. In the US, the level of imports is lower, currently at around twenty-five per cent of oil needs; however, in a global market shortage of supply affects the price that everyone pays.

Demand for oil is rising around the world. Developing nations are generating steadily increasing demand for energy and this demand focuses on oil and gas. A British admiral told me once that it would not be many decades before we saw Chinese aircraft-carriers seeking to protect Chinese interests in the Gulf. That senior officials are even bandying such notions about indicates the reality behind the theory that conflict results from competition for scarce resources. Securing these supplies is seen as vital by the industrialised nations, and some leading US decision-makers such as Paul Wolfowitz see US control of Persian Gulf oil as a means of controlling the policies of other major nations such as Japan and China.

In 2003 the industrialised world is as dependent on Gulf oil as it was in the 1970s. And now dependence on imports of gas has also become a key strategic issue.

Security of supply

As we have seen, in future Britain will have to import more and more of gas to make up its electricity generation shortfall, ninety per cent of this gas will be delivered through a very few pipelines, initially from Norway, but later from west Africa, the Middle East and former Soviet republics. If future gas supplies are interrupted, we would have major difficulty in keeping the lights on. Maintaining these supplies has a large current cost in shaping our policies towards supplier nations. These costs include the impact of fluctuating oil prices and the military and foreign policies of trying to secure the supply.

One unquantifiable cost is the way Western states forget their commitment to human rights when it comes to getting their hands on the oil needed to keep their economies going. For example, two major oil producers, Nigeria and Russia, appear to escape criticism for their internal human-rights abuses, because of the imperative of ensuring oil supplies. In both countries the government engages in widespread abuses of human rights, according to organisations such as Amnesty International. These values are often given by Western leaders as key ones to be supported in foreign policy. Unfortunately, the desire to obtain access to the oil mutes attention to reform of human rights.

Western governments do consider worst-case scenarios for the interruption of supplies of oil, but these assume that the disruptions will be short-lived. This assumption relies on the belief that (a) oil-supplying nations will always want to sell their oil regardless of the ideology of the people in charge, and (b) if an extremist government does try to 'hold the West to ransom' then the West can invade and seize control of the oil supplies. It is easy to imagine a situation where the government of one or more major oil-producing nations wished to withhold supplies as a means of attacking the industrialised world. In such a situation even a massive invasion might not get the oil wells and pipelines flowing and the tankers sailing again.

The experience in Iraq shows that six months after the invasion in March 2003, oil production had fallen from the 2002 level of two million barrels per day to less than a quarter of that. At the time of writing, production had gradually been restored to pre-war levels mostly from the peaceful southern oilfields around Basra, but it was proving very hard to export oil safely from the northern oilfields. Even 150,000 troops in a country of twenty million people had proved unable to forcibly extract oil.

Will governments in key oil-producers ever refuse to sell the oil? It is possible. With its huge reserves and large proportion of world oil production, Saudi Arabia is the most important nation where a political change would have a damaging impact. Some US present and past political and intelligence figures have been highly critical of the Saudi government and connections between Saudi Arabia and Al-Qaeda. The US needed to establish its military in Iraq as a means of being able to apply military/political pressure to the Saudi regime, according to James Woolsey, former US Director of Central Intelligence. The relationship of Saudi citizens to the attacks of 9/11 was considered so sensitive by President Bush that he insisted that twenty-six pages dealing with these matters be censored from the US

Congress's report on US intelligence operations before the attacks of 9/11. This potential problem is discussed in the section 'Could Al-Qaeda win?' in Chapter 2.

It is not necessary to say how great this type of a risk to oil supplies might be to realise that it is a risk that should be avoided if at all possible. History is full of surprises, such as the fall of the Soviet Union, and the only thing certain about the future is that there will be surprises. When I have discussed the problem of severe disruption of Gulf oil with government officials in London and Washington the usual reply is that since there is no option other than oil we must just make the best of things. When I questioned an expert on the US National Security Council about the lack of any 'Plan B' if the existing political strategy in the Gulf (Plan A) failed, he merely explained that America's Plan B was to make sure that Plan A worked.

So how serious a political and economic impact would major interruptions to supplies of oil and gas have on the industrialised world? In 2002, Robert 'Bud' McFarlane, National Security Adviser to President Ronald Reagan, answered the question 'What could go wrong?[4] by explaining that with world oil consumption at around seventy-six million barrels per day (mbd), a 'US move against Iraq' might interrupt 2mbd, the collapse of the Saudi regime 8mbd and the collapse of Kuwait 2mbd. In addition, McFarlane mentioned possible attacks on shipping in the Strait of Hormuz at the mouth of the Persian Gulf and in the Strait of Malacca between Indonesia and Malaysia, as well as sabotage of oil ports and refineries at places such as Rotterdam and in the Gulf of Mexico. Since 9/11 there have been several attacks on oil tankers. These occurred in the Gulf, in the Malaccan straits and off Sri Lanka. None had a wider impact beyond the ship, but some security sources interpret this to mean that the attacks were training exercises for planning a more devastating attack. Such is the concentration of supply routes that massive damage to a very few locations would cause years of economic disruption. Professor David Fisk of Imperial College London is of the view that because car use is so much more pervasive than even in the oil crisis of the 1970s, 'an oil shortage would not now be an inconvenience. Because transport has become such a basic commodity, it would be near catastrophic.'[5]

A study by the US Brookings Institution soon after the attacks of 9/11[6] illustrated the potential economic impact of several scenarios and provides a good example of some of factors that need to be considered. The study's worst-case scenario, written in early 2002, describes an economic disaster for the world as a whole:

> *Finally, as a worst case, assume extremists exert control over the entire 21.7 mbd production in Arab Muslim nations, and that they cut this production by 10 mbd. Iraq could be expected to join such an initiative. How plausible is this? Bin Laden and other extremists want most of all to overthrow the Saudi monarchy and the other dynastic rulers in the region. On the other hand, the United States would be expected to use military force to prevent it. Although a US military occupation of the region could maintain oil supplies, it would have imponderable consequences for our relations with the wider Muslim world and could prove unsustainable. Furthermore, apart from the particular scenario sketched above, 10 mbd of supply could conceivably be lost to some other combination of political takeover*

*or coercion, destruction of facilities, and interruption of
distribution. So its consequences are worth examining.*

The study included analysis of the impact of the worst-case scenario
and concluded:

> *The worst case brings devastating economic problems. Oil
> prices rise to $161 per barrel driving gasoline price to $4.84
> per gallon (without tax). The increase in the nation's bill for
> products of crude oil rises by about 10 percent of GDP,
> which adds perhaps 15 percent to the inflation rate in the
> first year. And the recession is the steepest and deepest of the
> post-war period, with GDP declining nearly 5 percent the
> first year.*

These scenarios all involve great changes in wealth. Assume some Al-
Qaeda-like government not only gains control over the production of
oil, but aquires control of the revenues from that production. The first
two scenarios give control of up to $74 billion a year. The third, which
includes all of the Arab Gulf oil, gives control of over $198 billion a
year, rising to $689 billion as the reduced production raises prices.

It would be very misleading to think that governments have put
no measures in place at all to respond to shortages of oil supplies. In
response to the oil crisis of 1973 the governments of the industrialised world created the International Energy Agency (IEA), and the
US has increased its military investment in the Gulf region to the
present deployment of an army.

The IEA's members are bound by treaty to support its emergency
mechanisms. These include storing several months' supply in

strategic reserves, preparing to use these when supplies are interrupted and procedures for cutting back on demand. These procedures were used both during the Iran–Iraq war in 1980 and after Saddam attacked Kuwait in 1991. After 9/11 some countries took further steps and Japan led south-east Asian nations in creating regional emergency reserves.

However, there are worrying inadequacies in the IEA emergency procedures, which themselves only deal with short-term problems. The European Commission has stated that the mechanisms were created in response to the circumstances of 1973 and are little changed today. In particular, any of the major industrial nations in the agreement can block implementation of the procedures; some countries do not even keep their allocated reserves; and there are no procedures at all for gas. Perhaps most worrying is that a review of some key questions has revealed that although the world has acknowledged the problem of oil dependency since the 1970s there has been no change in the level of that dependency over the last thirty years. The world got thirty-five per cent of its energy from oil in 2000, about the same level as the thirty-seven per cent of 1990, but gas increased from eighteen to twenty-two per cent in the same period.

The military subsidy of oil prices

The highly political nature of judgements on cost was well illustrated in a discussion some years ago in the US Senate. In a decidedly tetchy exchange, Senator Jesse Helms, then chairman of the Foreign Relations Committee, questioned Jeff Gottbaum, a senior official of the Clinton administration, about the costs of securing Gulf Oil during the 1991 war.[7]

Sen. Helms: All right, Mr Gottbaum, I have just a few seconds. It costs a bundle – meaning it costs the taxpayers of the United States a bundle – to protect foreign suppliers. We all agree on that, do we not? That is the reason we went to the Persian Gulf, et cetera, et cetera. That cost a lot of money. Have you ever computed or would you go back and have your people compute what it costs per barrel of imported oil to protect the producers of this oil?

Mr Gotbaum: Actually, Mr Chairman—

Sen. Helms: Do you understand the question?

Mr Gotbaum: Oh, I understand the question, absolutely. I think part of the reason I am here is because I, in fact, asked the question just the way you did, sir.

First let me say a couple of things just so that there is no miscommunication between us. Desert Storm (the reconquest of Kuwait in 1991), in addition to costing many lives, had a total estimated incremental cost of about $57 billion. Of that $57 billion, our estimate, almost $54 billion, over 90 per cent, was reimbursed to the United States either by cash contributions or in kind contributions. So, when I at least asked the question of my staff, well, what does this mean on a per barrel basis, the view we took is that we ought to look at the total cost of Desert Storm, say round figures, $60 billion. But since that was really there to protect world oil demand, we ought to look at it divided by something like the world oil supply over a period of years. If you take your

> *$60 billion and you take demand, if you will, which is about 24 billion barrels a year, say, over a 10-year period, that works out to be about 25 cents a barrel.*
>
> *Now, what I personally came away with was not that that meant that it was only worth 25 cents a barrel to us to have security in the Middle East. That is like saying that because a seat belt only costs $3, a human life is only worth $3. But it seemed to us that it said to us it is worth somewhat north of that, sir.*

As we shall see, a reasonable estimate of the military cost of attempting to secure Gulf oil is far higher than the extra cost of the 1991 Gulf War. The US Congressional Research Service (CRS) periodically reviews the economic and security effects on the US of oil imports. It made the assessment that 'in terms of military expenditures related to the Middle East, even if oil imports from the region could be minimized, US geopolitical interests there relate to far more than oil.'[8] The CRS also takes the view that the security cost of Gulf oil imports

> *is either insignificant or ponderous, depending on the assumptions made. ... If only those military activities are tallied which would not be undertaken in the absence of oil in the region, then the cost of defending the oil would be very small. If any military activity is counted that, undertaken for whatever reason, contributes to the security of the region the cost calculation becomes much larger.*

This fence-sitting is not especially helpful. The US has one other official interest in the Middle East other than oil and that is the security of Israel. However, Israeli security assistance is achieved directly by grants to the Israeli state and by Mediterranean-based military forces, not included in calculations of US forces in the Middle East. It is possible to argue that US and Western conflict with Iran and Iraq would exist regardless of the presence of major concentrations of oil. However, this argument is hard to sustain when the historical context of nearly a century of oil-driven politics is taken into account.

Comparing US and Western approaches to the Gulf with security in other regions indicates the weakness of the argument that military expenditures would remain about the same without the oil factor. If we look at the areas of east and north Africa it is clear that there is no large Western military commitment to securing the nations of Somalia, Ethiopia and Kenya on the one hand and Morocco, Tunisia and Algeria on the other. This is the case even though each region has more than its fair share of internal, cross-border and anti-Western conflict. The 'we would spend this much anyway' argument does not stand even a brief examination.

America's annual spending on the military and intelligence was around $400 billion and $40 billion respectively in 2004/5. About a quarter of this – or $120 billion – is focused on securing Middle East oil supplies.

In the early 1970s after OPEC's rapid increase in the oil price, the US first began to plan for the occupation of Saudi Arabia to secure oil on favourable terms, and, according to documents recently released and reported in the *Financial Times*,[9] in the 1970s and 1980s this requirement was part of broader US military planning against the Soviet Union.

For the United States, the fall of the Shah in the 1979 Iranian revolution created a greater requirement to get an army to the region quickly. Until then Iran had been both a bastion against communism and a counterweight to more anti-Western governments in the Arab world. After 1979, US military planners not only had to consider Iran a hostile power in its own right but also needed to consider Iran's potential to attack its much smaller and weaker, but oil-rich, neighbours in the monarchies along the southern shores of the Gulf. These considerations and the long Iran–Iraq war created a political demand in the US for a huge build-up of US forces in the Gulf itself and in bases such as the British-owned island Diego Garcia in the Indian Ocean. This build-up intensified after the 1991 war and the US established large bases in Kuwait and Saudi Arabia.

After the collapse of the Soviet Union, US military strategy focused on having enough forces for two possible major regional wars, one in the Gulf and one in Asia. Following the 1991 Gulf War, new fleets of transport ships and planes capable of moving an army to the Gulf in a few weeks were built. US troops practised flying into their bases in Kuwait, opening their sand-proofed, vacuum-packed tanks and driving to defend Kuwait's border with Iraq, which would be followed by exercises for the long drive north to Baghdad. These preparations were codified in the Pentagon's Operational Plan 1040 and were put into practice in early 2003. An exaggerated view of US spending on the Gulf would attribute half of all costs to supporting this contingency; however, allowing for a quarter would allow for other areas of spending such as nuclear weapons, headquarters and training.

In addition to the US's annual costs associated with Gulf oil, there are other military costs closely related to securing the region's oil. These include a proportion of the military spending of US allies in

NATO such as Britain and France, each of which spend more than $40 billion on the military each year.

Last, but by no means least, are the costs of the wars in the region in which oil played a strong if not determining factor. These include the decade-long Iran–Iraq war, the Iraqi invasion of Kuwait in 1990 and its subsequent expulsion in 1991, and the recent 2003 invasion of Iraq. Precise figures for all these factors are not available, but US figures for its military costs in these wars are more than $200 billion and rising. A somewhat conservative estimate would average this out at perhaps $10 billion a year. The larger cost of the lives lost is not calculable, while the proportion of the costs to the regional economy of the various wars is a complicated calculation, but the sums involved cannot be small.

It is also clear that oil wealth produces dramatically greater increases in military spending even within a region of considerable tension, according to data for 2002 from the London-based International Institute for Strategic Studies. Syria, which is still at war with Israel, spent $107 per person, with a total of $1.8 billion. For Saudi Arabia the figures are $981 per person and $20 billion per year respectively. The states bordering the Persian Gulf, not including Iraq, spent a total of over $35 billion in 2002.

Consequently, an estimate of the non-US annual oil-related military costs to both US allies and adversaries in the region of some $30 billion seems quite conservative.

This sum includes, an annual security cost attributable to Gulf oil of $120 billion for the US, $10 billion for the contribution of Britain, France and other Western states, $10 billion for the annualised costs of the various actual wars and $10 billion of the military spending of the Gulf states themselves; adding up to the sum of $150 billion a year.

Annual military spending, $US billion, 2001

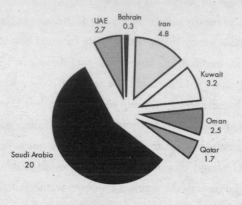

UAE
2.7

Bahrain
0.3

Iran
4.8

Kuwait
3.2

Oman
2.5

Qatar
1.7

Saudi Arabia
20

Total Middle East Spend US$35.2 Billion

SOURCE: *The Military Balance 2003–2004*, International Institute for Strategic Studies

What of the amount of oil that this spending is supposed to secure? At a maximum one could count the entire reserves in the region together with those elsewhere in the world. The argument for saying that the military security of the Gulf is in fact a protection of all oil is based on the fact that the world price is affected strongly by what happens in the Gulf. A minimum assessment would only count the amount of oil imported by the US and other states directly concerned. On the other hand, if one supports the idea that the US should keep global dominance by control of the Gulf, then the value assured to the US gets better for its huge investment in controlling oil. An intermediate position would be to include the oil produced by states under US protection, namely Bahrain, Kuwait, Oman, Saudi Arabia, Qatar and the United Arab Emirates. This amounts to some six billion barrels of oil per year.

It is reasonable to conclude that the $150 billion is spent trying to secure some six billion barrels a year. That is more than $20 a barrel or around $1 a gallon. Even half this figure, $75 billion, is still a large subsidy.

The global economic impact of fluctuating oil prices

In addition to the military subsidy to the price of oil, another and much larger cost of oil to the world economy is the cost of price fluctuations. These are sudden spikes and subsequent falls in the oil price caused by instability.

The price of oil has varied between $4 and $40 a barrel since 1970. This scale of fluctuation is quite common in world markets. Some rare minerals and climate-sensitive crops such as coffee also fluctuate unpredictably in price. Some other commodities such as platinum are critical to the world economy and are located in only a few places around the world. But only oil has such a huge quantitative role in the global economy through its near monopoly of providing fuels for transportation.

It is reasonable to expect that the economic impact of oil price fluctuations is great, but how great? Some $14 thousand billion (trillion) over a thirty-year period to the world as a whole; $7 trillion to the US economy alone according to the US Department of Energy Oak Ridge National Laboratory, in a study published in 2000:

> Oil dependence remains a potentially serious economic and strategic problem for the United States. This report updates previous estimates of the costs of oil dependence to the US economy and introduces several methodological enhance-

ments. Estimates of the costs to the US economy of the oil market upheavals of the last 30 years are in the vicinity of $7 trillion, present value 1998 dollars, about as large as the sum total of payments on the national debt over the same period. ... The costs of oil dependence have been large under almost any plausible set of assumptions. These cost estimates do not include military, strategic or political costs associated with US and world dependence on oil imports.[10]

I have not attempted to apply Oak Ridge's exhaustive analytic techniques to the world economy as a whole. Clearly there will be regional differences. However, it seems reasonable to assume that the rest of the world experiences comparable economic impact from price fluctuations to that recorded in the Oak Ridge study for the US. The US economy has made up around one-third of the global economy for some time so a global figure of triple the US cost is possible, but even if we assume that the costs to the US were a larger proportion of the total cost to the world, the global total still reaches $14 trillion over thirty years or an average of $467 billion a year. One reason for a lower global cost is that part of the cost to the US and other oil-consumers is simply transferring their wealth to the sellers of the oil. However, the Oak Ridge study estimates that the vast majority of the cost is caused by lower economic activity, recession, caused by the high cost of oil.

Shimon Awerbuch of Sussex University has analysed the problem of the relative costs of oil and of renewable energy and concludes that the cost of oil is normally calculated using obsolete methods based upon what is called the 'engineering economics' approach. Awerbuch argues that other industries use a well-established 'capital asset pricing' model for capital budgeting and project valuation.[11] When applied to oil and gas, he claims, they produce far higher estimates of the past and future costs of these products than those used by the IEA.

Awerbuch also provides a convincing summary of other studies that show the negative impact of oil price fluctuations in causing the main global recessions since 1945 and stock market slumps. For example, the rise in oil prices after the Arab–Israeli war of 1973 produced a global economic recession, and a similar recession was triggered after the Iranian revolution in the early 1980s. These rises in the cost of imported oil were an important factor in creating the debts now still burdening many third-world nations.

Getting out of oil and gas: asymmetric geopolitics

Since 9/11 there has been much discussion amongst strategists and in the media of 'asymmetric war and strategy', by which is meant unusual ways of fighting and of organising power. However, imagine for a moment that a shift from oil and gas could be made in the same way that the Victorians shifted from horse and sail to steam ships and trains. Were such a change to shift to decentralised and plentiful energy sources then the prospects for peace would be much improved.

- For a start, the imperial vision of the US conservatives would look as relevant as a Victorian general's obsession with cavalry and coaling stations. There would be no point for any nation to try to run the world through controlling oil, and little need to fight about Gulf oil or pipelines across Afghanistan and Armenia.
- A decision to shift transport away from oil would also remove the possibility that extremist regimes in the Gulf could cripple the

industrialised world and that any further US-inspired gun battles in the region would risk blowing up the world's petrol station.

- Supporters of the EU can also use a fast track out of oil for transport as the quickest and most cost-effective means of both reducing reliance on the US military to secure Europe's oil and providing greater freedom of action to disagree with Washington.

- While turning from oil and gas into renewable energy may make us safe from having the power blackout, it may even allow us to undermine the military-industrial complex. The term 'military-industrial complex' is no invention of left-wing pacifists. Indeed, it is a network whose threat to society was first drawn to public attention by President Dwight D. Eisenhower, a man who as General Eisenhower had led the D-Day landings and the liberation of Western Europe:

> This conjunction of an immense military establishment and a large arms industry is new in the American experience. ... We recognise the imperative need for this development. Yet we must not fail to comprehend its grave implications.... In the councils of government, we must guard against the acquisition of unwarranted influence, whether sought or unsought, by the military-industrial complex. The potential for the disastrous rise of misplaced power exists and will persist.[12]

At present, governments from Tokyo to Berlin and Brussels bite their tongues when thinking of criticising Washington. They used to do so because they felt they needed the US as a balance to the USSR. Today, they assume that US military might controls Gulf oil. The crudeness of this relationship is shown most clearly in the member-ship of the Iraq reconstruction council in mid-2003. The US only allowed countries to take part in reconstruction contracts if they are helping in the military occupation. So Poland got to join, but not Iraq's neighbours Syria and Iran as they are not friends of the US. And of course France, Germany and Russia did not get invitations.

An existing strategy for reducing the security impact of depend-ence on Gulf oil has been to seek new sources of supply. However, even though Russia is now producing almost as much oil as Saudi Arabia, its reserves are still less than ten per cent of those in the Middle East. Few of the new oil and gas finds are in politically stable areas, and most are in states with Islamic populations increasingly alienated by the West. Getting out of oil may be desirable, but is it practical?

Perhaps the whole idea of a rapid transition to renewable energy is no more than a fantasy that we can run our cars on cow farts. Before we take a technical tour of the options, just think about diesel cars for a moment. A few years ago diesels were for buses and Land Rovers. Today, the car magazines are loaded with the latest sports turbo diesels, every car comes in a diesel version. This change has come simply because governments have put less tax on diesel, and why? Because diesel puts less greenhouse gas, carbon dioxide (CO_2), into the atmosphere.

The sports diesel is just one of a range of changes in fuels and engines for transport that has been developed in response to global warming. A review of these technologies reveals that they are well advanced. Nevertheless, governments and industry are assuming that the technology will not be implemented for another thirty-odd years. This need not be the case.

A transition to hydrogen will need to address four main issues. These are how to produce it, how to distribute it to filling stations, how to get public acceptability and how to produce high-performance vehicles. The following discussion provides some answers to these questions. Hydrogen would be best produced using renewable electricity, and though this is a huge task it is achievable over a decade or two. Distribution is often cited as an almost insurmountable obstacle although, based on some evidence from industry, these costs are lower than might be imagined. It is also clear that industrial leaders appear to believe that vehicles can be made that have sufficient performance to appeal to the public.

Before we dive into some of the technicalities, I think it is important not to be too easily put off by sceptics. For example, I noticed a 2003 study for the IEA on considering a transition to hydrogen. It is scathing about efforts by political leaders around the world who are trying to support such a transition. To remove any room for doubt the study takes the example of France and claims that to support vehicles with hydrogen would require producing as much electricity altogether as France now produces. It conjures up a picture of 350,000 windmills and one per cent of the surface area of the country covered in solar panels. Fortunately, I had to hand an EU assessment on offshore wind energy[13] – windmills at sea – which stated that the capacity to produce electricity from this source alone from around the shores of Europe was equal to whole of current European electricity production: 'In 1995, electricity production in the EU amounted to 2384 terawatt hours. The annual offshore resource is estimated to be in excess of 2500 terawatt hours.'

How can we turn an analysis of the benefits of shifting to renewables into a practical programme? There is no space in this book to give a detailed technical and political programme. Nevertheless, I think it is important to set out some concrete targets that governments can and should meet and to sketch out the current technical and political context that should provide the base for a rapid transition to renewable electricity and hydrogen.

A key target is for governments to announce that in five years they will only purchase vehicles that are either hybrid oil/electric or hydrogen powered, and that they will immediately seek such vehicles to provide for emergency services and public transport. These targets can be set by individual countries but would ideally be set at a global or regional level through such organisations as the UN, G7, the EU, the African Union and the Association of South East Asian Nations. The advantage of this approach is that governments have enormous purchasing power in the market and thus an ability to provide manufacturers with somewhere to sell innovative vehicles. In California, such an initiative has been adopted by the state government. A second target would be to aim to complete a transition to renewable hydrogen by 2020. Present planning in governments tends to assume that such a transition would just be starting around 2020.

As we have seen, it is essential to pursue a prompt transition for security, environmental and economic reasons. It is no use leaving such issues hanging in the air. They have to be brought down to earth with a tough discussion about prompt change. To sustain that argument we will now take a swift jog through the technical and political details.

The technical fixes: engines and fuels

New engines and fuels include the replacement of the internal-combustion engine in vehicles and the introduction of wind and solar sources to provide electrical power. In addition, energy specialists are able to demonstrate that considerable energy savings can be made through the increased efficiency of household electrical appliances and insulation and more efficient oil-powered vehicles. However, the implementation of new engines and fuels for transport and improved methods of producing electricity are the essential changes that are needed.

The 'hydrogen economy' is a phrase used to describe an almost complete transition to a fuel cell-driven economy by the middle of the twenty-first century. Jeremy Rifkin's *The Hydrogen Economy* provides a route map to a mid-century transition. The key techno-logical idea is to dispense with the internal-combustion engine and replace it with a chemical system that transfers hydrogen into elec-tricity. This system needs no moving parts comparable to the cylinders filled with exploding petrol or diesel that power the internal-combustion engine. A different or interim approach is to replace oil and diesel with fuel from plants and produce hybrid vehicles using both internal-combustion and fuel cell engines.

Key questions that have to be settled are: will the fuel cells work? Where will the hydrogen come from? Are other fuels like vegetable oil viable? And how much will it all cost?

Environmentalists working to reduce climate change caused by CO_2 production from oil burned in vehicles, are concerned that hydrogen may actually make things worse. The argument runs that if the hydrogen is produced using electricity from oil- and gas-fired power stations then there will be no benefit at all to the environment. Indeed, the shift to hydrogen might be seen as a scam to pretend that the problem of these greenhouse gases has been fixed when in fact it has not.

A German speaker, Dr Gert Eisenbeiss, expressed a strong and sceptical view at an IEA conference in 2003.[14] He derided the political desire to see a rapid transition to hydrogen on the grounds that it was too difficult to make and introduce soon. In particular he expressed a concern common amongst environmental groups that moving to hydrogen may simply mean using oil and gas to make the hydrogen or using crops to create bio-fuels when the moral choice is to produce more food for the world's starving people.

There are a number of potential solutions to this problem. For example, the Borax company is looking at means of producing hydrogen by means of non-toxic, non-CO_2-emitting chemical reactions. A second solution is to massively expand the production of solar and wind-generated electric power to produce the needed electricity; and finally, where oil- and gas-produced electricity is used, the problem of controlling CO_2 emissions will have been transferred from millions of exhaust pipes to hundreds of factories. Where the task has been concentrated it may be easier to tackle, both technically and financially.

An additional option, under development by Shell, is to use photovoltaic cells to break up water into hydrogen and oxygen. At present the costs involved are considered to be too great; however, were the technology considered as important to the nation's defence as the need to maintain a high-tech military industry, then the cost would be regarded as much more manageable.

In addition to hydrogen there are two other solutions to the problem of alternatives to oil for transport fuels. The first is to produce vehicles with combined electric and internal-combustion engines. Major car manufacturers are now producing and developing these hybrid vehicles – Ford, GMC, Chevrolet, Toyota and Honda have cars in production – although in Europe manufacturers such as Volkswagen are concentrating on getting diesels to achieve more than 100 mpg. The first models looked and were cramped and heavy. Newer models, such as the Toyota Prius, look and perform more like mainstream cars. They cut demand through fuel efficiency as they are able to produce a combined fuel consumption of around seventy miles per gallon.

The second solution is to find other fuels for the traditional internal-combustion engine. One type of fuel used is liquefied gas; however, although these vehicles minimise the production of CO_2, the use of gas merely transfers the problem of fuel importation from the oil problem to the gas problem. A second major type of fuel is derived from plants. These bio-fuels include recycled vegetable oil or chip fat, and there was a lot of publicity about people converting their cars to run on this fuel. Some diesel vehicles are reported to run well without technical modification on a combination of ninety per cent diesel and ten per cent vegetable oil. In the United States, there are already taxpayer subsidies for farmers to produce ethanol fuel derived from maize (corn).

UK bio-diesel advocates explain an example of what can be achieved:[15]

> *The environmental benefits of bio-fuels are well proven. UK agriculture could produce over 5 per cent of fuel needs in fairly short order from existing crops and technology. In a 10-year time span this could rise to 10 per cent if new crop technology were brought into use and sufficient land was available after the core function of food production had been met.*

Many environmentalists are sceptical over the effectiveness of subsidising bio-fuels compared to wind and solar power. Nevertheless, bio-fuels offer a quite quick if partial solution to oil dependency.

The introduction of hybrid electric/internal-combustion cars may well offer an important bridge out of oil dependency, but the real prize would be to begin an accelerated shift out of dependence on oil and gas altogether.

The competitive price of wind and solar power

Potential stumbling blocks in the proposed transition from oil to electricity produced from renewable hydrogen include the cost of producing the hydrogen and, as we have discussed, the problem of not adding to greenhouse gases. So, how cheap does the hydrogen need to be?

In a presentation at the Royal Institute for International Affairs,[16] Professor Bragi Arbason of the University of Iceland explained that production of renewable hydrogen by passing electricity through water – electrolysis – which releases the H2 from the O, costs around 2 US cents per kilowatt hour (kWh) for the electricity, using Iceland's abundant supplies of hydro-electric power. This electricity price is between two and three times the price of imported petrol. However, since fuel cell engines are between two and three times more efficient than internal-combustion engines the prospect of commercial viability is in sight.

Assuming that a target cost of electricity is in the range of 2–3 cents/kWh, can such a price be obtained from the renewable sector? A study by the European Wind Energy Association in 2003[17] stated that wind power production costs were already down to below 3 cents/kWh. This is a fall from around 15 cents in the 1980s, around 6–8 cents in the 1990s and 4–5 cents at the turn of the century. Some studies are recording that economies of scale produced by much larger turbines are already bringing the price below 2 cents. An additional factor with dispersed energy supplies is that less is lost by being transported along powerlines.

An assessment made at Imperial College London[18] indicated that, particularly for wind energy, prices would fall considerably further by around 2020. The study concluded that by 2020 the following cost ranges were likely:

- Onshore wind: 1.5–2.5p/kWh
- Offshore wind: 2.0–3.0p/kWh
- Photovoltaic: not competitive until between 2020 and 2025
- Wave and tidal stream: 4.5–6.0p/kWh is likely in the short term (3–4 years)
- Energy crops: 2.5–4.0p/kWh.

An important part of this study was including estimates of the decrease in price resulting from economies of scale. It did not, however, include any additional financial or regulatory input from governments on grounds of national security.

It should also be noted that the use of solar power simply to generate heat and use it as a source for hydrogen is a far shorter router to solar derived-hydrogen than photovoltaics, especially along the coastlines of hot countries. For example, Volker Quaschning and Franz Trieb found that 'prices in the range of 5 to 8 cents/kWh of generated electricity can be expected in the medium term for solar only operated thermal power plants'.[19]

Political initiatives for renewable energy

The major drive for renewable energy has come from the environmental movement, concerned to reduce damage to humans and the world as whole resulting from a man-made change in the weather.

Climate change became a major centre of action for governments and pressure groups around the world. This effort created the UN agreement known as the Kyoto protocol that sets targets for governments to meet that limit of the amount of CO_2 released into the atmosphere. Some governments, including the US, have refused to agree to this measure and have not implemented comparable unilateral actions themselves. Amongst the states that have agreed to reduce CO_2 emissions, there has been an upsurge of investment in renewable energy technologies, particularly in wind power. For the first time major government incentives and industrial investment are being applied to renewable technology. It is this political process that provides the background for the current progress on renewable energy.

By itself the limitation and prevention of damaging climate change will make an important contribution to global security by reducing social and political dislocation and human destitution. In addition, the work done as a result of environmental concerns provides a powerful technical and political base that can be strongly reinforced by the security argument made in this chapter for a rapid shift away from oil and gas.

Since the oil price rise of 1973 there have been isolated voices in and out of Western governments calling for an end to dependency on Middle Eastern oil and for a new energy strategy. Now, at least in the United States, there is the growth of a broader strategy. A US group involving both the legal adviser to President George Bush Snr and the White House Chief of Staff to President Clinton along with Senator Tim Wirth is leading a new and integrated approach through the Energy Futures Coalition.[20] They defined the coalition's strategy this way:

A strategic energy policy will unite diverse political constituencies and forge common cause among stakeholders that are often at odds ... Most of all, a collaborative strategic approach holds out hope for ending dependence on oil, eliminating excess carbon dioxide emissions, and providing clean and reliable energy services and agricultural opportunity to the world's poor. The result would be to 'hurry the future' by unleashing a torrent of innovation that will stimulate economic growth, create new jobs, improve productivity, and increase prosperity and security for the United States and the world.

Government initiatives for the hydrogen economy

It is in Japan that the greatest effort is being made towards a shift to hybrid engines and hydrogen. This is not surprising given Japan's disastrous dependency on oil in the Second World War and its present reliance on oil from the Persian Gulf, an unstable area of the world over which it can exert little direct influence.

The Japanese government and associated agencies are investing around ¥100 billion a year (£500 million) in the shift to hydrogen. It projects that by 2020 some five million vehicles will be driven by hydrogen. The Japanese programme envisages a development phase ending in 2005 with proven technologies and new industry standards for the new fuels. In the period 2005–10 Japanese planning envisages the gradual introduction of the infrastructure to install hydrogen alongside diesel and petrol in filling stations. The Japanese see government-owned vehicle fleets leading industry and the public towards the widespread use of hydrogen-powered vehicles. Government-owned vehicles include as a matter of course large numbers of cars, light vans, buses and trucks. A government-led purchasing policy would entail announcing to industry that as of a certain date the government will only purchase vehicles meeting the new specifications. Government power as the largest consumer in society would provide a major competitive impetus to industry, all in the spirit of the old saying 'the customer is always right'.

In the EU the Commission President, Romano Prodi, created an advisory 'High Level Group on Hydrogen and Fuel Cells' in 2002 to look at the transition to hydrogen. The EU already has a target of meeting twenty per cent of vehicle fuel needs from alternative sources by 2020, including hydrogen. In September 2003 the EU announced a four-year research programme totalling 300 million. This is barely a tenth of the level of Japanese central support and, even allowing for national research efforts within the EU, the Union is far behind the Japanese in this area of research.

The most recent EU policy on security of supply has been heavily criticised by some leaders of the renewable energy community[21] for failing to take the opportunities offered by renewable technology and not meeting the real security challenges.

In the United States, President Bush launched a new Hydrogen Initiative that aims to assist the transition to a hydrogen economy. President Bush's multi-year commitment of $1.7 billion to research into the hydrogen economy is insignificant compared both to the current expenditures on oil-related defence costs and to a serious transition to hydrogen. A key problem in the Bush proposals is that it seeks to use gas to produce the hydrogen, which would not reduce greenhouse gas emissions and would increase the pressure on global gas supplies, especially as the gas comes partly from oil and coal production.

In the UK the government has launched an ambitious and practical plan to reduce greenhouse gas emissions through the development of wind power for electricity, and is also sponsoring an international effort to assist renewable technology in the developing world. However, in the area of transport it is merely participating in the EU pilot city study on hydrogen fuel cell buses.

The industrial effort

Research and development into hydrogen-powered fuel cells is also being carried out by industrial corporations in several sectors. These include vehicle manufacturers such as DaimlerChrysler, General Motors, Honda, Renault and Toyota, fuel companies including BP and Shell, and specialist fuel cell-builders including Ballard, Rolls-Royce and Siemens. Total industry investment in fuel cells totals around $4 billion.

Reuters Report From Tokyo, 6 October 2003[22]

Just last Thursday, Japan's top auto maker, Toyota Motor, invited journalists to tour the production site of its new Prius hybrid to demonstrate how cheaply they could be built by sharing an assembly line with conventional mass-market cars.

But Larry Burns, GM's vice-president of research, development and planning, said zero-emission fuel cell vehicles (FCV) will eventually make gasoline-electric hybrids obsolete, rejecting Toyota's view that hybrids will remain on the road even after FCVs become affordable for the average consumer.

The race needs to be judged with a long-term view – the goal is to get automobiles out of the environmental debate altogether, he told Reuters in an interview.

Japan's Toyota and Honda Motor became the first to put a saleable FCV on the road last year, but the cars are only on lease since they still cost millions of dollars to produce.

If you look at the growth of economies in the world – whether it be the US, Japan, Europe, or Brazil, Russia, India, China and Korea – commensurate with that is the growth in energy consumption, he said.

And with many countries relying almost 100 percent on foreign oil, they would eventually want vehicles that don't use conventional gasoline combustion engines in the interim before FCVs take over.

California has long been a leader in environmental technologies and it is there that some of the first prototype fuel cell vehicles can be found on the roads. Toyota has a fuel cell sports utility vehicle and GM a light van.

The biggest single factor holding back the introduction of hydrogen is lack of investment. BP estimates that the total global investment in the hydrogen economy is around $1.5 billion a year:[23] a huge amount but barely one per cent of the military-industrial research budget of the EU and the US, which totals some $150 billion per annum.

Making the shift to renewable hydrogen for vehicles

The IEA claims that $16,000,000,000,000 – 16 trillion – of investment will be required up until 2030 to provide for the world's energy needs. According to the IEA projections, just nine per cent of this investment will be towards renewable sources of energy. The assumption is that larger investments in renewables are too complex, lack political will and would be too costly. But is this the case?

At present major oil companies such as BP have limited objectives for hydrogen, but nevertheless BP provides a useful overview of the types of assistance that may be provided by governments. These could include:

- policy incentives to accelerate the transition;
- long-term strategy promoting vehicles and fuels with reduced carbon burden across the full life cycle;
- support for early adopters;
- prolonged period with zero tax on fuel;
- prolonged incentive to buy zero-emission vehicles;
- capital allowances towards infrastructure costs;
- education and public perception and awareness;
- local regulatory approval: bodies adopt and support developing codes and standards.[24]

As we have demonstrated already, renewable electric power and renewable electricity/hydrogen for fuel cells are rapidly becoming cost comparable to the existing cash cost of petrol, diesel and natural gas for electricity. So what estimate can be made for the total cost of installation of the new technologies? If such costs are already included in the IEA's $16 trillion estimate of global energy investment – only directed to oil and gas production – the main point may be the introduction of national and international steering mechanisms to move the market away from oil and gas and towards renewables. These can include tax incentives and other short-term subsidies, regulations, and removal of support for old technologies.

Wind Force 12, a study by the European Wind Energy Association, estimates a global cost of $628 billion to achieve a world wind energy output of twelve per cent of the electricity needs estimated by the IEA for 2020, some 3,000 terawatt hours (TWh). World wind resources are far larger, though not evenly distributed around the world. Nevertheless, the following data indicates a massive potential for the use of wind energy. The total world wind resource potential is 53,000TWh in comparison to a world electricity demand of 14,000TWh in 1998, rising to an estimated 27,000TWh in 2020. Just for the sake of argument, suppose the target was ten times as great; not twelve per cent, but 120 per cent of electricity needs, over 30,000 TWh. The cost would be huge, some $6 trillion ($6,000,000,000,000) over the next fifteen years, or $400 billion a year: comparable to around eighty per cent of currently planned investment, but with great additional benefits. A comparable effort should be considered for the use of solar electricity. In combination there would be enough electricity to support hydrogen for transport as well as dramatically reducing the requirement for natural gas imports.

A shift to renewables for both electricity and transport would need to resolve a number of major logistical issues. The cost of installing hydrogen in petrol stations is one example of the changes that are needed. At first sight it may seem an insurmountable task. But not according to the evidence provided by BP to the US Congress.[25] They argue that in a transition phase to hydrogen before pipelines across country had been established, 'the cost to BP alone to add hydrogen to all our retail sites in the US would be $6.8 billion.' BP's market share of US petrol stations is around 14 per cent, thus a cost for all of the US could be $50 billion for changing an entire infrastructure around. Compare this to the $87 billion President Bush allocated to one year's security and reconstruction in Iraq. A global capital cost of even $150 or $200 billion to install hydrogen is a small price to pay for the benefits of the transition.

These are gigantic numbers to bandy about. However, before we let them panic us, consider the following:

1. a move from oil dependency will result in a phasing out of the military 'khaki cost' of defending oil and gas supplies of around $150 billion a year;

2. a phasing out of an annual cost of price fluctuations that is in the region of $400 billion a year for the global economy;

3. in addition to the phasing out of the combined military cost and impact of oil price fluctuations of close to $1 trillion a year, the global economy would have the benefit both of these resources and of an environment in which it was possible to plan business on the basis of stable electricity and fuel transport prices.

Oh, and a marked reduction in conflict in the region; a reduction in the potential for Islamic extremists to hold the industrialised world to ransom and conversely in the industrialised world's wish to maintain control of oil-rich Islamic states; a reduction in the US domination of allied states; greater political freedom of action for the EU and other powers reliant on US-controlled oil supplies; and increased freedom all round.

Along with the global economic and security benefits of a shift from oil, a rapid move to renewable energy will also:

• provide cheaper and decentralised electricity generation capacity for the developing world;

- remove the concern over increased greenhouse gas emissions from the developing world;
- reduce greenhouse gas emissions.

To summarise: an emergency move out of oil into renewable energy would have huge benefits in terms of global security, economic stability, economic development and environmental policy. A similar but less urgent shift from gas would have similar benefits.

These are the advantages that can be gained from governments announcing that they will only buy hybrid or hydrogen vehicles five years from now, and that the transition to hydrogen-powered vehicles should take fifteen years. Without this proposed shift out of oil and gas, economic indicators point to increasing global competition for a gradually decreasing resource. Such competition will tend to increase the occurrence of war over oil. At present such potential for war would not be much limited by any controls over armaments. On the contrary, if past experience is any indicator of the future, competition and war over oil and gas will lead to a new build-up of armaments. The regulation and removal of weapons is the theme of the next chapter and would ideally go hand in hand with the shift out of oil and gas so that as the demand for the weapons is decreased, so the weapons themselves are swept up and scrapped.

As for renewable energy, it should be clear by now that in the fruit machine called 'World Politics', when the windmills and solar panels all line up, there is a peace and economic jackpot.

Eight

Scrapping the weapons

B-52 aircraft were scrapped in accordance with the START arms limitation treaty, being subjected to a giant guillotine that effectively cut the fuselage and control cables, rendering the airframe unusable.

US State Department

So far this book has set out a programme of economic and democratic reform that should take the steam out of present and future conflicts. This chapter faces up to the challenge of dealing with the weapons of war.

Scrapping and regulating all the major weapons in the world is practical. A lot of the work has already been done in existing treaties. These have already ensured that tens of thousands of weapons were regulated and scrapped.

This chapter discusses the main arguments for managing weapons, especially weapons of mass destruction (WMD), and then outlines how we could regulate and scrap the major weapons in the world. This can be done by using the most effective parts of existing treaties as components in a comprehensive, verifiable and enforceable system. The chapter ends by outlining what I have called a Strategic Concept for Regulating and Removing Arms and Proliferation. Which, astonishingly, turns into the handy acronym SCRRAP. This is in the spirit of existing acronyms such as START, cooked up by Ronald Reagan's spin doctors, to indicate that something was being done about the arms race back in the days of Cold War.

The problem

In Part 1, I showed the huge dangers we all face from modern weaponry. Many world leaders express their concerns over weapons of mass destruction (WMD), small arms and other armaments. However, the major powers only suggest controls on small parts of the world's arsenals and, with a rather childish simplicity, they usually propose controlling other people's weapons rather than their own. There are two main strategies for dealing with WMD. One approach involves the use or threat of force, the second focuses on the control and elimination of these weapons. For most of the last fifty years, these strategies have been used together, sometimes in contradiction, sometimes in mutual support. In the 1950s Winston Churchill simultaneously tried to broker US–Soviet negotiations and set about creating Britain's own H-bomb. He hoped that the idea of deterrence would mean that the weapons would not be used. The issues of states and individuals trying to get WMD and the stocks already built by some states are interconnected. A key reason that people want to get hold of WMD is that they fear and envy those that have them already.

Deterrence, rogue states and 'Star Wars'

Deterrence has been central to United States and NATO military and political planning for fifty years. Its supporters believe that it prevented war with the Soviet Union. However, deterrence and indeed war depend on having someone to shoot at. The problem with guerrilla groups and suicide fighters is that they do not present a target. In tackling such independent groups our own WMD are at best irrelevant. The only useful strategy is prevention.

During the Cold War, a circular argument was used to justify more weapons. It was acknowledged that if a deterrent is so terrible that no one will ever use it, it lacks credibility and therefore more usable deterrents are needed. In a climate of secrecy and paranoia the Soviet Union and US-led NATO built all sorts of nuclear weapons, including Hiroshima-size bombs that could be fired from artillery guns and dropped on submarines by helicopters. Weapons became faster and more accurate, more capable, more of a deterrent. In short, the more dangerous things were, the safer we were.

The terms 'deterrence', 'war', 'fighting' and 'defences' often get confused. In particular, the word 'deterrence' is used to describe many different ideas and weapons. This has best been explained by Lee Butler, the general who commanded US nuclear forces for President George Bush Snr and who was ordered to develop nuclear options during the first Gulf War. If you have ever seen a movie about nuclear war, you will recall that there is usually a general on the phone to the President poised to fire thousands of nuclear weapons. This was Butler's task in real life. He remarked in a speech criticising deterrence that

> as nuclear weapons and actors multiplied, deterrence took on too many names, too many roles, overreaching an already extreme strategic task. Surely nuclear weapons summoned great caution in superpower relationships ... The exorbitant price of nuclear war quickly exceeded the rapidly

depreciating value of a tenuous mutual wariness. Invoking deterrence became a cheap rhetorical parlor trick, a verbal sleight of hand. Proponents persist in dressing it up to court changing times and temperaments, hemming and re-hemming to fit shrinking or distorted threats ... It gives easy semantic cover to nuclear weapons, masking the horrors of employment with siren veils of infallibility ... How is it that we subscribed to a strategy that required near perfect under-standing of an enemy from whom we were deeply alienated and largely isolated? ... **Deterrence was a dialogue of the blind with the deaf. In the final analysis, it was largely a bargain we in the West made with ourselves** *[emphasis added]. At best it is a gamble no mortal should pretend to make. At worst it invokes death on a scale rivalling the power of the creator.*[1]

Nevertheless, in a formal statement of US national policy, one of Butler's successors explained that even now, with respect to Russia, 'stability equates to parity in war-fighting capability'.[2] The US's war-fighting strategy is explicit and formalised in Major Attack Option 1 of the Single Integrated Operating Plan (SIOP MAO1) for the use of US nuclear weapons.[3] This plan is designed to destroy Russian and Chinese weapons before they can be launched. The strategy is often called counterforce, first strike or first use because it involves coun-tering the other side's forces by striking first as soon as it is clear that war has in fact started.

As Butler explains so well, a key problem in any crisis is that decision-makers are in charge of complex systems and in relationships they can neither predict nor control. A clear example of the potential for misunderstanding comes from Bruce Blair, President of the Center for Defense Information in Washington. Blair was a launch control officer for US Intercontinental Ballistic Missiles. After the Cuban missile crisis, when the US and the USSR came close to nuclear war, the US government introduced a system of physical locks and launch codes that had to be given by the President before any missile could be launched. But as Blair explains: 'The locks had been installed but everyone knew the combination. And so the "secret unlock code" during the height of the nuclear crises of the Cold War remained constant at 00000000.'[4] I have always used the same number on the combination lock of my suitcase, because it always seemed too much to bother with. The US Air Force took the same approach to the desire of elected politicians to control the use of nuclear weapons. Thus, for years, US presidents thought things were safer than they really were. In Russia and other nuclear states comparable problems exist as well.

Notwithstanding the potential for stumbling into nuclear war, both Russia and the US each keep about 2,500 hydrogen bombs ready to fire in less than forty-five minutes. The US, other NATO nations and Russia all reserve the legal right to start a nuclear war. US and Russian nuclear weapons are designed to be accurate enough to target the other side's weapons. The Russian arsenal was always technically inferior to the American one. The Russian arsenal has deteriorated and the US has kept its own in prime condition.

The incoming Bush team supported strengthening nuclear warfighting capabilities by adding supporting systems. Several of the people President Bush appointed to key positions sought to integrate nuclear weapons with 'defences' and smart conventional weapons.[5] Though it is worth recalling that even under President Clinton new roles were found for nuclear weapons, and the Pentagon included 'non-state actors' among the list of likely targets for US nuclear forces.

The US is also spending large amounts of money on non-nuclear weapons designed to negate opposition nuclear missiles and satellites. These are called missile defences. In theory, the US is trying to have the same decisive advantage that a gladiator with both a sword and a shield has over one who only has a sword. In practice, as we have already seen, this comparison does not give the full picture as no sword threatens to blow up the entire Coliseum.

Building on present US supremacy, the Bush administration is implementing a policy of deploying defences that has had powerful support over many years within the US. They are determined to build up a full range of missile shields targeted not only at incoming missiles but also at non-US satellites. Satellites are becoming ever more important in civilian and military communications and in electronic eavesdropping, satellite photography and remote sensing of the atmosphere. In fact, the proposed lasers in space – which may be tested in a few years' time – will be far more effective against these satellites than against enemy rockets. In the language of US Space Command, lasers are weapons for dominating the full spectrum of conflict. Increasing numbers of states are launching satellites or buying satellites that other states launch for them.

A clearer picture of the implication of missile 'defences' emerges when these defence systems are considered in the context of how a war with a 'rogue state' might be fought. For example, if the US ever went to war in Korea, the US Army and Air Force would fight alongside their South Korean partners with strong support from the US Pacific fleet, the Marines, and US-based air power. Missile 'defence' would be there to pick off any missiles that survived US conventional or nuclear strikes. Missile 'defence' is to be used as part of fighting wars, not just as a defensive shield.

Another example of the planned offensive use of missile 'defence' is in combination with smart conventional weapons. US security planners have long sought to give the President an option to win a nuclear war without tossing the entire planet into the incinerator of a nuclear holocaust. What better way than to use smart conventional weapons to destroy the other side's nukes? The Clinton administration spent some energy working this out and even tested the navy's Trident missiles with conventional warheads. US conventional weapons could destroy Russia and China's nuclear arsenals today. China's force is small but even Russia's four hundred or so nuclear missile-launchers might be overwhelmed by the thousands of conventionally armed cruise missiles and stealth bombers in the US arsenal. A few might survive and be used in retaliation, but if they could be shot down by the proposed missile 'defences', the US would be able to make it impossible for Russia and China to retaliate without having to use its own nuclear weapons. The smart weapons Washington is developing to track and destroy command bunkers and mobile missiles like the Scud would also be useful for destroying Russian and Chinese targets. Some officials in Washington call this 'humane' deterrence.

Advocates of missile 'defences' usually discuss them as if they existed in a box by themselves; once they are examined in the context of other weapons, their use in offensive operations becomes easy to see. Indeed, historically, offensive and defensive weapons have been used together in the attack. A common analogy is that defences add the shield to the sword, giving a great advantage to the man with both. But adding the shield did not stop the arms race or resolve conflict. Commentators who ignore the 'offence–defence' connection are either disingenuous or incompetent.

Everyone wants to be defended but the policy described above risks war, is certainly no defence and may lead to an arms race. Ambassador Evan Galbraith, Donald Rumsfeld's personal representative to NATO, believes that such an arms race may be no bad thing: 'I know the detractors, many in this room, will undoubtedly continue to groan about the arms race. "Don't start an arms race." I might add we won the last one and I think that probably wasn't a bad idea.'[6] Galbraith was for many years chairman of the *National Review* – a very conservative and influential US journal whose support was important to Governor Bush's successful candidacy.

There are a number of other arguments for and against missile 'defence' aside from its use in offensive operations. One of the arguments in favour is that missile 'defences' are only intended for use in the case of so-called rogue nations, such as Libya, Iraq, North Korea and Syria. This is because they are so unpredictable and therefore unamenable to deterrence, and we should not be subject to blackmail by their WMD. These nations, however, only have small numbers of mostly short-range weapons, and these only travel around 500 kilometres.[7] 'Rogue state' missiles all use the same engine design invented by Werner von Braun, which was used first in the Nazi V2, then in the Soviet Scud and most recently in North Korea's No Dong. Ranges of around 1,500 kilometres have been achieved by placing one V2 engine on top of another in a second stage. While these ranges are adequate for Iran and the Arab states to threaten one another and Israel, when fired from Iran they can barely reach the European Union, let alone the US. There is no major military-industrial complex in 'rogue states' able to build these weapons. They would have to rely on supplies from Russia, China or NATO members. The lack of any more powerful missile technology than the V2 is a testament to the success of non-proliferation efforts and an indication that the problem of missiles in the hands of 'rogue states' is exaggerated.

The term 'rogue state' is designed to convey the idea that these states are beyond reason. This is untrue. There have been successful negotiations with North Korea and Iran. Saddam Hussein was a Western ally until 1990. It is possible that the West would not have acted to remove Saddam from Kuwait if he had been known to have nuclear weapons or, as he in fact did have, chemical and biological weapons. It is more likely, however, that in this case Israel and the US would have acted earlier. Advocates of missile 'defence' would be more convincing if they also supported arms control and engagement efforts.

The other argument in favour of missile 'defences' is that they are just to protect us from an accidental missile launch if deterrence fails. This is a fine idea by itself, but as we have seen they are designed to work with offensive weapons, and an adversary is unlikely to see it any other way.

One of the arguments against missile 'defence' is that it will cost too much, but if there is a good reason for having the weapons then it may be that the money would be well spent. In fact, the offensive nature of plans for missile 'defence' means that they are a poor idea, regardless of cost. Another argument is that missile 'defence' will never work. Ted Postol of the Massachusetts Institute of Technology has argued that there are key problems with the essential physics involved – especially in trying to distinguish between real and fake incoming warheads. Finally, there is an argument that missile 'defence' is inevitable and that Europeans should just ensure that it fits in with deterrence. This misses the point. The entire purpose of missile 'defence' is to prevent the 'other side' from being able to strike at all. Thus, we deter them but they do not deter us. People can call this deterrence if they want to. A more accurate word is 'domination'.

All these problems with missile 'defences' led the US to negotiate an agreement with the Soviet Union to control them back in the 1970s. They introduce a further level of complicated calculation to a world where, as General Butler describes, rationality is in short supply.

Just to make the future look even more cheerful, factor in not just a confrontation between two countries, but one with several: the US, China, Russia, India, North Korea and perhaps Japan. The problem is well described by Robert Cooper, the senior EU foreign policy official and former adviser to Tony Blair:

> An international system in which several countries held nuclear weapons would no longer function along classical balance-of-power principles. In fact we do not know how it would function. In such a world the search for a new international equilibrium by the usual process of trial and error would have devastating consequences.

And this is the world that we are now entering. The US has just agreed to supply Japan and Taiwan with missile defences and to station its own in Alaska.

As we have seen, the reality behind the word 'deterrence' is a world of preparations for fighting nuclear war. The idea that such preparations can exist indefinitely without war is naive, and a risk that should not be run if there is any possible alternative.

Weapons management and threat elimination

The second major approach to WMD is arms control and disarmament or, as I prefer to describe it (to get away from the language of the Cold War), weapons regulation and removal. The control of armaments can be designed to produce a stable state between nations or as a step towards weapons elimination.

The last few years have seen a huge change in international relations on the control of armaments. Until the Bush administration came to office there had been a general international consensus that the control of weapons through treaties was a good thing. There was also continuing, albeit unsuccessful, pressure on the states with nuclear arms to get rid of them from those without them. The Bush administration then either withdrew from or failed to carry forward a bookshelf of treaties. Its argument, which we have already discussed, was that treaties should not be allowed to restrict US power, and were in any case ineffective.

The great lesson of 2003 was that weapons regulation and removal under international agreements worked in Iraq, Iran and Libya – all states that US conservatives had alleged were 'rogues' who would always fool the naïve inspectors of the UN. The UN inspectors in Iraq got it right about Saddam's programmes and effectively demonstrated that containment can prevent proliferation. 'Wimpy' European negotiations succeeded in bringing Iran's covert programmes into the open and may secure its non-nuclear status.

One of the most widespread untruths spread about the failure of the UN inspectors in Iraq concerned the biological–weapons programme, as the then head of the programme, Rolf Ekeus, explained:[8]

> *Take Iraq's biological weapons program, often cited as evidence of Baghdad's ability to deceive weapons inspectors. In his speech to the UN General Assembly on Thursday, President Bush attributed the successful uncovering of the bioweapons program to the fortuitous defection of a senior Iraqi weapons official in 1995 ... In fact, in April 1995, four months before the Iraqi official defected, UN inspectors disclosed to the Security Council that Iraq had a major biological weapons program, including a sizable production facility ... the inspection team, known as the UN Special Commission on Iraq, or UNSCOM, added details about Iraq's research into weapons that could spread anthrax, botulism, aflatoxin and gas gangrene. The discovery of Iraq's bioweapons program was the work of smart inspectors, not a godsend. UNSCOM searched normally innocent institutions such as hospitals, university labs, health centers and veterinary centers, and slowly a picture emerged of a major weapons program. UNSCOM profited from breakthroughs in genetic analysis to discover traces of biological weapons in samples obtained earlier at suspect facilities. If, in the face of Iraq's total denial and non-cooperation, the inspectors could find that kind of carefully concealed activity, that should give us reason to trust a renewed UN inspection system.*

Libya's long-standing attempt to negotiate with the West was finally responded to. Its chemical and nuclear capacity and missile capacities were handed over to the US and the UN authorities. While Tony Blair and George Bush have claimed that this occurred in response to the attack on Iraq, the facts contradict them. The US official responsible for negotiations with Libya under President Clinton was Martin Indyk. He wrote in the *Financial Times* after the Libyans had handed over their WMD materials that 'in fact, Libya offered to surrender WMD programmes four years ago, at the outset of secret negotiations with US officials. In May 1999, the offer was formally conveyed to US officials – at the peak of the "12 years of diplomacy with Iraq" that Mr Bush now disparages.'[9] The Clinton administration considered the Libyan programmes to be unimportant and concentrated instead on resolving the issue of Pan Am 103, the airliner blown up over Scotland.

President Bush himself began a multilateral initiative in early 2003. He tore up his own political prayer book of ritual assaults on the UN and the International Atomic Energy Agency (IAEA) and launched an initiative to strengthen the UN Non-proliferation Treaty (NPT) and the IAEA, albeit in ways that would best suit the US. But this belated conversion was a very partial approach to the problem posed by WMD, though a welcome decision to at least resume talking the same language as the civilised world.

Blair and Bush argue that it was only the attack on Iraq that produced a negotiating process. There seems to be little evidence to support this. North Korea, Iran and Libya had all previously been engaged in dialogue. However, negotiations have always taken place in a context of hard political pressures. The anti-arms control position as exemplified by Colin Gray is that treaties are simply a delusion to ensnare gullible Western liberals. The key point, as discussed in Part 1, is that getting a workable cooperative agreement is worth cutting deals because such agreements are essential to survival. Gray's argument is really not much more than that of the US gun lobby applied to WMD. That is to say, all controls are bad, the bad guys will always be armed and the good guys will be defenceless. The reality is that the 'good guys' have most of the weapons anyway and that agreements are proven to scrap weapons and help improve relations.

Those opposed to all disarmament agreements are sweeping aside the achievements of the past and of the present day, ignoring the contribution of weapons regulation and removal have made to peace and stability. Too many others have forgotten they exist. The argument that these old-fashioned approaches do not tackle the contemporary problems of terrorism and rogue states is common and invalid. At the same time the sceptics of agreements argue that it is rogue states from which terrorists may obtain weapons. The focus is on the supposed rogue states at the expense of a universal system of controls. While terrorist weapons are undoubtedly a problem, so too are long-standing and re-emerging concerns over the behaviour of countries. The ownership of WMD by Britain, China, France, Russia and the US along with the relative newcomers India, Israel and Pakistan cannot rationally be regarded as no longer a problem.

In reality, attempting to tackle WMD by focusing only on the small potential of third-world states and terrorists ignores the full extent of the crisis in human affairs. This wider problem includes the unfinished business of disarming the Cold War stockpiles and bringing the existing and potential nuclear states into a global security structure.

Disarming Cold War stockpiles also relates to the problem of potential terrorist acquisition of nuclear weapons and radioactive material. The huge stocks of surplus WMD and related materials in Russia are, despite major efforts by the US, still a huge problem. It is only because of the dedication of underpaid and underresourced Russian officials supported by the US 'threat-reduction' programmes that the country has not yet become a car boot sale of WMD.

A new overall approach is needed to assist the international community in developing concrete and comprehensive plans to re-energise the effort to regulate and remove weaponry. It can include measures to assist in implementing the key disarmament provisions of the Non-Proliferation Treaty. The approach suggested here draws upon existing global, regional and bilateral agreements to help develop international debate and policy.

The new approach proposed in this book is intended to directly increase security through controls of the enormous amounts of weaponry in the world owned by states and consequently to build greater consensus for combined international actions against terrorists and states that truly hold out against the international community. This concept, detailed below, describes the existing successful agreements for the regulation and destruction of weaponry and enumerates how they can be used as building blocks for a comprehensive structure of weapons management and elimination. The concept encompasses space weapons, WMD, missiles, conventional weapons, small arms and light weapons.

Such a concept is a tool that shows how to manage global disarmament. It is a policy equal to the task of achieving world peace. And a challenge to those who pay lip service to controlling WMD.

The SCRRAP concept

This is not the first time the world has faced crises over WMD. They occurred during the Cold War with unpleasant frequency. Each crisis produced a positive backlash leading to concrete disarmament measures. These measures included the Partial Test Ban Treaty of 1963, and some stabilising US–Soviet agreements on nuclear arms in the 1970s, including the Strategic Arms Limitation Agreements, the Anti-Ballistic Missile Treaty and the Nuclear Non-proliferation Treaty. These achievements came in the wake of the Cuban missile crisis of 1961. This was a time when the US and USSR came close to nuclear war after the USSR based nuclear arms in Cuba.

Between 1987 and 1996 there was an unprecedented succession of agreements on almost all kinds of weapons. They are described below, but they include the Intermediate Nuclear Force and Strategic Arms Reduction Treaties, the Conventional Forces in Europe Treaty and the Comprehensive (nuclear) Test Ban Treaty. These became law during a period of renewed confrontation between the US and the USSR. There is still profound disagreement over what happened and why. Some argue that a strong policy by the US forced Soviet concessions and collapse. Others argue that the great public fear felt around the world over nuclear war forced both sides to a more reasonable course of action and that the Soviet Union was, in any case, far weaker than portrayed by US conservatives.

Unfortunately, today the achievements that came out of these crises have mostly been forgotten. They are no longer part of public political discussion and anyone becoming interested in international affairs today would have to look long and hard to find out about them. National officials and NGOs who have spent a lifetime working to these ends have found themselves in retreat.

People who seek a better response to present problems than the 'war on terror' are not being offered a unified approach to either the problems of proliferation or those posed by the advocates of the war on terror, by politicians, arms control academics or by pressure groups. Indeed, few people are even aware that weapons can be, and have already been, controlled with great success and that therefore more can be done in the future.

Ironically, the world has already created the components and prototypes of a comprehensive, global system to manage and eliminate weapons of all kinds. Such an approach has crucial advantages. A comprehensive approach would close loopholes through which it would be possible to pursue some other type of weapons. For example, some states see Western concern over WMD as merely a way of preserving Western supremacy in conventional armaments. The late Les Aspin, who served as President Clinton's first Secretary of Defense, remarked on this. He was one of the first to say that third-world countries wanted WMD to counter US conventional supremacy, much as NATO had used them to counter Soviet superiority in tanks. An approach that covered both conventional weapons and WMD would offer something to both the weak and the strong.

Another, historical, example makes the point that without a comprehensive approach, new technologies can allow one state or another to sidestep the terms of an agreement to seek an advantage. Back in 1972 the first US–Soviet Strategic Arms Limitation Treaty limited missiles, but not the nuclear warheads on them. At the time the US believed it had scored a diplomatic coup, for in secret it had built a missile (the Poseidon) that carried a dozen nuclear weapons, each able to attack a separate target. But in the end, as Henry Kissinger admits, this achievement was a disaster as the Soviet Union built the same technology and there were then far more nuclear weapons on missiles than ever.

It is tempting to start from scratch with a new set of procedures unencumbered with the history and bias of past agreements. However, this would be to continue to ignore the significant existing achievements in the area of weapons control.

This concept considers the existing measures for the regulation and removal of weaponry and demonstrates that these measures contain the models, prototypes and building blocks of a comprehensive structure of weapons management. In outline the concept would arrange for the universal application of the core provisions of the following agreements:

- Biological Weapons Convention, draft verification protocol
- Chemical Weapons Convention
- Nuclear Non-proliferation Treaty and related IAEA safeguards
- Regional Nuclear Weapon-Free Zone Treaties
- Strategic Arms Reduction Treaty (START) and Intermediate Nuclear Force (INF) Treaty
- Anti-Ballistic Missile Treaty
- Comprehensive Test Ban Treaty
- Organisation for Security and Cooperation in Europe (OSCE)'s Conventional Forces in Europe (CFE) Treaty
- OSCE's Open Skies Treaty and Confidence and Security Building Measures
- UN and various international organisations' programmes on small arms and light weapons
- The proposed Arms Trade Treaty
- Informal export control regimes including the Missile Technology Control Regime, the Wassenaar agreement, the Australia group, the Nuclear Suppliers Group and the Zangger Committee.

Reduction by destruction (emphasis added)

Decision of the Joint Consultative Group on Additional Procedure for Reduction by Destruction of Armored Combat Vehicles Limited by the Treaty on Conventional Armed Force in Europe.

Pursuant to Section I paragraph 5 of the Protocol on Procedures Governing the Reduction of Conventional Armed Forces in Europe of 19 November 1990, hereafter referred to as the Protocol on Reduction, the Joint Consultative Group decided on 29 June 1993 that the additional procedure for reduction of armored combat vehicles by destruction, as Specified in paragraphs 2 to 6 of this decision, shall be deemed sufficient to carry out the reduction of conventional armaments and equipment limited by the treaty.

Procedure for destruction by deformation and severing: The armored combat vehicle, including the hull, turret and integral main armament, if any, shall be placed in a large capacity cutting machine, and it shall be deformed and severed so that none of its parts measure more than 500 millimeters in width, 500 millimeters in height, and 1000 millimeters in length.

* * *

US State Department statement on the destruction of intermediate missiles.

As for destruction of the missiles affected by the INF Treaty, ... the US Air Force cut them apart with chain saws ... crushing the motors and other portions of the missiles with bulldozers.

Most of SCRAAP can be demonstrated to have been effectively implemented in some part of the world. Almost all nations support the bans on biological and chemical weapons and nuclear weapons test explosions. Over fifty nations, including the US and Russia, allow each other to carry out airborne inspections of one another's countries under the Open Skies Treaty. Around fifty countries in Europe have their armies and air forces controlled under the CFE Treaty, which scrapped more than fifty thousand weapons. The US and Russia destroyed thousand of missiles under the START and INF treaties. UN inspections and government export controls have limited proliferation. In Africa several countries have rounded up and crushed thousands of guns such as AK-47s.

Many of these agreements were made quite recently, between 1987 and 1996. Before this period they seemed too difficult to make. Indeed earlier efforts had been much less ambitious. For example, the comprehensive ban on testing came more than thirty years after the agreement of a partial ban. The Conventional Forces in Europe Treaty came after years of less ambitious yet fruitless talks on mutual and balanced force reductions. And START achieved reductions after previous agreements had only managed limitations in future build-up!

At the time that these ambitious agreements were made many people were sceptical that the practical and political difficulties could be overcome. Yet they were. Nevertheless, one cannot simply print off the existing treaty documents, stack them up and demand that they be implemented globally. Building a new security structure based upon existing achievements will leave some large gaps to be filled, notably in the areas of space warfare and new technologies.

It would be silly to dismiss the huge political obstacles to disarmament that exist in international politics at present. But the historical record of the agreements made between the Soviet Union and the West should be taken as a sign that what seems impossible can become possible. It is also worth remembering that some of the key elements of the Reagan administration's policies were criticised by arms control groups as too far-reaching to be achievable. These included the 'zero option' of eliminating the entire class of INF land-based missiles. Similarly, there were those who argued that some partial limit on nuclear testing was all that was realistic. In fact, a comprehensive ban was achieved, and has so far been maintained.

It is necessary to carry out considerable research and policy development involving governmental and non-governmental representatives to develop SCRAAP. Fortunately, there now exists in many countries considerable expertise in weapons management and elimination, not least in the nations of Europe and North America and in South Africa. It is here that the hard work of helping manage the end of the Cold War was carried out with great success. This experience can be drawn upon for further bilateral, regional and global agreements.

It would be a tragedy if once again an opportunity for disarmament arose and was lost because the best advocates of disarmament were too fragmented and demoralised to take that opportunity, and because a new generation were simply unaware of the practical relevance of the treaties made by their predecessors in the 1960s and 1980s.

Of the three types of WMD, chemical weapons have a system of global verification in place; biological weapons have a system that has been tested in trials but is not in force; and nuclear weapons in the hands of the states with them should be subject to controls that are presently used to stop new states from getting them. Missiles with ranges between 500 and 5,500 kilometres are subject to US and

Russian treaties that can serve as models for international application.

In essence, the countries with nuclear weapons will need to agree to something very like the provisions in the START and INF Treaties – with a timetable leading to zero, while their bomb factories and stores will be subjected to the same scrutiny so conveniently practised in Iraq, Iran, Libya and a few years ago in South Africa.

The regulations on conventional army and air force weapons in the CFE Treaty already apply to a quarter of the nations on earth.

Filling the gaps in the existing treaty structure

The previous discussion of existing regulations covering weaponry shows that there are working examples in some parts of the world of the effective regulation and removal of almost all kinds of weaponry.

The two largest gaps are weapons in space and small arms. These catagories are at the top and bottom of the scale of weapons, both geographically and technologically. Small arms are generally low tech, involved in low-level violence from gun crime and civil wars to infantry fighting, while space weapons use the highest technology, would be used in high level global conflict and are, as some Americans say, up on the High Frontier. The other area without any control at present is weapons at sea.

Naval vessels

Compared to land-based weapons governed by the CFE and INF Treaties, naval ships and submarines are large and hard to hide, few in number and based in only a few ports. These factors make verification of their numbers, location and weaponry a far easier task than is the case for land-based conventional arms, which are already governed successfully in international treaties. Ironically, despite the ease of the verification task, there is total refusal by the dominant naval power, the US, to contemplate any limitations. A far-reaching intermediate step would be achieved merely by controlling missiles and aircraft aboard ships. The relevant provisions of the CFE and INF Treaties could be used as models.

Naval arms control has something of a bad name, because of ill-fated naval agreements before the Second World War. The US and UK were at a disadvantage when Japan broke out of the agreements; however, it is worth recalling that the mere fact of its breaking out provided some warning of aggressive intent, as did Hitler's decision to break controls established on Germany after the First World War. Agreements can provide an early warning, even when they break down, that is clearer than would exist if there were no controls in place.

Small arms

On the world's ground floor and scattered around the back garden, so to speak, are small arms and light weapons. These exist in the hundreds of millions and are easy and cheap to make. They are being used to kill people all the time. The enormous quantities involved, the low technology needed and the ease of hiding them make regulation the necessary first stage.

There is a draft agreement at the UN on controlling unauthorised use and trade in these weapons. In addition Amnesty International, Oxfam and an international coalition have written a proposed text for an arms trade treaty and are now campaigning to have it adopted by the nations of the UN. The UK's Department for International

Development has committed considerable funding to supporting efforts to control small arms in conjunction with its European partners and recipient countries. Prior to the UN conference on small arms in 2001 a number of states in Africa conducted symbolic destruction activities.

Weapons burned across the region

A number of West African countries conducted symbolic arms destruction ceremonies this week to coincide with the UN conference on small arms, which opened in New York on Monday.

Members of the Economic Community of West African States (ECOWAS) signed a small arms moratorium in 1999 with a view to controlling the flow of small and light weapons within countries and across the region's borders. The availability of such weapons has been recognised as a strong factor in the instability affecting West Africa.

Mali, which began its weapon destruction on Monday at two sites, destroyed over 500 weapons. At Lere, southwest of Timbuktu on the border with Mauritania, some 230 small arms were burned, according to the UN Programme of Coordination and Assistance for Security and Development (PCASED) in Bamako.

'In Lere a local committee was formed by mainly women in the area and Muslim groups. They organised an awareness campaign and reached members of the community through local radio,' Napoleon Abdullai, disarmament expert at PCASED, told IRIN on Friday. The residual ore from the destroyed weapons will be used to build a monument in a 'Garden of Peace', and whatever is left over will be used for agricultural implements, he added.

At the second site, Dire, some 90 km southwest of Timbuktu, 277 weapons were destroyed, Abdullai said. A 'weapons-for-development' programme, involving the exchange of arms for agricultural tools, started last year in the mainly agricultural area populated by sedentary farmers who grow rice and livestock-rearing nomads.

Meanwhile, Nigeria began the destruction of its stockpile of illicit weapons on 6 July by setting fire to 2,421 guns of various types in the northern city of Kaduna. Weapons destroyed included submachine guns, automatic and pump-action rifles, double-barrelled shotguns and pistols. They were seized from armed robbers, illegal dealers and participants in recent communal conflicts.

In the Ghanaian capital, Accra, 874 weapons were destroyed on Monday.

* * *

In Niger, some 1,200 weapons were destroyed in August 2000 in recognition of the restoration of peace between the state and Tuareg and Toubou rebel movements while, in 1999, Liberia destroyed some 19,000 weapons and two million rounds of ammunition left over from its seven-year civil war, according to UNREC. Other countries, including Sierra Leone, have ongoing weapons destruction programmes.

It is estimated that there are eight million illicit small arms and light weapons in circulation in West Africa, according to UNREC.

UN-IRIN Weekly West Africa Update, 13 July 2001

Space weapons

Up on the roof of the world are space weapons. These are future weapons, very expensive, few in number and using very advanced technology such as lasers.

There is no evidence that any state has yet put them in space. However, the US in particular has an official policy of dominating space, regarding it as a future battlefield comparable to the great ocean spaces that influenced politics in years gone by. Other states, including China, also regard space as a potential future battleground. There is a discussion at the UN (Conference on Disarmament) on this matter and China has proposed a treaty banning weapons in space. Fortunately, checking up on space weapons would be quite easy. It would involve checking space launch missiles on the ground. There are very few space launch sites in the world and the capsules and satellites they launch are very small and so full of kit that it would be easy to spot an illicit weapon.

*

So far this chapter has outlined the different approaches to managing weapons and proposes a new and far-reaching concept to regulate and remove weapons of all kinds. Numerous treaties have been mentioned.

They involve a great deal of technical detail and required considerable political pressure. To help fill in some of the background of the SCRRAP proposal I have itemised below the major existing agreements and pointed to ways that their achievements can contribute to a broader system of regulation and removal.

Nuclear weapons

The Nuclear Non-Proliferation Treaty (NPT)

The NPT is discussed in chapter two in outline, it includes the existing International Atomic Energy Agency safeguard agreements[10] that provide a verification systemn for nuclear materials which could be applied universally, not only, as it is at present, to the non-nuclear weapon countries in the NPT with different levels, and in a limited form, to the nuclear weapons states in the Treaty (Britain, China, France, Russia and the US).

Nuclear Weapons Free Zones (NWFZ)

The treaties in Latin America, the South Pacific and South East Asia effectively ban nuclear weapons from large parts of the globe. An African NWFZ Treaty has been signed by forty-nine states but has yet to come into force. The states that have agreed to them are all signatories of the NPT as well, and the NWFZ Treaties serve to underpin the NPT. Some of the NWFZ Treaties also contain undertakings by states not to allow other countries to base nuclear weapons in their countries. The NWFZ Treaties act as political indicators of public rejection of nuclear weapons and as a system of mutual reassurance between the states concerned and could, moreover, act as the foundation for building other agreements for regional arms regulation and removal, using some of the agreements made in Europe on conventional weapons as models. New agreements in Africa and central Asia have been agreed in principle recently but have yet to come into effect.

The Comprehensive Test Ban Treaty (CTBT)

The CTBT has banned states from carrying out test explosions since it was agreed in 1996, and five countries that used to test have stopped.

They are Britain, China, France, Russia and the US. These five have each made the political decision to stop testing and Britain, France and Russia have made this commitment formal by completing the process of making the Treaty national law in their countries. India and Pakistan tried a few nuclear weapons out in 1998 but none have been exploded since. China and the US have signed the Treaty and are abiding by it, but have refused to ratify it, a process necessary for it to pass it into national law. The verification system involves many nations around the world and is an excellent way of providing assurance that no weapons have been exploded. Previously, Russia and the US had carried out thousands of test explosions, the others far fewer.

The test ban has prevented new types of weapons from being developed. However, there are continuing political pressures from weapons advocates to try out new and old weapons (to see if they still work). These pressures are mainly in China and the US.

There are some concerns over the effectiveness of the Treaty. As long ago as 1945, the US developed and used the bombs dropped on Hiroshima and Nagasaki with only one test. In France, the UK and the US, billions of dollars are being spent trying to use computer modelling as a substitute for explosive testing. It is noteworthy that those who argue that stopping testing has achieved little can often be found arguing to start exploding them again. Nevertheless, the CTBT has put a stop to half a century of explosions and put great limitations on the ability of nations to build weapons. This international norm contributed to the small scale of these countries' tests by institutionalising a taboo against nuclear explosions. It is a key part of a global structure for reducing and removing weaponry.

To get the Treaty we have today it was necessary to get agreement amongst the most heavily armed and economically powerful nations in the world as well as from scores of smaller states. The problems associated with getting states outside the Treaty to come into it are considerable but they are far less than those overcome by the international community in agreeing to the Treaty as it exists at present.

The CTBT is a powerful agreement with near-universal acceptance at present, even though it is under threat from a possible US resumption of testing. It provides a crucial building block in the strategic concept of regulating and removing armaments. It includes effective verification of the testing of the world's most dangerous weapons of mass destruction and an agreement that they should never be tested again.

Chemical weapons
The Chemical Weapons Convention (CWC)
Almost all countries in the world have agreed this convention. The CWC is an organisation for checking up on activities going on in particular countries. It is unique in the way it requires intrusive inspections to ferret about looking for suspect activities. It is served by an international secretariat based in The Hague, and has an Executive Committee charged with implementing the Treaty and adjudicating on problems. Both Russia and the US have found that technical and resource issues have so far prevented them from completing the destruction of the enormous stocks they built up between 1945 and 1990.

The verification provisions of the CWC provide a major contribution to the process of checking up on other types of WMD.

Biological weapons
The Biological Weapons Convention (BWC)
The BWC has been agreed by most countries in the world, but it has no verification component. An extensive negotiation on a verification

protocol produced an agreement that many nations thought would be effective in preventing the development of these weapons. The Bush administration vetoed the agreement and the negotiations themselves. Nevertheless, the draft agreement could be brought into effect without waiting on Washington. One way would be for a state to introduce it as a resolution at the UN General Assembly. This tactic was used by Australia to bring in the CTBT when India was blocking consensus in the regular negotiating committee in Geneva. Another alternative would be for a regional organisation such as the EU to put the BWC verification process into effect and then encourage other groups of countries to join in.

Missiles
The Intermediate Nuclear Forces Treaty (INF)

The INF Treaty applies to the US and Russia. It requires that these states have no ballistic or cruise missiles that can be fired from the ground to targets more than 500km, and less than 5,500km, away. The INF Treaty does not govern missiles fired from warplanes, ships and submarines. Uniquely, it eliminated a whole class of missiles.

The INF Treaty contains very detailed requirements for checking that there are no such missiles and for checking that the 2,692 missiles that existed at that time were destroyed. The Treaty contains the vital technical provisions that would be needed for a global treaty banning all intermediate-range cruise and ballistic missiles. The verification procedures were completed and closed in 1992.

The US eliminated its last ground-launched cruise missile on 1 May 1991. The last Pershing II was destroyed on 6 May 1991. The Soviet Union destroyed the last of eighty SSC-X-4 non-deployed cruise missiles on 5 October 1988 and the last of six SS-5s on 16

August 1989. With the destruction of the last declared SS-4 on 22 May 1990, the only remaining Soviet intermediate-range system enumerated in the Treaty was the SS-20 until its final elimination on 12 May 1991.

> *Continuous portal-monitoring operations began in both countries in July 1988. At Magna, Utah and Votkinsk, Russia, permanent communities of up to thirty inspectors each are located outside the gates of former INF missile production and final assembly plants to check exiting vehicles for Treaty-limited items ... Continuous portal-monitoring operations at Votkinsk and Magna are proceeding with rotations of portal inspectors occurring at three-week and monthly intervals, respectively.*
>
> *As for destruction of the missiles affected by the INF Treaty, Soviet officials indicated they would burn most of their weapons in pits but also may launch some for disintegration in the upper atmosphere. The US Air Force planned to fly its cruise missiles, deployed in Europe, to Davis-Monthan Air Force Base, Arizona, and cut them apart with chain saws. The Army decided to transport its Pershing II missiles, deployed in Europe and stored in the US, to two Army installations located in the US for destruction – the Pueblo Depot Activity and the Longhorn Ammunition Plant cited above. It will destroy all of the Pershing 1a models at their present location, the Pueblo Depot Activity. The destruction procedure calls for burning the solid fuel propellant and crushing the motors and other portions of the missiles with bulldozers.*[11]

In both Russia and the US some experts believe that the Treaty stops them from having weapons necessary for fighting other nations and propose scrapping it altogether.

To globalise the INF, the necessary amendments would include adding additional manufacturers and brands of missile to the existing lists, and including those that could be fired from warplanes and naval vessels. It would be advisable to lower the range limit from 500km to 0km in order to be comprehensive. Technical arrangements on the shortest-range missiles would need to be slotted into provisions on conventional forces in the CFE Treaty.

The Strategic Arms Reduction Treaty I (START I)

START I governs US and Russian ballistic missiles with ranges over 5,500 km, and long-range bombers. It provides for checks that certain missiles were destroyed and that those that remain conform to certain technical specifications. Its provisions built on the achievements of earlier treaties. These were the first and second Strategic Arms Limitation Treaties (SALT). Because START allows thousands of weapons to remain it contains many details to prevent cheating and, in common with other treaties of the same historical period, was made in such a way as to ensure support from the most diehard US sceptics of the reliability of verification. Consequently, it provides a very reliable model that can be applied globally.

In combination with the INF Treaty, START I contains the key provisions for a global treaty that could regulate and remove all missiles.

The Anti-Ballistic Missile Treaty (ABM)

The ABM Treaty used to apply to the US and Russia. It prevented either country from building large numbers of missiles designed to shoot down other missiles of the types controlled under the START and SALT agreements. Its purpose was to stop the action-reaction cycle of building missiles, and anti-missile missiles. President George W. Bush withdrew the US from the Treaty and it is no longer in effect. The Bush administration believes that it is necessary to have a missile defence against rogue states and that the old idea of a balance of terror, the famous Mutually Assured Destruction (MAD) or deterrence theory, amounts at best to being blackmailed. At worst, they argue, deterrence can result in being left defenceless in face of a madman who is not deterred by the threat of being hit back. Nevertheless, for decades, the US, Russia, the countries of NATO and the entire UN referred to the ABM Treaty as essential to global stability because strategists believed that the stand-off inherent in MAD provided the best security available. It was not until Ronald Reagan denounced deterrence as vulnerable to accident and amounting to accepting a permanent Russian roulette that the arguments long made by anti-nuclear campaigners hit the mainstream.

The ABM Treaty contains most of the necessary technical details for a global ban on anti-ballistic missiles. In a missile-free world it would have less importance. However, it is important to note that missiles made to shoot down other missiles are very good at shooting down satellites. This is because satellites have a much more predictable flight path, and like ducks in a fairground shooting gallery, if you miss, you can have another try when they come back the next time.

Informal international agreements on WMD
There are a host of secret intergovernmental bureaucracies invloving mostly Western states that are designed to stop the bad guys getting hold of weapons. Appropriately enough they all have names that

would sell well on the cover of an airport thriller. The London Club seeks to place export controls on items which could be turned to military purposes in the nuclear area. The Wassenaar agreement, the Australia Group, the Zangger Committee, the Proliferation Security Initiative and the Missile Technology Control Regime are all agree-ments to control detailed lists of materials that might be used to make nuclear, chemical and biological weapons and missiles. At present these agreements tend mostly to involve Western countries agreeing not to sell to some nations that are considered potentially threatening. Many developing states complain at the UN that the agreements prevent them from buying equipment for normal commercial activity that the Western states are continuing to supply to each other.

These agreements can form the basis for a comprehensive set of global controls on WMD formalised as part of an international treaty. As part of a system of regulation and prevention of WMD-related international technology transfers, the lists of technology would form part of a system of international controls rather than the present selective and secret system.

Conventional weapons
The Conventional Forces in Europe Treaty (CFE)
The CFE Treaty sets limits on the numbers of warplanes, helicopters, tanks, armoured vehicles and artillery guns owned by more than forty countries in Europe, including US forces stationed in Europe, Russian forces and the nations of the Caucasus. The Treaty sets out in intricate detail the definitions of the different types of military equipment, the procedures for checking who has what, and the procedures for destroying weapons in excess of specified limits. Although originally structured as a NATO–Warsaw Pact treaty it still remains a force for peace.

Robert Cooper has explained the revolutionary nature of the CFE Treaty. Cooper is a senior official of the EU's foreign affairs section and was a senior adviser to Tony Blair. In describing how Europe has evolved into what he calls a 'post-modern' condition in which states abandon old ideas of balance and secrecy in favour of sharing their security in common, he says:

> *It is important to realise what an extraordinary revolution this is. The normal, logical behaviour of armed forces is to conceal their strength and hide their equipment from their enemies. Treaties to regulate such matters are an absurdity in strategic logic.*
>
> *By the end of the 40-month reduction period prescribed by the Treaty, the 30 CFE States Parties completed and verified by inspection the destruction or conversion to other uses of more than 50,000 battle tanks, armored combat vehicles, artillery pieces, combat aircraft and attack helicopters as required by the Treaty. In addition, the States Parties conducted and accepted some 2,300 intrusive on-site inspections.*[12]

Tens of thousands of weapons were destroyed under the provisions of the Treaty.

The CFE Treaty provides a highly developed political, technical and bureaucratic basis from which to create a global treaty regulating and removing all these types of weapon. CFE is more than a model, a prototype or a foundation stone. It is a structure of control that encompasses the armed forces across the continent of Europe.

CFE has already been used as a basis for one additional agreement. This is the arms control section of the 1995 Dayton accords. The

Dayton accords settled the war in Bosnia-Herzegovina in the western Balkans. They provide for detailed checks on the weapons held by the Serb, Croat and Bosniak forces engaged in that civil war.

In general there are few complaints from any side over the provisions of the CFE Treaty or the way it has been implemented. The main breach of the Treaty was Russia's build-up of forces in Chechnya during the civil war of the early 1990s. In addition some analysts have criticised the way excess stocks of equipment were 'cascaded' to less well-equipped nations in Europe and on to the international arms market. The existing challenge is to bring in the Baltic states, who were part of the Soviet Union when the Treaty was signed but are now independent and part of NATO.

Landmines and inhumane weapons

Formally known as the Convention on the Prohibition of the Use, Stockpiling, Production and Transfer of Anti-Personnel Mines and on Their Destruction (APL Ban Treaty) and the Convention on Prohibitions or Restrictions on the Use of Certain Conventional Weapons Which May Be Deemed to Be Excessively Injurious or to Have Indiscriminate Effects (CCWC), these two agreements regulate some of the most brutal forms of killing.

The APL Ban Treaty controls anti-personnel landmines. Most countries in the world support it. It appears to have brought a halt to the production and use of these weapons by most states. Some critics argue it endangers their security and they, including the US, have not agreed to it. From a different perspective some NGOs argue that its loopholes permit cluster bombs and anti-vehicle landmines.

The CCWC is without any verification regime and yet has been quite effective in preventing the introduction of some weapons, notably bullets that explode on contact with the body rather than 'merely' passing through. The Convention has been used to ban using blinding lasers and is an important framework for banning new technologies.

Confidence- and security-building measures
The Open Skies Treaty

The Open Skies Treaty applies in Europe. It allows for unarmed over-flight of the entire territory of participating states using a variety of sensors. The Treaty aims to promote transparency in military activities and to enhance confidence- and security-building whilst facilitating monitoring of compliance with other arms control agreements.

The Open Skies Treaty specifically allows any country to join in the system. As it covers the borders of areas of tension such as the Middle East and central Asia, the countries in these areas could be brought into an international system.

The Treaty is, like the others described here, tried and tested and should become a global treaty or could serve as a model for regional agreements in other parts of the world.

Open Skies

The following fact sheet describing a typical observation mission under the Open Skies Treaty was released by the State Department's Bureau of Arms Control in April 2001.[13]

The Treaty on Open Skies is one of the most wide-ranging international arms-control efforts to date to promote openness and transparency in military forces and activities. It dramatically advances confidence-building and enhances national security in the new circumstances of the post-Cold War world. Observation flights under the Open Skies Treaty are conducted with unarmed, fixed-wing aircraft outfitted with a suite of Treaty-permitted sensors. For its missions, the US plans to fly the OC-135B aircraft (a modified WC-135B), a military version of the Boeing 707 formerly used for weather reconnaissance and capable of accommodating 38 personnel. An Open Skies logo on the tail signifies the aircraft's historic task.

Initial Notification of a Flight:

An Open Skies flight is conducted on short notice and the observed State Party has no right of refusal. Observation teams do not arrive unannounced: one Treaty Party notifies another that it intends to conduct an observation flight at least 72 hours before it plans to arrive at the POE (point of entry). All other States Parties are notified at the same time of the request. A notification indicates an ETA (estimated time of arrival), the POE where the observation team will arrive, and the designated 'Open Skies Airfield' from which the mission will launch. Also identified are the names and functions of the observation team from a master list previously supplied to all States Parties.

The 1999 Organisation for Security and Cooperation in Europe, Vienna document

This agreement under the auspices of the OSCE provides for information-sharing about military policies and practices. It is not an agreement about hardware; however, it is one of the ways states can start to build and sustain confidence between one another.

It is important to recognise that much valuable security can be achieved with even partial measures. For example, the process of exchanging information can build confidence. In addition, merely freezing levels of weapons under effective verification can do a great deal. The actual process of reduction and removal to destruction can be phased in over a longer period of time.

A dialogue now needs to begin about adopting a comprehensive approach to weapons management regionally and globally. There should be a leading role for the European security institutions of the EU, NATO and the OSCE in these matters. This is for two reasons. First of all, a significant part of the global pool of expertise in implementing weapons regulation and removal exists within the staff of European governments. In addition, a key region of tension, the Middle East, is Europe's neighbour. In addition to treaties, great progress can be made nations deciding on their own to scrap weapons – the first President Bush and Mikhail Gorbachev removed all the thousands of battlefield nuclear weapons from their ships and armies in this way.

SCRRAP around the world

The Middle East stands out as a region of high tension and military rivalry. There have long been private discussions between Arabs and Israelis about a WMD-free zone in the Middle East. Recent progress in the Arab world and in Iran presents an opportunity to develop such a proposal that might include the states from Egypt to Iran. A key factor would be prohibitions on Western states bringing forces into the region. A early start might be made by extending the Open Skies Treaty to the region and looking at way of bringing new states into the CFE Treaty. There is rising interest in the Middle East in solving the problems presented today by Iran and Israel with a comprehensive approach to arms control. European nations should meet the challenge by offering their expertise and political will to make such a process work through producing a synthesis of key provisions of the existing treaties described above as a ready-made package that can be used in other regions.

In Europe there remains an abundance of armaments and no conceivable threat. As long ago as 1990 I argued for rapid further reductions in a *Washington Post* article I wrote with former Director of Central Intelligence William Colby. Little did we realise how soon the West would lose interest in controlling weapons once the Soviets had disappeared. A leaner European defence force should be of considerable interest to European tax payers and finance ministries, who are now paying to keep up a Cold War arsenal of warships, submarines, fighter jets and tanks when there is no one to fight, and when even a newly angry Russia would have first to rebuild its army and then travel hundreds of miles even to reach Poland. The one possible exception to this positive picture is the Russian border with the new NATO members in the Baltic states.

South Asian security is characterised by the India–Pakistan confrontation. Each country's armed force owes much to UK influence and today each draws on Western ideas for its nuclear policy. The new attempts at a settlement of long-standing arguments over Kashmir present an excellent opportunity to draw on the lessons of the OSCE CFE, Confidence- and Security-Building Measures and Open Skies agreements to manage the regulation and removal of armaments along their common border. In east Asia the growing tensions between the Koreas, China, Japan and the US present a good opportunity to introduce preventive diplomacy in the region with a strong emphasis on confidence-building measures and the regulation of weapons.

The SCRRAP proposal also maps out a practical way to implement fully Article VI of the NPT, which covers the legal commitment of the nuclear powers to disarm and which is a critical deal at the heart of the global non-proliferation regime. The article reads: 'Each of the Parties to the Treaty undertakes to pursue negotiations in good faith on effective measures relating to cessation of the nuclear arms race at an early date and to nuclear disarmament, and on a Treaty on general and complete disarmament under strict and effective international control.' This is a legally binding commitment on all the nations that are party to the Treaty. It is the only legally binding commitment to nuclear disarmament. Traditionally, states and pressure groups favouring nuclear disarmament have emphasised this aspect of the article. Conversely, opponents have tended to focus on what they view as a necessary unsavoury link between nuclear and overall disarmament. This linkage is usually regarded as creating a goal so utopian that it can safely be forgotten. In recent years, especially in the 'unequivocal commitment' made by all the states with nuclear weapons to nuclear disarmament, nuclear weapons have been regarded separately. States in favour of disarmament have usually baulked at the huge challenge presented by the whole of Article VI; the SCRRAP proposal is designed to meet this challenge.

What sort of timescale should be set as a target? One useful consideration is how fast agreements can be made when the political will exists to get the job done. The most complex of the existing treaties are the CFE and CWC agreements covering conventional arms and chemical weapons. The first involved all the nations of NATO and the then Warsaw Pact and governs tens of thousands of weapons. The second had to get to grips with inspecting normal chemical factories around the world. Each of them involved decades of fruitless discussions followed by two to five years of real hard political and technical work. On this basis a target of five years to agree to a global SCRRAP treaty seems appropriately ambitious.

What might be agreed at that five-year point?

The first phase would involve: the exchange of data on weapons systems, which should be completed within a year; the final date for ordering new equipment in the specified categories of weapons; continuing mutual observation of military activity. The second phase would involve a period of verification lasting an additional twelve months. The third phase would entail the progressive regulation through destruction of weapons in each type down to zero or some specified new maximum. This could be done in stages over, say, a total of ten years. The overall programme of negotiation and reductions should have a target date for completion of fifteen years.

Taken together with comparable objectives for the energy sector described in the previous chapter, these proposals provide a focused programme to achieve disarmament and development in the context of the programmes for economic justice and enhanced democracy described earlier.

Conclusion

War and chaos are not inevitable. Peace and freedom are practical. These are the messages of this book. But I can already here the cries of 'Don't be unrealistic!'

As if what governments are doing at the moment is realistic. The war on Iraq: realistic or naïve? No back-up plan if Osama bin Laden gets his hands on the oil: realistic or naïve? No global programme to irradicate weapons of mass destruction: realistic or naïve? Hoping corporations will act like charities: realistic or naïve? If ever there was a time when we needed large-scale ideas for change in politics, economics and military affairs then this is it.

Even if the ideas themselves are realistic, perhaps it is unrealistic to try to challenge the powerful. This is the perfect argument for doing nothing but moan at the world in general and await your fate. Getting rid of apartheid? Supporting dissidents against communism? Equal rights for women? Banning nuclear tests? A UN agreement on global warming? Well, all of these were achieved despite the cynics.

These achievements did not come from isolated efforts. Education, links between like-minded governments and international pressure groups, mass demonstrations; these all played their part in these achievements. One of the beauties of the internet is that it is now easier for activists to communicate than it is for govern-

ments, hidebound as they are by chains of command and bureaucratic procedures.

Whether or not the proposals in the book suit you, I hope it is clear
that it is essential to have a new set of objectives for the reform of
military, economic and political policy. The ideas I offer are far-reaching
but they are rooted in the values of those who fought and won what
Malise Ruthven calls the 'Jihad against Fascism'. We need to rediscover
that vision and revitalise their agenda to resolve the issues we face today.
Set within that perspective, our task becomes clearer and more feasible.

The proposals in this book are intended to be useful at once on a small
scale and capable of being built into a mutually supporting and broader
political platform. For example, any community or school group can
discuss the relationship between pre-emptive war and vigilante action.
You can find out more at my website www.danplesch.net.

A comprehensive approach to armaments is overdue in the short
term in south Asia and the Middle East. Worldwide regulation and
destruction could and should be under way within five years using
the proven techniques built into existing treaties. We may not meet
these targets, but by setting them we may at least slow down the
schedule of new weapons deployments.

Any home, business or community can start to install renewable
energy, helping at a micro level to build support. Political party and
national policies moving away from oil and gas will immediately send
a signal to all those fighting over these resources that they will soon be
irrelevant. The twin targets of changing government vehicle purchases
to hybrid and hydrogen designs in five years and then moving to a full
transition away from oil in a generation are practical and essential.

In Britain, schoolchildren and local communities may find new
role models by tracking down their Chartist and Suffragette

ancestors. Similar efforts in other countries will reveal a parallel democratic history.

Any party, any country, any local council or even your email can begin the argument for the direct election of national representatives to world institutions.

Similarly, the case to bring shareholders down to earth by removing their privileges can begin and gather pace from anywhere. The demand for restoring equality before the law is an issue of human rights. It can be used ultimately to reform limited liability, and in the short term to counter demands for removing regulations that protect such essentials of a socially secure society as public services and environmental protection. Restoring legal accountability to capitalism will increase social consensus in both the industrialised world and in states where corporate culture has only recently become prevalent.

Taken together these programmes have the capacity to damp down the fires of war in many parts of the world. A decision to move away from oil would immediately take the urgency out of the underlying competitions for power in Iraq, Iran, Saudi Arabia and the other Gulf states. Even the self-styled realists would no longer have an incentive to provide Western support for repressive actions against human rights in oil-producing states including Nigeria, Angola, Georgia and Indonesia. Decentralised electricity production would reduce the threat from terrorism to national power supplies and enable sustainable development throughout the poverty-stricken developing world.

By 2020, where might all this effort have got us? The United Nations would have greater authority and relevance as it was evolving, de facto, into a parliament of national representatives as would the EU, WTO and other institutions. Corporations and their shareholders would have at least returned to the mixed economy of social democracies with a balance of rights and privileges amongst social groups. In the developing world the tyranny of wealth protected by limited liability would be ending, increasing social cohesion. These real political changes as well as a better sense of history would help revive engagement in political life. The global economy would be shifting to renewable electricity and hydrogen vehicles, so enabling sustainable development, signalling the irrelevance of oil wars and reducing global warming. The process of regulation through destruction of weaponry around the world would be well under way.

In these circumstances the major causes of national and civil wars would be muted. Grievances would be being addressed, the rule of law upheld. Fewer and fewer people would be attracted to joining an Islamist global guerrilla war. The military-industrial complex would be cut down to size. Utopia? No. A huge improvement on the way we are now? Most certainly.

And without a programme comparable to the one I have outlined, can we expect just to muddle along? Only if we are very lucky.

Present trends of increasing violence look set to continue. Without the prospect of economic and political change fewer and fewer people will vote, creating societies of greater social division and anxious apathy – a fertile ground for extremists of every stripe. With the present level of aggressive incompetence, the battles in Palestine, Iraq and Afghanistan are likely to continue to grow and merge into a world in full-scale civil war. Who would take a bet that bin Laden and friends will not control a major oil-producing state?

Further attacks on the scale of 9/11 or Madrid may have far more devastating effects. In these conditions this programme will both be harder to discuss, yet even more important to implement.

It is easy to construct outlandish Hollywood scenarios for World War Three and easy to get carried away. But, what we can see clearly is that without a strong and coordinated effort, those forces spoiling for a scrap in the US and in the Islamic world may all get their dreams coming true.

Winston Churchill described the Second World War as an unnecessary war; the same will be true of wars in the twenty-first century. I could write pages more about a doom-laden, fearful future. Looking at the newspapers and the bookshelves, perhaps I should. Fear sells. But as Franklin Roosevelt put it, we have nothing to fear except fear itself.

Appendix I

Surrender of Italy

Instrument of Armistice and surrender of the Italian Forces to the Commander-in-Chief of the Allied Forces, Gen. Dwight D. Eisenhower. Sicily, 3 September 1943.

The following conditions of an Armistice are presented by General DWIGHT D. EISENHOWER, Commander-in-Chief of the Allied Forces, acting by authority of the Governments of the United States and Great Britain and in the interest of the United Nations, and are accepted by Marshal PIETRO BADOGLIO, Head of the Italian Government:

1. Immediate cessation of all hostile activity by the Italian armed forces.
2. Italy will use its best endeavors to deny, to the Germans, facilities that might be used against the United Nations.
3. All prisoners or internees of the United Nations to be immediately turned over to the Allied Commander-in-Chief, and none of these may now or at any time evacuated to Germany.

4. Immediate transfer of the Italian Fleet and Italian aircraft to such points as may be designated.

Proclamation by Genral Eisenhower on the surrender of Italy. United Nations Radio. 8 September 1943.

This is Gen. Dwight D. Eisenhower, Commander in Chief of the Allied Forces.

The Italian Government has surrendered its armed forces unconditionally. As Allied Commander in Chief, I have granted a military armistice, the terms of which have been approved by the Governments of the United Kingdom, the United States and the Union of Soviet Socialist Republics. Thus I am acting in the interest of the United Nations.

The Italian Government has bound itself to abide by these terms without reservation. The armistice was signed by my representative and the representative of Marshal Badoglio and it becomes effective this instant.

Hostilities between the armed forces of the United Nations and those of Italy terminate at once. All Italians who now act to help eject the German aggressor from Italian soil will have the assistance and the support of the United Nations.

Surrender of Germany

German surrender document

I. We, the undersigned, acting by authority of the German High Command, hereby surrender unconditionally to the Supreme

Commander, Allied Expeditionary Force, and simultaneously to the Soviet High Command, all forces on land, sea, and in the air who are at this date under German control.

II. The German High Command will at once issue orders to all German military, naval, and air authorities and to all forces under German control to cease active operations at 2301 hours Central European Time on 8 May and to remain in the positions occupied at that time. No ship, vessel or aircraft is to be scuttled, or any damage done to their hull, machinery or equipment.

III. The German High Command will at once issue to the appropriate commanders and ensure the carrying out of any further orders issued by the Supreme Commander, Allied Expeditionary Force, and by the Soviet High Command.

IV. This Act of Military Surrender is without prejudice to, and will be superseded by, any general instrument of surrender imposed by, or on behalf of, the United Nations and applicable to Germany and the German Armed Forces as a whole.

V. In the event of the German High Command or any of the forces under their control failing to act in accordance with this Act of Surrender the Supreme Commander, Allied Expeditionary Force, and the Soviet High Command will take such punitive or other action as they deem appropriate.

Appendix II

The United Nations Millennium Declaration, 8 September 2000.

I. Values and principles

1. We, heads of State and Government, have gathered at United Nations Headquarters in New York from 6 to 8 September 2000, at the dawn of a new millennium, to reaffirm our faith in the Organization and its Charter as indispensable foundations of a more peaceful, prosperous and just world.

2. We recognize that, in addition to our separate responsibilities to our individual societies, we have a collective responsibility to uphold the principles of human dignity, equality and equity at the global level. As leaders we have a duty therefore to all the world's people, especially the most vulnerable and, in particular, the children of the world, to whom the future belongs.

3. We reaffirm our commitment to the purposes and principles of the Charter of the United Nations, which have proved timeless and universal. Indeed, their relevance and capacity to inspire have increased, as nations and peoples have become increasingly interconnected and interdependent.

4. We are determined to establish a just and lasting peace all over the world in accordance with the purposes and principles of the Charter. We rededicate ourselves to support all efforts to uphold the sovereign equality of all States, respect for their territorial integrity and political independence, resolution of disputes by peaceful means and in conformity with the principles of justice and international law, the right to self-determination of peoples which remain under colonial domination and foreign occupation, non-interference in the internal affairs of States, respect for human rights and fundamental freedoms, respect for the equal rights of all without distinction as to race, sex, language or religion and international cooperation in solving international problems of an economic, social, cultural or humanitarian character.

5. We believe that the central challenge we face today is to ensure that globalization becomes a positive force for all the world's people. For while globalization offers great opportunities, at present its benefits are very unevenly shared, while its costs are unevenly distributed. We recognize that developing countries and countries with economies in transition face special difficulties in responding to this central challenge. Thus, only through broad and sustained efforts to create a shared future, based upon our common humanity in all its diversity, can globalization be made fully inclusive and equitable. These efforts must include policies and measures, at the global level, which correspond to the needs of developing countries and economies in transition and are formulated and implemented with their effective participation.

6. We consider certain fundamental values to be essential to international relations in the twenty-first century. These include:

- Freedom. Men and women have the right to live their lives and raise their children in dignity, free from hunger and from the fear of violence, oppression or injustice. Democratic and participatory governance based on the will of the people best assures these rights.
- Equality. No individual and no nation must be denied the opportunity to benefit from development. The equal rights and opportunities of women and men must be assured.
- Solidarity. Global challenges must be managed in a way that distributes the costs and burdens fairly in accordance with basic principles of equity and social justice. Those who suffer or who benefit least deserve help from those who benefit most.
- Tolerance. Human beings must respect one other, in all their diversity of belief, culture and language. Differences within and between societies should be neither feared nor repressed, but cherished as a precious asset of humanity. A culture of peace and dialogue among all civilizations should be actively promoted.
- Respect for nature. Prudence must be shown in the management of all living species and natural resources, in accordance with the precepts of sustainable development. Only in this way can the immeasurable riches provided to us by nature be preserved and passed on to our descendants. The current unsustainable patterns of production and consumption must be changed in the interest of our future welfare and that of our descendants.
- Shared responsibility. Responsibility for managing worldwide economic and social development, as well as threats to international peace and security, must be shared among the nations of the world and should be exercised multilaterally. As the most universal and most representative organization in the world, the United Nations must play the central role.

7. In order to translate these shared values into actions, we have identified key objectives to which we assign special significance.

II. Peace, security and disarmament

8. We will spare no effort to free our peoples from the scourge of war, whether within or between States, which has claimed more than 5 million lives in the past decade. We will also seek to eliminate the dangers posed by weapons of mass destruction.

9. We resolve therefore:

- To strengthen respect for the rule of law in international as in national affairs and, in particular, to ensure compliance by Member States with the decisions of the International Court of Justice, in compliance with the Charter of the United Nations, in cases to which they are parties.

- To make the United Nations more effective in maintaining peace and security by giving it the resources and tools it needs for conflict prevention, peaceful resolution of disputes, peacekeeping, post-conflict peace-building and reconstruction. In this context, we take note of the report of the Panel on United Nations Peace Operations and request the General Assembly to consider its recommendations expeditiously.

- To strengthen cooperation between the United Nations and regional organizations, in accordance with the provisions of Chapter VIII of the Charter.

- To ensure the implementation, by States Parties, of treaties in areas such as arms control and disarmament and of international humanitarian law and human rights law, and call upon all States to consider signing and ratifying the Rome Statute of the International Criminal Court.

- To take concerted action against international terrorism, and to accede as soon as possible to all the relevant international conventions.

- To redouble our efforts to implement our commitment to counter the world drug problem.

- To intensify our efforts to fight transnational crime in all its dimensions, including trafficking as well as smuggling in human beings and money laundering.

- To minimize the adverse effects of United Nations economic sanctions on innocent populations, to subject such sanctions regimes to regular reviews and to eliminate the adverse effects of sanctions on third parties.

- To strive for the elimination of weapons of mass destruction, particularly nuclear weapons, and to keep all options open for achieving this aim, including the possibility of convening an international conference to identify ways of eliminating nuclear dangers.

- To take concerted action to end illicit traffic in small arms and light weapons, especially by making arms transfers more transparent and supporting regional disarmament measures, taking account of all the recommendations of the forthcoming United Nations Conference on Illicit Trade in Small Arms and Light Weapons.

- To call on all States to consider acceding to the Convention on the Prohibition of the Use, Stockpiling, Production and Transfer of Anti-personnel Mines and on Their Destruction, as well as the amended mines protocol to the Convention on conventional weapons.

10. We urge Member States to observe the Olympic Truce, individually and collectively, now and in the future, and to support the International Olympic Committee in its efforts to promote peace and human understanding through sport and the Olympic Ideal.

III. Development and poverty eradication

11. We will spare no effort to free our fellow men, women and children from the abject and dehumanizing conditions of extreme poverty, to which more than a billion of them are currently subjected. We are committed to making the right to development a reality for everyone and to freeing the entire human race from want.

12. We resolve therefore to create an environment – at the national and global levels alike – which is conducive to development and to the elimination of poverty.

13. Success in meeting these objectives depends, inter alia, on good governance within each country. It also depends on good governance at the international level and on transparency in the financial, monetary and trading systems. We are committed to an open, equitable, rule-based, predictable and non-discriminatory multilateral trading and financial system.

14. We are concerned about the obstacles developing countries face in mobilizing the resources needed to finance their sustained development. We will therefore make every effort to ensure the success of the High-level International and Intergovernmental Event on Financing for Development, to be held in 2001.

15. We also undertake to address the special needs of the least developed countries. In this context, we welcome the Third United Nations Conference on the Least Developed Countries to be held in May 2001 and will endeavour to ensure its success. We call on the industrialized countries:

- To adopt, preferably by the time of that Conference, a policy of duty- and quota-free access for essentially all exports from the least developed countries;
- To implement the enhanced programme of debt relief for the heavily indebted poor countries without further delay and to agree to cancel all official bilateral debts of those countries in return for their making demonstrable commitments to poverty reduction; and
- To grant more generous development assistance, especially to countries that are genuinely making an effort to apply their resources to poverty reduction.

16. We are also determined to deal comprehensively and effectively with the debt problems of low- and middle-income developing countries, through various national and international measures designed to make their debt sustainable in the long term.

17. We also resolve to address the special needs of small island developing States, by implementing the Barbados Programme of Action and the outcome of the twenty-second special session of the General Assembly rapidly and in full. We urge the international community to ensure that, in the development of a vulnerability index, the special needs of small island developing States are taken into account.

18. We recognize the special needs and problems of the landlocked developing countries, and urge both bilateral and multilateral donors to increase financial and technical assistance to this group of countries to meet their special development needs and to help them overcome the impediments of geography by improving their transit transport systems.

19. We resolve further:

- To halve, by the year 2015, the proportion of the world's people whose income is less than one dollar a day and the proportion of people who suffer from hunger and, by the same date, to halve the proportion of people who are unable to reach or to afford safe drinking water.
- To ensure that, by the same date, children everywhere, boys and girls alike, will be able to complete a full course of primary schooling and that girls and boys will have equal access to all levels of education.
- By the same date, to have reduced maternal mortality by three quarters, and under-five child mortality by two thirds, of their current rates.
- To have, by then, halted, and begun to reverse, the spread of HIV/AIDS, the scourge of malaria and other major diseases that afflict humanity.
- To provide special assistance to children orphaned by HIV/AIDS.
- By 2020, to have achieved a significant improvement in the lives of at least 100 million slum dwellers as proposed in the 'Cities Without Slums' initiative.

20. We also resolve:

- To promote gender equality and the empowerment of women as effective ways to combat poverty, hunger and disease and to stimulate development that is truly sustainable.
- To develop and implement strategies that give young people everywhere a real chance to find decent and productive work.
- To encourage the pharmaceutical industry to make essential drugs more widely available and affordable by all who need them in developing countries.
- To develop strong partnerships with the private sector and with civil society organizations in pursuit of development and poverty eradication.
- To ensure that the benefits of new technologies, especially information and communication technologies, in conformity with recommendations contained in the ECOSOC 2000 Ministerial Declaration, are available to all.

IV. Protecting our common environment

21. We must spare no effort to free all of humanity, and above all our children and grandchildren, from the threat of living on a planet irredeemably spoilt by human activities, and whose resources would no longer be sufficient for their needs.

22. We reaffirm our support for the principles of sustainable development, including those set out in Agenda 21, agreed upon at the United Nations Conference on Environment and Development.

23. We resolve therefore to adopt in all our environmental actions a new ethic of conservation and stewardship and, as first steps, we resolve:

- To make every effort to ensure the entry into force of the Kyoto Protocol, preferably by the tenth anniversary of the United Nations Conference on Environment and Development in 2002, and to embark on the required reduction in emissions of greenhouse gases.
- To intensify our collective efforts for the management, conservation and sustainable development of all types of forests.
- To press for the full implementation of the Convention on Biological Diversity and the Convention to Combat Desertification in those Countries Experiencing Serious Drought and/or Desertification, particularly in Africa.
- To stop the unsustainable exploitation of water resources by developing water management strategies at the regional, national and local levels, which promote both equitable access and adequate supplies.
- To intensify cooperation to reduce the number and effects of natural and man-made disasters.
- To ensure free access to information on the human genome sequence.

V. Human rights, democracy and good governance

24. We will spare no effort to promote democracy and strengthen the rule of law, as well as respect for all internationally recognized human rights and fundamental freedoms, including the right to development.

25. We resolve therefore:

- To respect fully and uphold the Universal Declaration of Human Rights.

- To strive for the full protection and promotion in all our countries of civil, political, economic, social and cultural rights for all.
- To strengthen the capacity of all our countries to implement the principles and practices of democracy and respect for human rights, including minority rights.
- To combat all forms of violence against women and to implement the Convention on the Elimination of All Forms of Discrimination against Women.
- To take measures to ensure respect for and protection of the human rights of migrants, migrant workers and their families, to eliminate the increasing acts of racism and xenophobia in many societies and to promote greater harmony and tolerance in all societies.
- To work collectively for more inclusive political processes, allowing genuine participation by all citizens in all our countries.
- To ensure the freedom of the media to perform their essential role and the right of the public to have access to information.

VI. Protecting the vulnerable

26. We will spare no effort to ensure that children and all civilian populations that suffer disproportionately the consequences of natural disasters, genocide, armed conflicts and other humanitarian emergencies are given every assistance and protection so that they can resume normal life as soon as possible.

We resolve therefore:

- To expand and strengthen the protection of civilians in complex emergencies, in conformity with international humanitarian law.

- To strengthen international cooperation, including burden sharing in, and the coordination of humanitarian assistance to, countries hosting refugees and to help all refugees and displaced persons to return voluntarily to their homes, in safety and dignity and to be smoothly reintegrated into their societies.
- To encourage the ratification and full implementation of the Convention on the Rights of the Child and its optional protocols on the involvement of children in armed conflict and on the sale of children, child prostitution and child pornography.

VII. Meeting the special needs of Africa

27. We will support the consolidation of democracy in Africa and assist Africans in their struggle for lasting peace, poverty eradication and sustainable development, thereby bringing Africa into the mainstream of the world economy.

28. We resolve therefore:

- To give full support to the political and institutional structures of emerging democracies in Africa.
- To encourage and sustain regional and subregional mechanisms for preventing conflict and promoting political stability, and to ensure a reliable flow of resources for peacekeeping operations on the continent.
- To take special measures to address the challenges of poverty eradication and sustainable development in Africa, including debt cancellation, improved market access, enhanced Official

Development Assistance and increased flows of Foreign Direct Investment, as well as transfers of technology.

- To help Africa build up its capacity to tackle the spread of the HIV/AIDS pandemic and other infectious diseases.

VIII. Strengthening the United Nations

29. We will spare no effort to make the United Nations a more effective instrument for pursuing all of these priorities: the fight for development for all the peoples of the world, the fight against poverty, ignorance and disease; the fight against injustice; the fight against violence, terror and crime; and the fight against the degradation and destruction of our common home.

30. We resolve therefore:

- To reaffirm the central position of the General Assembly as the chief deliberative, policy-making and representative organ of the United Nations, and to enable it to play that role effectively.
- To intensify our efforts to achieve a comprehensive reform of the Security Council in all its aspects.
- To strengthen further the Economic and Social Council, building on its recent achievements, to help it fulfil the role ascribed to it in the Charter.
- To strengthen the International Court of Justice, in order to ensure justice and the rule of law in international affairs.
- To encourage regular consultations and coordination among the principal organs of the United Nations in pursuit of their functions.

- To ensure that the Organization is provided on a timely and predictable basis with the resources it needs to carry out its mandates.

- To urge the Secretariat to make the best use of those resources, in accordance with clear rules and procedures agreed by the General Assembly, in the interests of all Member States, by adopting the best management practices and technologies available and by concentrating on those tasks that reflect the agreed priorities of Member States.

- To promote adherence to the Convention on the Safety of United Nations and Associated Personnel.

- To ensure greater policy coherence and better cooperation between the United Nations, its agencies, the Bretton Woods Institutions and the World Trade Organization, as well as other multilateral bodies, with a view to achieving a fully coordinated approach to the problems of peace and development.

- To strengthen further cooperation between the United Nations and national parliaments through their world organization, the Inter-Parliamentary Union, in various fields, including peace and security, economic and social development, international law and human rights and democracy and gender issues.

- To give greater opportunities to the private sector, non-governmental organizations and civil society, in general, to contribute to the realization of the Organization's goals and programmes.

31. We request the General Assembly to review on a regular basis the progress made in implementing the provisions of this Declaration, and ask the Secretary-General to issue periodic reports for consideration by the General Assembly and as a basis for further action.

32. We solemnly reaffirm, on this historic occasion, that the United Nations is the indispensable common house of the entire human family, through which we will seek to realize our universal aspirations for peace, cooperation and development. We therefore pledge our unstinting support for these common objectives and our determination to achieve them.

Appendix III

Napoleon's secret instructions to conquer Haiti. From Die Kolonialpolirik Napoleon I, *Gustav Roloff (Munchen und Leipliz: Drud und Berlag von R. Oldenbourg, 1899) pp. 244–257, translation by Jacques C. Chicoineau, Webster University, August 1990, edited by Bob Corbett, Webster University, April 2003. Professor Corbett's website on Haiti can be found at http://www.webster.edu/~corbetre/haiti/haiti.html.*

Chapter 1

The general-in-chief in St. Domingue is necessarily the Major General. Should General Leclerc die, General Rochambeau will succeed him as General-in-Chief and from that time onwards as Major General. The latter dying, General Dugua will succeed him as General-in-Chief and Major General. Then, after this one, General Boudet.

Fleet
Admiral Villaret Joyeuse is named General Commander of all naval forces of the Republic in America and is in charge of all the first dispositions relating to the landing.

He will follow his mission in America with part of his squadron only when the Major General will be so well established that he would not need any more the assistance of crews to maintain the garrison in the places. It is therefore necessary that we should have taken the Cap, Port au Prince, Port de la Paix, Puerto Plata, the Mole, Fort Dauphin, the Cayes, Sto. Domingo, Gonaives, St. Marc, Jeremie and that the five divisions which are the main part of the army had arrived.

Then, Rear Admiral Latouche will be promoted Commander of the Cruises of St. Domingue and Admiral Villaret will go with five or six ships, among those which will be the better organized, in the seas of the United States in order to get some supplies and to display his colors in the main harbors. After that he will manage his return to St. Domingue where he will receive his orders, either to go back to France, or to go to take over Martinique, according to the progresses of the negotiations in Europe.

The Major General and the Admiral should act in concert for their operations. The Rear Admiral, commander of the cruises of St. Domingue, will be under the orders of the Major General.

Land Army

The land army is made of 7,000 men embarking in Brest, 3,000 who embark in Rochefort, 1,200 in Nantes and Lorient, 1,000 in Le Havre, 1,500 in Cadix, 3,000 in Toulon, 1,500 in Flessingue, 800 in Guadeloupe, 19,000 in total.

The three divisions of Brest, Lorient, and Nantes and Rochefort will meet and leave together. If the ones of Le Havre and Flessingue are not ready to leave with these three divisions, they will get under way within ten days.

Before being in sight of the land at St. Domingue they will send two frigates with 400 men, under the command of General

Kerversau, having on board the Government Commissioner in the Spanish part.

These two frigates will proceed to Santo Domingo, will take over the city, will move the inhabitants of the country against the negroes of the French part, will publish the printed proclamations joined to the present instruction.

In the event when, in view of the great number of Toussaint's troops, and feeling not strong enough to help the inhabitants, one would judge that it would not be appropriated to land, the frigates will cruise in front of the harbor, cut off all communications, will not let any ship enter or go out, and will establish secret correspondence in the country, waiting for the effect which it will have on the garrison Toussaint had left in Santo Domingo in the view of taking over of Cap.

A frigate, from the same point of departure will be sent to the Mole with a field officer who would have secret correspondence with the negroes who, in that country, are Toussaint's enemies. He will take possession of the Mole.

The squadron of Rear Admiral Latouche, with the forces embarked from his squadron, and all those reunited within the army and which make more than 8,000 men, that one judges necessary to the division of the Cap, will go straight to Port au Prince.

When arrived at the Cap, one will immediately take possession of the Ile de la Tortue, by sending there a vessel, and establishing there a base.

The squadron will arrive at the Cap, under a secure wind, in such manner that it would be possible to disembark during the same day that the squadron had been seen for the first time.

Two frigates will present themselves to the Cap and the Admiral and the Major General will instruct the General Commander of the place of their arrival in the colony. A frigate will present itself very close to Fort Piccolet in order to assure itself about the state of mind of the garrison at that fort, and if, as everything inclines to presume, one is received as friends, or if, at this unexpected moment the Republic should find some at St. Domingue, didn't have time to prepare their defense, the squadron will enter the harbor, disembark some troops and take over the city. The attack would consist in arriving three leagues from the Cap before sunrise, and to have 6,000 men on the ground before sunset.

If by any accident, it would happen that Toussaint would be warned of the arrival of the fleet, and be able to receive the army at the Cap, and that from that time onwards the Admiral judged that the squadron would be in danger to confront the fire of the batteries and the forts, the army would be able to disembark on the beach in front of fort Piccolet or in the Acul bay, in case one would suspect some resistance.

Being masters of the Cap, one will placard and publish the printed proclamations. One would make the teacher of Toussaint's children to leave with his two children, and will mail the letter enclosed with the present instructions. Some vessels from the squadron will go in front of Port de la Paix, Fort Dauphin, and all other points of the Island in order to take possession of them, or to blockade them, to communicate everywhere and diffuse some proclamations.

All the whites of the Cap, the colored men and the faithful men among the blacks should be armed and organized.

All the coastal batteries will be disarmed meanwhile in such manner that they could be promptly rearmed if some unforeseen circumstances would make it that we would lose superiority at sea.

The army will occupy positions in order to cover all Cap's plain and, if one judges it convenient, the plain of Plaisance.

It is only then that it will be possible for the Major General to see if he must decide to send by sea 1,200 men in order to occupy the post of the Gonaives, so as to find himself there in communication with the Division of Port au Prince; or, if he would content himself with the blockade of the Gonaives by some frigates, he might prefer to keep his forces together and occupy the Gonaives by a detachment backed by his advanced guard.

The Rear Admiral Latouche, who should take possession of Port au Prince, will dispatch a vessel and two frigates carrying at least 500 men of French troops, being careful to assign several officers knowing the country. These troops will go to the Cayes. This separation will be made out of sight of land and at a point from where they can arrive at the Cayes one or two days after the arrival at Port au Prince.

The Rear Admiral Latouche will take possession of the Ile La Gonave before arriving at Port au Prince in order to establish a base. The landing at Port au Prince will be conducted in the same spirit as at the Cap. Masters of the city and of the fort, they will secure Leogane and Gonaives. They will establish cruises in front of St. Marc and, if they have sufficient forces, will take over that post at the same time as Port au Prince. Everywhere they will diffuse the proclamation and organize the national guard, arm the whites, the colored men, and use the negroes on whom they can count.

The General Commander of the expedition at Port au Prince, when disembarked, will write to General Toussaint in order to let him know that the Major General disembarked at the Cap should have written to him in order to invite him to surrender.

The division which will arrive at Cayes will occupy the Ile des Vaches, Cayes, Fort St. Louis, and will arm the whites, the colored men and the faithful negroes and will manage to communicate by land with Port au Prince.

If the inhabitants behave well a part of the vessel crews can hold garrison at the post of the Cayes and 500 troops will rejoin by land the General who would have occupied Port au Prince.

Be careful to take possession of Jeremie and to keep small armed ships on cruise in front of the posts occupied by the rebels.

At time when different reinforcements will arrive, it seems that the organization of the army can be managed in five divisions of 3,000 men each: two in the Northern part, one in St. Marc, one in Port au Prince and the fifth in the Spanish part.

The squadron will provide 6,000 men from the detachment of its vessels, taken among the crews if necessary. These 6,000 men will have a garrison at Cap, Fort Dauphin, Port de Paix, the Mole, Gonaives, St. Marc, Port au Prince, Jeremie, Cayes, St. Domingue, Porto de la Plata, etc. The reserves of the divisions will also have a garrison in the different harbors. The division in the Spanish part of St. Domingue will reunite at St. Yago, part landing in Sto. Domingo, part in Porto Plata.

In order to understand the instructions, it is necessary to divide the time of the expedition in three periods:

The first will cover the 15 to 20 first days, necessary in order to occupy the places, to organize the national guards, to reassure the well disposed, reunite the ships under escort, to organize the artillery transport, to accustom the mass of the army to the customs and to the physiognomy of the country and take possession of the plains.

The second period is the one when the two armies being separated, one would pursue the rebels to the knife, one would "take them out of the nest", first in the French part, and successively in the Spanish part.

If the French part was an island, the rebels would soon be brought into submission; but one presumes that it will be in the Spanish part, where one will be far from the harbors, that they will try to hold for a longer time. The main resources must be then the colored men of the Spanish part. It seems that one wages war to the blacks almost the same way that in the Alps, eight or ten columns at the same time, combining their movements to a single position. The strength of these columns seems not to be over 3 to 400 men.

The posts of St. Yago, of Plaisance, of the Croix, of the Bouquets are indicated as the main points where it would be good to have entrenched posts, secured from the forays of the blacks. Not knowing the art of attack and the art of fortification, it is necessary to use against the blacks the ancient fortifications, towers, defensive walls which can be built promptly and which inspire more respect than the fortifications at the level of the ground.

The third period is the one when Toussaint, Moyse and Dessalines will not exist any more and when 3 to 4,000 blacks, withdrawn in the hillock of the Spanish part will form what is called in the islands the Maroons and whom one can succeed in destroying them with time, steadfastness and a well-combined system of attack.

Chapter 2

Instructions on foreign policy relating to the Americans and the neighboring powers

The Spaniards, the British and the Americans are equally worried to see a Black Republic. The Admiral and the Major General will write memorandums to the neighboring establishments in order to let them know the goal of the government, the common advantage for the Europeans to destroy the black rebellion and the hope to be seconded.

If one needs it, one must ask for some supplies in America, in the Spanish islands or even in Jamaica. One must ask at Havana if one needs a thousand or so men, in order to help to occupy the Spanish part of St. Domingue.

One must sequester for the benefit of the army, all the goods found in the harbors, and which belong to the blacks, until one knows the conduct they will display.

Declare the state of blockade of all the harbors where the rebels will be, and confiscate all the vessels which will enter or go out.

Jefferson has promised that as soon as the French army would arrive, all dispositions will be taken in order to starve Toussaint and to help the army.

Chapter 3

Instructions on internal policy relating to the blacks and their leader
The French nation will never give irons to men it had recognized as free. Therefore all the blacks will live in St. Domingue as they are today in Guadeloupe.

The conduct to be observed relating to the three periods of which it was spoken above:

During the first period, one will disarm only the blacks who would be rebels.

During the third, one will disarm all the blacks.

During the first period one will not be exacting: one will negotiate with Toussaint, one will promise everything he may ask for, in order to take possession of the places and to get in the country.

When that first goal will be achieved, one will become more exacting. One will intimate to him the order to categorically answer the proclamation and my letter. One will enjoin him to come to the Cap.

In the interview which one can have with Moyse, Dessalines and the other generals of Toussaint, one will treat them well.

Win over Christophe, Clairveaux, Maurepas, Félix, Romain, Jasmain etc. and all the other blacks well disposed towards the whites. During the first period, confirm them in their grades, and their employments. During the third period, send all of them to France with their grades if they well served during the second.

All the principal agents of Toussaint, whites and colored men, must, during the first period, be indistinctly heaped by kindness, confirmed in their grades, and, during the last period, be all sent to France, with their grades, if they had behaved during the second period, and as deported if they misbahave during that same period.

All the blacks who are in place must, during the first period, be flattered, well treated, but generally one should try to take out their popularity and their power. Toussaint, Moyse and Dessalines must be well treated during the first period and sent to France during the last period, arrested or with their grades, depending on the behavior they will display during the second.

Raymond has lost the trust of the government, one will seize him and one will send him to France, at the beginning of the second period, as a criminal.

If the first period lasts 15 days, there will be no drawback. If it will last longer, one would be duped.

Toussaint will be subdued only when he will come to the Cap or to Port au Prince, amidst the French army, to pledge fidelity to the Republic. That day, it is necessary, without any scandal, without any insult, but with honor and consideration, to put him on board of a frigate and send him to France. If possible, arrest at the same time Moyse and Dessalines, or pursue them to the bitter end and, then, send to France all the white followers of Toussaint, all the blacks having had positions and suspected of malevolence. Declare Moyse and Dessalines traitors to the country and enemies of the French people. The troops will take the field, and take no rest before getting their heads and disperse and disarm all their partisans.

If after the first 15 or 20 days it is impossible to bring back Toussaint, it is necessary, in a proclamation, to declare that if during so many days, he is not coming to take the oath to the Republic, he is declared traitor to the country and, at the end of the delay, one will start war to the knife.

A few thousands blacks, wandering in the hillocks and looking for refuge in these rustic lands, must not prevent the Major General from considering the second period as ended and to arrive quickly to the third one. Then the moment to assure for ever the ownership of the Colony to France had arrived. And the same day, one must on all points of the Colony, arrest all the men in place who would be suspected, whatever their color be, and embark at the same time all black generals whatever their manners, their patriotism, and the services they had rendered, observing meanwhile to let them go with their grades, and with the assurance that they will be well treated in France.

All the whites who served under Toussaint, and who, in the scenes of St. Domingue, were covered with crimes will be sent to Guyana.

All the blacks who behaved, but that their grades don't allow any more to remain on the island, will be sent to Brest.

All the blacks or colored men who misbehaved, whatever their grades, will be will be sent to the Mediterranean sea and dropped in a harbor of the island of Corsica.

If Toussaint, Dessalines or Moyse would be taken bearing arms, they will be within 24 hours judged by a military commission and shot by a firing squad as rebels.

Whatever would happen, one thinks that during the third period, one must disarm all the negroes, whatever the party they will be, and to put them back to cultivation.

All the individuals who signed the Constitution should, at the third period, be sent to France, some as prisoners, the others free as having been compelled to do so.

The white women who prostituted themselves to the blacks, whatever their rank will be, will be sent to Europe. The flags of the regiments of the National Guard will be taken away; new flags will be distributed and the regiments will be reorganized. One will reorganize the "gendarmerie." Do not accept that any black, having had a grade above captain, remains in the island.

The Ile de la Tortue will be used as depot for the black prisoners. Some warships or frigates can serve for the same purpose.

Chapter 4

Internal policy relating to the former Spanish part of St. Domingue
There will be in the Spanish part a general Commissioner who will not be dependent of the Colonial Prefect

The General-in-Chief will be the Major General of the two parts of St. Domingue. He will be able to ask a general officer to replace him in the Spanish part, who will be Major General of the Spanish part and who will remain under his orders.

There will be in that part a justice commissioner who will not depend upon the one in the French part. If the political goal in the

French part of St. Domingue should be to disarm the blacks and to make them farmers, but free, one must in the Spanish part also disarm them but put them back into slavery. One must retake possession of that part, the taking possession by Toussaint being null and void.

The French part is divided into departments and municipalities. The Spanish one must remain divided in dioceses and jurisdictions. Administration, commerce, justice, everything must be different from the French part in the Spanish one. One would not attach himself too much to the principle that, to establish a difference of manners, and even a local antipathy, is to keep live the influence of the metropolis in that colony.

Chapter 5

Administration relating to the old landholders
The policy concerning the old landholders must related to the periods and will depend upon the events which will occur during the first, second and third periods The Colony is not supposed to be French. No landholder is supposed to be in the enjoyment of his possessions and everything else as under Toussaint's administration. The product of the plantations is used to pay, feed and equip the army.

After the third period the proclamation which declares at last the island of St. Domingue returned to the Republic, one will give back to all the landholders who are in France, and who never emigrated, their possessions.

Every landholder who would not stay in St. Domingue or in France during the war, and who would have lived in America, England or any other foreign country, will be able to regain ownership of his possession only by a decree of the Government. No former landholder of St. Domingue will be allowed to enter the Colony if he is coming directly from England, Spain or any other country without having passed through Paris and having obtained the authorization, not only to recover his possessions but also to enter the Colony.

All donations made by Toussaint are null, but this declaration should be publicized only during the third period.

Every private possession in St. Domingue should be submitted to taxation. The amount of these taxes must be such that it will be sufficient to cover the needs of the Colony and the maintenance of the troops, etc.

Chapter 6

Administration relating to civil servants, military personnel, public education, clergy, commerce

The individuals, military or civil, composing the army are divided into two classes.

Into men having already fought the war at St. Domingue, knowing the country. These men will receive, after the third period, orders to return to France with rewards and tokens of satisfaction suited to services they would have rendered

The Major General should not accept any vacillation in the principle of these instructions and any individual who would discuss the right of the blacks, who shed the blood of the whites, will be, under any pretext, sent back to France, whatever his rank or services will be.

No public education of any sort will be established in St. Domingue and all the creoles will be compelled to send their children in France to have them raised there.

It will be announced that 3 French bishops will be installed in the French part of St. Domingue. They will receive the canonical investiture from the Pope, and will soon go to the Colony. The parish priests will be re-installed, and a certain number of priests, who will accompany the bishops in order to reorganize the clergy, will be sent from France.

Generally speaking, every priest who served Toussaint will be sent back to France, meanwhile some others will arrive in order to replace them.

Commerce must, during the first, second and third periods be accessible to Americans, but after the 3rd period, Frenchmen only will be admitted and the ancient rules from before the Revolution will be put back into force.

During the same first, second and third periods, any ship from Bordeaux or from an other harbor in France, which would carry flours, wines, and other goods necessary to the Colony, and which purchase would have be done in the name of the Republic, with the funds collected in the Colony, will have preference over the Americans.

The Major General and the Colonial Prefect should even take some dispositions, in such manner that even when the goods coming from France would make up a loss of 15 percent for the Colony over the objects purchased from the Americans, they will still give preference, considering these 15 percent as a necessary premium to foster our renascent commerce.

Notes

Introduction

1 Webber, R. (ed.) *Dad's Army: The Complete Scripts* (Orion, London, 2003), p. 490.

2 Hobbes, T. *Leviathan*, pt I, ch. 4.

2 Hirst, P. and Thompson, G. *Globalization in Question: The International Economy and the Possibilities of Governance* (Polity, Cambridge, 1996).

4 UK and USA, the Atlantic Charter, August 1941.

3 Haass, R. *The Reluctant Sheriff: The United States after the Cold War* (Council on Foreign Relations Press, New York, 1998).

4 Brzezinski, Z. *The Grand Chessboard: American Primacy and Its Geostrategic Imperatives* (Basic Books, New York, 1997), p. 40.

7 Chilton, P., Nassauer, O., Plesch, D. and Patten, J. *NATO, Peacekeeping and the United Nations*, British American Security Information Council, Report 94-1 (Berlin Information Centre for Transatlantic Security/British American Security Information Council, Berlin, London and Washington, 1994).

8 See for example Alinsky, S. *Rules for Radicals* (Vintage, New York, [1971] 1989) and Moyer, B. *Doing Democracy* (New Society, Gabriola Island, BC, 2001).

9 Speech to the Federalist Society, Washington, 1997.

10 US Constitution, Article VI, clause 2.

11 Kagan, R. *Paradise and Power* (Atlantic, London, 2003), pp. 62–3.

12 The Nuclear Non-Proliferation Treaty.

13 Speech on Iraq and the threat of international terrorism, 5 March 2004.

14 Speech at the Britain in the World Conference, 29 March 1995, cited in Cooper, R. *The Breaking of Nations* (Atlantic, London, 2003).

15 Remarks by the US President on Haiti, South Grounds, 1.05 p.m. EST, 29 February 2004.

16 *Independent*, 22 March 2004.

17 Admiral Lord Boyce, Lords Hansard, 10 February 2004.

18 *Time*, 8 December 2003.

19 Third Infantry Division (Mechanized) After Action Report, Operation Iraqi Freedom, 2003, available at www.globalsecurity.org.

20 *New York Times*, 26 February 2003.

21 Ibid.

22 *Washington Post*, 30 March 2003.

23 Record, J. *Bounding the Global War on Terrorism* (Strategic Studies Institute, US Army War College, Carlisle, PA, 2003).

24 Haldane, Lt-Gen. Sir J. *The Insurrection in Mesopotamia* (W. Blackwood & Sons, Edinburgh and London, 1922).

Chapter One

1   Lord Moran, *Winston Churchill: The Struggle for Survival 1940–1965* (Constable, London, 1966), p. 186.

2   Nato Basic Documents, www.nato.int.

3   Mandela, N. *Long Walk to Freedom* (Abacus, London, 1994), p. 110.

4   Williams, E. F. *A Prime Minister Remembers* (Heinemann, London, 1961), p. 54.

5   www.usaaf.net/chron/42/mar42.htm.

6   President Franklin Delano Roosevelt, *Fireside Chat*, 12 October 1942, 'Ships and Shipping'.

7   Hoopes, T. and Brinkley, D. *FDR and the Creation of the U.N.* (Yale University Press, New Haven and London, 1997).

8   John Bolton, Under Secretary for Arms Control and International Security, The Federalist Society 2003 National Lawyers Convention, 13 November 2003.

9   Moran, *Winston Churchill: The Struggle for Survival*, p. 280.

10 Telegram sent to prominent Americans, 24 May 1946, published in the *New York Times*, 25 May 1946. In the *Oxford Dictionary of Modern Quotations*.

11 Winston Churchill, The Hydrogen Bomb, speech, House of Commons, 30 March 1954, in Churchill, Sir W. *Complete Speeches, 1897–1963* (ed. Rhodes James, R.) (Chelsea House/R. R. Bowker, New York and London, 1974), 8 vols, p. 8551.

12 Gray C. *Weapons Don't Make War: Policy, Strategy and Military Technology* (University Press of Kansas, Lawrence, 1993), p. 146.

13 Ibid., p. 165.

14 Schell, J. *The Gift of Time: The Case for Abolishing Nuclear Weapons Now* (Granta, London, 1998).

15 www.stimson.org.

16 Burke, J. *Al-Qaeda: Casting a Shadow of Terror* (I. B. Tauris, London, 2003).

Chapter Two

1   Prof. Sir Joseph Rotblat, speech at the Royal United Services Institute, London, 8 January 2003.

2   If you want to get an overview of all the wars around the world today I can recommend one short and very clear book: Smith, D. *Atlas of War and Peace* (Earthscan, London, 2003), which provides a brief and graphic survey of the world at war and current peace-building efforts.

3   Voice of America, 12 February 2003.

4   Perle, R. and Frum, D. *An End to Evil: How to Win the War on Terror* (Random House, New York, 2003).

5   www.brad.ac.uk/acad/sbtwc/other/disease.htm.

6   Pinkston, D. A. and Saunders, P. C. 'Seeing North Korea Clearly', *Survival*, 2003, vol. 45, no. 3, pp. 79–102.

7   Nuclear weapons were built to be fired from an astonishing variety of equipment, including artillery guns, tanks, helicopters, planes, ships and submarines.

8   Sigal, L. *Disarming Strangers: Nuclear Diplomacy with North Korea* (Princeton University Press, Princeton, 1998), p. 113.

9   www.worldtribune.com, 17 October 2003.

10 22 January 2004.

11 Self, B. and Thompson, J. (eds) *Japan's Nuclear Option: Security, Politics, and Policy in the 21st Century* (Henry L. Stimson Center, Washington, 2003).

12 US Joint Chiefs of Staff, Joint Doctrine 3-1-12, Theatre Nuclear Operations.

13 Butcher, M. *US Counterproliferation Policy* (Physicians for Social Responsibility, Washington, 2003).

14 Morland, H. *The Secret That Exploded* (Random House, New York, 1981).

15 Cooper, R. *The Breaking of Nations: Order and Chaos in the Twenty-first Century* (Atlantic, London, 2003).

16 Wells, H. G. 'The Stolen Bacillus', *Pearson's Magazine*, 1905, in Russell, A. (ed.) *The Collector's Book of Science Fiction by H. G. Wells*, (Castle, Secaucus, NJ, 1978).

17   Ruthven, M. *Fury for God: The Islamist Attack on America*, rev. ed. (Granta, London, 2004).

18   *Atlantic Monthly*, May 2003.

19   Ruthven, M. *Islam in the World*, 2nd ed. (Penguin, London, 2000).

20   *Guardian*, 16 February 2004.

21   'Measuring Poverty at the Global Level', PovertyNet, World Bank, 2002.

22   *Independent*, 7 December 2003.

Chapter Three

1   www.strategy.gov.uk/output/Page4392.asp.

2   Kitson, Gen. F. *Bunch of Five* (Faber & Faber, London, 1977), pp. 283ff.

3   Gwynn, Maj. Gen. Sir C. *Imperial Policing*, 2nd ed. (Macmillan, London, 1939).

4   Lowther-Pinkerton, J. and Wight, A. 'The Future Shape of Global Counter-terrorism', Royal United Services Institute/University of California Seminar, 14 February 2002.

5   International Commission on Intervention and State Sovereignty, *Responsibility to Protect* (International Development Research Centre, Ottawa, December 2001).

6   Halliday, F. *Islam and the Myth of Confrontation: Religion and Politics in the Middle East* (I. B. Tauris, London and New York, 1995)

Chapter Four

1   Hutton, W. *The World We're In* (Abacus, London, 2003).

2   Hansmann, H. and Kraakman, R. 'The End of History for Corporate Law', Working Paper #CLB-99-013 (New York University Center for Law and Business, New York, January 2000).

3   Soros, G. *George Soros on Globalization* (PublicAffairs, Oxford, 2002).

4   Herman, E. and Chomsky, N. *Manufacturing Consent: The Political Economy of the Mass Media*, rev. ed. (Pantheon, New York, 2002).

5   Hines, C. *Localization: A Global Manifesto* (Earthscan, London, 2000).

6   *Financial Times*, 21 June 1999.

7   A. Michaels, *Financial Times*, 27 August 2003.

8   N. FitzGerald, *Financial Times*, 8 September 2003.

9 'The Charity/Business Duet: Harmony or Discord?', Allen Lane Lecture, London, 11 February 2003.

10 Friedman, M. *Capitalism and Freedom* (University of Chicago Press, Chicago, 1962).

11 *Corporate Governance 1999* (OECD, Paris, 1999).

12 Howard Davies, Chairman, Financial Services Authority, 'Corporate Governance and the Development of Global Capital Markets', China Securities Regulatory Commission, Beijing, 22 April 2002.

13 Smith, A. *An Inquiry into the Nature and Causes of the Wealth of Nations* (University of Chicago Press, Chicago, [1776] 1976). An excerpt (Book V, ch. 1, pt iii, art. i, pp. 280-82).

14 Micklethwait, J. and Wooldridge, A. *The Company: A Short History of a Revolutionary Idea* (Weidenfeld and Nicolson, London, 2003).

15 Korten, D. *When Corporations Rule the World* (Kumarian Press/Berrett-Koehler, West Hartford, CT and San Francisco, 1995).

16 Griffiths, M. 'Lifting the Corporate Veil', Kensington Business School, London, 2003.

17 Recent Court Decision Favorable for Corporate Shareholders on CERCLA Liability:

The United States Court of Appeals for the Sixth Circuit, which hears decisions from Ohio, Michigan, Kentucky and Tennessee, recently issued a decision on November 17, 1997 which is favorable for corporations and their shareholders with respect to when liability can be imposed on shareholders under the federal superfund law, CERCLA. The troublesome issue of a shareholder being an owner or operator of a contaminated facility has plagued businesses for some time. The Sixth Circuit has cleared up the issue, at least for courts within the Sixth Circuit's jurisdiction.

In *Donahey v. Bogle*, 1997 U.S. App. LEXIS 32146 (6th Cir. 1997), the court, in an *en banc* 10-2 decision, held that a shareholder of a corporation is not liable as an operator as defined under 107(a)(2) of CERCLA unless circumstances justify piercing the corporate veil. The court also reaffirmed the principle that the applicable state law must be used by federal courts to determine the veil-piercing standards. In this case, the shareholder was the sole shareholder of the corporation and was only involved with the financial aspects of the company. The day-to-day affairs, including the waste disposal activities, were handled by the hired managers who did not need the approval of the shareholder to execute their duties. As a general rule, state law corporate veil-piercing standards favor corporations.

Two justices dissented in the decision. The dissenting justices would not apply the veil-piercing standards to a sole shareholder who is active in the corporation, but instead would find direct liability under the CERCLA statute without first having to pierce the corporate veil. They expressed their concern that a savvy polluter can form a closely held corporation of which he owns 100% of the shares, play an active role in the company, but follow a 'don't ask, don't tell policy' regarding disposal of environmental toxins and not be considered an owner or operator of the facility. The dissent also stated that it was reserving judgment on whether persons should be held liable under CERCLA who own less than 100% of the shares or are not active in management of the facility. However, the dissent offers no guidance on where it would draw the line for shareholder personal liability, except to state that an appropriate inquiry should be whether the corporate individual could have prevented or stopped the hazardous waste discharge.

The *Donahey* decision closely follows *U.S. v. Cordova*, 113 F.3d 572 (6th Cir. 1997), in which the Sixth Circuit recently held that under CERCLA, a parent corporation is liable for the environmental harms done by its subsidiary only if the elements necessary to pierce the corporate veil are present. The *Cordova* decision has been appealed to the U.S. Supreme Court, but the Court has not yet ruled whether it will accept the case for decision. Many of us that have followed these issues expect that the High Court will accept the case because of the split in authority around the United States. We would not be surprised to learn that the *Donahey* decision will also be appealed to the U.S. Supreme Court since it has been hotly debated for years. These two cases provide a good opportunity for the Court to address these important CERCLA-related corporate issues. From www.vssp.com

18 Hansmann and Kraakman, *The End of History for Corporate Law*.

19 BBC History Timeline on the Limited Liability Act of 1855.

20 Weinstein, M. *Share Price Changes and the Arrival of Limited Liability in California* (University of Southern California Law School, Los Angeles, 2002).

21 Evans, L. and Quigley, N. 'Shareholder Liability Regimes, Principal-Agent Relationships, and Banking Industry Performance', *Journal of Law and Economics*, 1995, vol. 38, no. 2, pp. 497–520.

22 Weinstein, *Share Price Changes*.

23 House of Lords, 24 January 2004.

24 Wolff, E. 'How the Pie Is Sliced: America's Growing Concentration of Wealth', *American Prospect*, 1995, vol. 6, no. 22.

25 Glasbeek, H. 'The Invisible Friend', *New Internationalist*, July 2003, no. 358. Prof. Glasbeek is Professor Emeritus and Senior Scholar, Osgoode Hall Law School, York University, Toronto, and author of *Wealth by Stealth: Corporate Crime, Corporate Law, and the Perversion of Democracy* (Between the Lines, Toronto, 2002).

26 Kingsnorth, P. *One No, Many Yeses: a journey to the heart of the global resistance movement* (Free Press, London, 2003).

Chapter Five

1 Howard, M. *The Invention of Peace. Reflections on War and International Order* (Profile, London, 2000).

2 Jones, T. et al. *Who Murdered Chaucer?* (Methuen, London, 2003).

3 Adams, D. *The Hitch-Hiker's Guide to the Galaxy* (Pan, London, 1979), p. 29.

4 New Internationalist Publications, London, 2003.

5 www.gatswatch.org.

6 UN Security Council/General Assembly document A/50/79-S/1995/106, http://www.un.org/documents/ga/docs/50/plenary/a50-79.htm.

7 http://www.un.org/Depts/dhl/reform.htm

8 Ryan, S. *The United Nations and International Politics* (Macmillan, London, 2000); Coates, K. *Think Globally Act Locally: The United Nations and the Peace Movements* (Spokesman, Nottingham, 1988).

9 Murphy, J. T. *Labour's Big Three: A Biographical Study of Clement Attlee, Herbert Morrison and Ernest Bevin* (Bodley Head, London, 1948), p. 234.

10 Freedland, J. *Bring Home the Revolution: How Britain Can Live the American Dream* (Fourth Estate, London, 1998).

Chapter Six

1 *A Remonstrance of Many Thousand Citizens* (July 1646). Reprinted in Wolfe, D. (ed.) *Leveller Manifestoes of the Puritan Revolution* (Thomas Nelson & Sons, London and New York, 1944); *A Remonstrance of the Shee-citizens of London* (London, 1647).

2 Fortescue. J. W. *A History of the British Army* (Macmillan, London, 4 vols, 1899–1906), vol. 4, pt 1, pp. 565ff.

3   Pearce, E. *Reform!: The Fight for the 1832 Reform Act* (Jonathan Cape, London, 2003).

4   Linton, 'Who Were the Chartists?', *Century Magazine*, January 1882.

Chapter Seven

1   *Key World Energy Statistics 2002* (International Energy Agency, Paris, 2003).

2   An email from Yves Marignac, Director of WISE-Paris, gave this information:

The main study on the costs of this transition was carried out in 2000 for the then Prime Minister of France, Lionel Jospin. I was co-author of the main annexe report, with an expert from the French CEA (Commissariat à l'Énergie Atomique), on 'Le parc nucléaire actuel'. The purpose was to establish the material and economic balance of the existing nuclear fleet in France. Unfortunately, this report only exists in French. In case you can read it, you can download it (in three parts) from the web links below:

http://lesrapports.ladocumentationfrancaise.fr/BRP/014000107/0000.pdf
http://lesrapports.ladocumentationfrancaise.fr/BRP/014000107/0001.pdf
http://lesrapports.ladocumentationfrancaise.fr/BRP/014000107/0002.pdf

You can also get the full report, 'Report to the Prime Minister – Economic Forecast Study of the Nuclear Power Option', by Jean-Michel Charpin, Benjamin Dessus and René Pellat, downloadable in English from the address below:

http://fire.pppl.gov/eu_fr_fission_plan.pdf

Finally on that report, you'll find in an attachment a briefing, in English, that I prepared after the report was made public. It summarises the main methodological break-through (in the French context) and results of that evaluation. I sent it in two parts, text plus annexes ('BriefCDP-Eng-Main.doc' and 'BriefCDP-Eng-Annex.doc').

Now to conclude on the figures: you'll find in the second chapter of the report on 'Le parc nucléaire actuel' (paper pages 120 to 162) a comprehensive review of the various costs linked to the French nuclear programme, mostly based on primary data from the industry. A summary is given in the English main report, pages 54 to 64. For instance, on page 56, there is a figure of the total investments in Electricité de France's nuclear fleet of fifty-eight pressurised-water reactors, by year between 1971 and 1996. From these figures we estimated the total investment of France in its fifty-eight currently operating reactors to be worth 470 billion francs, or about €70 billion.

In addition, one must include R&D costs (100 billion francs), and 682 or 698 billion francs for decommissioning cost at the end of their lifetime. We also calculated costs related to operation, fuel cycle, etc. All the results are summarized in the table on page 161 (where the columns, numbers S1 to S6, correspond to scenarios slightly differentiated on operational lifetime and options or back end of the fuel cycle).

As a final result, France spent about the following on nuclear electricity generation between 1977 and 1998 (in billion francs):

Investment: 470

R&D: 55 (out of a total of 100 for the full lifetime of the fleet)

Operation: 300 (out of a total of 1,035, corresponding to about 14.4 by year on average)

Fuel cycle: 364 (271 + 93)

So in total, France spent about 1,189 billon francs – or roughly €180 billion – in the first twenty-one years of operation of its nuclear fleet, corresponding to an average of €8.6 billion per year.

If you look at the total cost, including the years to come before the end of the nuclear reactors' lifetime, the decommissioning, the long-term waste management, etc., the total is up to between 2,740 and 2,943 billion francs, say 2,850 on average – or €435 billion. As long as the operation runs from 1977 to 2049, this is about 6 billion by year. But I think it is more fair to use the figure of forty-five years equivalent of the whole nuclear fleet in operation.

Hence the rough figure is of about €10 billion for one full year of operation of the fifty-eight reactors.

3 Awerbuch, S. 'Determining the Real Cost: Why Renewable Power Is More Cost-competitive Than Previously Believed', *Renewable Energy World*, March–April 2003, vol. 6, no. 2.

4 Robert McFarlane, presentation on energy security, Royal United Services Institute, London, October 2002.

5 Prof. David Fisk, presentation on energy security, Royal United Services Institute, London, November 2002.

6 Perry, G. *The War on Terrorism, the World Oil Market and the US Economy*, Analysis Paper 7 (Brookings Institution, Washington, 2001).

7 'United States Dependence on Foreign Oil', Hearing before the Committee on Foreign Relations, United States Senate, 104th Congress, 1st Session, 27 March 1995 (US Government Printing Office, Washington, 1995).

8 *Oil Imports: An Overview and Update of Economic and Security Effects*, CRS Report for Congress (Congressional Research Service, Washington, 1997).

9 *Financial Times*, 2 January 2004.

10 Greene, D. and Tishchishyna, N. *Costs of Oil Dependence: A 2000 Update*, Oak Ridge National Laboratory (US Department of Energy, Washington, 2000).

11 Awerbuch, 'Determining the Real Cost'.

12 President Dwight D. Eisenhower, farewell broadcast, 17 January 1961, in *New York Times*, 18 January 1961, quoted in *Oxford Dictionary of Modern Quotations*.

13 European Wind Energy Association *Wind Energy – The Facts* (Office for Official Publications of the European Communities, 4 vols, Luxembourg, 1999), vol. 1: Technology.

14 Dr Gert Eisenbeiss, International Energy Agency, Paris, March 2003.

15 Memorandum submitted by the British Association for Biofuels and Oils (BABFO), Select Committee on Environment, Food and Rural Affairs, 2003.

16 'Delivering Climate Technology Programmes, Policies and Politics', Royal Institute for International Affairs/Carbon Trust, London, November 2003.

17 *Wind Force 12* (European Wind Energy Association/Greenpeace, Brussels, 2003).

18 Chapman, J. and Gross, R. (lead authors) *Technical and Economic Potential of Renewable Energy Generating Technologies: Potentials and Cost Reductions to 2020* (Imperial College London, London, 2003).

19 Quaschning , V. and Trieb, F. 'Solar Thermal Power Plants for Hydrogen Production', Hypothesis IV symposium, Stralsund, Germany, 9–14 September 2001.

20 Wirth, T., Gray, C. and Podesta, J. 'The Future of Energy Policy', *Foreign Affairs*, July/August 2003, vol. 82, no. 4.

21 Statement of Dr Hermann Scheer, President of EUROSOLAR, on the European Commission draft 'Proposal for a directive of the European Parliament and of the Council concerning measures to safeguard security of electricity supply and infrastructure investment', Berlin, 4 December 2003.

22 6 October 2003.

23 Dr M. D. Jones, Manager, Hydrogen Technology, BP, presentation to the IEA Renewables Energy Working Party Seminar, Paris, 3 March 2003.

24 Dr Jones, presentation to the IEA as above.

25 J. P. Uihlein, Fuels Project Manager, BP, evidence to US House of Representatives Subcommittee on Energy, 24 June 2002.

Chapter Eight

1 General Lee Butler's remarks at the National Press Club, 2 February 1998, 'The Risks of Deterrence: From Superpowers to Rogue Leaders', www.cdi.org/issues/armscontrol/butler.html.

2   Admiral R. W. Meiss, Senate Armed Services Committee Hearings on Defense Authorization Request for Fiscal Year 2000, pt 7, p. 365, 14 April 1999.

3   Natural Resources Defence Council study on the nuclear war plan, www.nrdc.org.

4   Bruce Blair's nuclear column at www.cdi.org.

5   These references are to a briefing on the Bush administration's Nuclear Posture Review and to the Report of the US Defense Science Board Task Force on Future Strategic Strike Forces. www.globalsecurity.org/wmd/library/news/usa/2002/us-020109-dod01.htm.

6   Ambassador Evan Galbraith, speech at the Royal United Services Institute, November 2001.

7   Wolterbeek, Lt-Col. C. *European Missile Defence and the Potential Ballistic Missile Risk*, Weapons of Mass Destruction Centre, NATO HQ, July 2001.

8   Rolf Ekeus, *Washington Post*, 15 September 2002.

9   Inyk. M. 'The Iraq War did not force Gadaffi's hand', *Financial Times*, 9 March 2003.

10 INFCIRC/540.

11 US State Department, INF Treaty. www.state.gov.

12 US State Department, CFE Treaty. www.state.gov.

13 US State Department, Open Skies Treaty. www.state.gov.

Index